D1797863

PROPAGANDA, THE PRESS AND CONFLICT

This volume analyses the use of the press for propaganda purposes during times of conflict, using the first Gulf War and the intervention in Kosovo as case studies. As the contemporary analysis of propaganda during conflict has tended to focus considerably upon visual and instant media coverage, this book is intended to redress the imbalance and to contribute to the growing discourse on the role of the press in modern warfare.

Through an innovative comparative analysis of press treatment of the two conflicts it reveals the existence of five consistent propaganda themes: portrayal of the leader figure, portrayal of the enemy, military threat, threat to international stability and technological warfare. As these themes construct a fluid model for the analysis and understanding of propaganda content in the press during conflicts involving British forces, they also provide the background against which the author can discuss general issues regarding propaganda. Amongst the issues which have become increasingly relevant to both recent academic debate and popular culture, the author tackles the role of the journalist in war coverage, the place of the press in a news market dominated by 'instant' visual media and the effectiveness of propaganda in specific cultural and political context.

This book will appeal to advanced students and researchers in war studies, media studies/propaganda and psychology.

David R. Willcox has recently completed his PhD, which forms the basis for this book, at the University of Kent at Canterbury.

CONTEMPORARY SECURITY STUDIES

PROPAGANDA, THE PRESS AND CONFLICT

The Gulf War and Kosovo

David R. Willcox

Routledge
Taylor & Francis Group

LONDON AND NEW YORK

First published 2005
by Routledge
2 Park Square, Milton Park, Abingdon, Oxon OX14 4RN

Simultaneously published in the USA and Canada
by Routledge
270 Madison Avenue, New York, NY 10016

Routledge is an imprint of the Taylor & Francis Group

Transferred to Digital Printing 2006

© 2005 David R. Willcox

Typeset in Times by BC Typesetting Ltd, Bristol

British Library Cataloguing in Publication Data
A catalogue record for this book is available from the British Library

Library of Congress Cataloging in Publication Data
A catalog record for this book has been requested

ISBN10: 0–415–36043–9 (hbk)
ISBN10: 0–415–40791–5 (pbk)

ISBN13: 978–0–415–36043–2 (hbk)
ISBN13: 978–0–415–40791–5 (pbk)

CONTENTS

CONTENTS

ACKNOWLEDGEMENTS

I would like to thank my PhD supervisor Professor David Welch for his guidance through the years and for the opportunity to continue my studies past the Propaganda MA. This book is a development of my PhD thesis and as such extensive gratitude is extended to those who have supported my academic progress. Specific mention must also go to Mark Connelly for his help, especially with regards to teaching. Posthumous gratitude is extended to Patricia Tweedie who enabled me to complete my A-Level studies. In addition to academic influences, the University of Kent provided funding, while the Royal Historical Society helped towards some research costs. Fundamentally, without the help of Andy McNab and the scholarship he provided neither my PhD nor this book would have been achievable.

The staff of the University of Kent has been wonderful over the many years, especially those in the History Office. Of the archives I have visited I must mention the Mass Observation Archive at Sussex University and the Imperial War Museum for access to material of great interest and benefit to this work.

On a personal note John, Sheila and Richard Willcox provided financial, emotional and nutritional support for which I am ever indebted. Old friends from school and university as well as the members of the new community put up with my varying stages of excitement and disappointment with admirable consistency. Special mention goes to Kat Albert who also had to live and eat with me for a year. Finally, Sarah Halfpenny provided invaluable emotional support and academic criticism during the most difficult stage of the work.

INTRODUCTION

The role of the British media in the dissemination of propaganda during conflict is a wide-ranging and multifaceted subject that has increasingly assumed a growing importance to those wishing to control public opinion. Since William Russell's reports for *The Times* during the Crimean War the media has had a role not only in relaying information about the events during war, but more significantly shaping the public perception of those events. While the nature of both the scope and proliferation of media and the conduct of conflict in the twentieth century have altered drastically, the use of propaganda in sustaining support for war has been consistently important. This book will examine the presentation of war coverage in Britain through the medium of the British press. The research will show that consistent propaganda themes are utilized to generate and sustain support for intervention in war. Five propaganda themes will be identified and each is applicable despite variances in the nature of conflict. Together they form a fluid model whereby the emphasis and importance placed upon each theme, by those advocating intervention, is shifted depending on the justifications required for involvement.

Government attempts to win not only domestic but, increasingly, global support for intervention in conflict are substantially conveyed through the media, making it a vital component for comprehending public understanding of crises. As the British media has expanded and become part of a wider global news network, television has succeeded in becoming the dominant conduit of news for the British public. Increasingly, the role of the British press has seemingly been diminished as a result of contemporary developments in modern electronic media. Arguably, the printed media could be perceived as an outdated mode of communication, immediately superseded by 24-hour news channels and the global capabilities of digital radio, television and the Internet. However, this monograph argues that the above interpretation is a superficial evaluation of the role of the British newspaper within the larger structure of mass media. It is necessary to reinterpret the relationship between the printed and visual media as one of a mutually compatible structure, rather than an adversarial one. Each has positive and negative attributes that suggest each will continue to constitute an important element of information dissemination.

The study of printed media in Britain in a contemporary period of history is important for a number of reasons. It is the object of this book to assess the propaganda content of newspapers during conflict, but also to place this wider context of printed media within mass media in general and to consider the role of the war reporter. As a result it will be demonstrated that the printed media retains a place as a complementary element of modern media and an important conduit for propaganda dissemination.

In an age of instant, visual news coverage the role of the British press could be overlooked. Arguably, the printed media cannot hope to compete with the rapid dissemination of news offered by television, radio and the Internet. However, there are a number of caveats to be assigned to this interpretation. For example, major British national newspapers now appear as on-line editions that expand their audience and facilitate up-to-date news coverage. This development allows global access to their news items and, by doing so, alleviates some of the antiquated associations levelled at the press.

More recently, a reappraisal of the desirability of continuous news coverage has questioned the benefits of instant broadcasting. The insatiable demand for information and pictures it creates does little to promote the production of news based upon informed opinion from reliable sources. The two are not exclusive, but continual updating and the need to produce swift and constantly updated coverage hinder the process of reflection and analysis. Instead of news based upon fact the demand for a stimulating visual image to accompany continually fresh information becomes paramount.

The supposed weakness of the press, its inability to produce rapid and constantly changing news, may in fact provide the very niche it requires to retain a substantial portion of the media market. Thus, any perceived victory of television over the press is a redundant concept. National newspapers still command wide readership and popularity amongst a cross-section of society and as such constitute a considerable section of the media.[1] Instead, the relationship the press has with the rest of the media network is one of a complementary, rather than of a conflicting, nature.

Newspapers also offer another fundamental difference in the media market, but worryingly this offers little hope to the seekers of diversity of opinion in British media. Traditionally the press has provided a forum for the interpretation of news by the utilization of opinion and political bias in the form of comment pieces by individuals and an overall editorial policy. The ability of newspapers to provide political bias in an overt manner appears to provide them with a significant opportunity to rival allegedly neutral television news coverage in a competitive media market. In this respect the existence of political propaganda during peace and war would seem inevitable. Yet, it is the very ability of newspapers to provide opinionated news coverage if required that makes their conformity with the pro-interventionist agenda and government ideology during conflict all the more difficult to justify.

Analysis of the British press enables a comparative element to be introduced into the methodology. Comparing a number of national newspapers offers the opportunity to demonstrate diversity of opinion, yet the propaganda in each is markedly similar. The five newspapers selected for analysis are *The Times*, *The Daily Telegraph*, *The Guardian*, *The Sun* and the *Daily Mirror*. In addition to comparison of the conflicts a selection of newspaper sources enables evaluation of propaganda content in relation to political and social considerations that are reflected in both the newspapers themselves and their readerships. By providing these comparative elements the strength of the conclusions, regarding consistent propaganda themes transcending the differences between newspapers and conflicts, is enhanced. The newspapers were selected to provide a balance between the political opinions they represent. More importantly the five newspapers chosen represent some of the best-selling titles. The five national newspapers also provide a balance between tabloid and broadsheet coverage. Ideally the research would have included all the major national British titles, however, a compromise was struck in an effort to retain a greater depth of analysis.

Similarly, the choice of the Gulf War 1990–91 and the Kosovo Conflict 1999 is significant for a number of reasons. The two conflicts demonstrate a number of differences in style and duration. These differences are intended to strengthen the argument herein that shows a large number of similarities between the propaganda seen during the two military interventions. To begin with, the Gulf War was heralded as the first 'live' war, fought in the spotlight of international media able to transmit 'live' images to domestic audiences. Meanwhile the Kosovo Conflict assumed the title of the first war involving British forces in the Internet era. This development extended the globalization of news coverage that had been accelerated by global television coverage. Both these 'firsts' demonstrate the rapidly changing nature of media technology in contemporary conflict. Within a decade the nature of conflict coverage had altered markedly, although the propaganda techniques employed remained recognizably similar.

Second, both crises occurred in the aftermath of the Cold War enabling distinctions to be drawn with previous conflicts fought within different global, diplomatic and military circumstances, as well as alternate technological environments. The Cold War had seen a marked rise in ideological tensions. These predominantly manifested themselves in an inactive war, fought to win 'hearts and minds' rather than physical territory. This information war has continued to manifest itself in propaganda campaigns since, despite the collapse of the Soviet Union.

INTRODUCTION

Third, the commencement of hostilities in each case varied greatly. The Gulf War had a well-defined trigger, namely the invasion of Kuwait, to herald the start of an international crisis and focus media and government attention on the issue. The escalation of events leading to intervention in Kosovo was less well defined, resulting in a more piecemeal representation of the growing crisis in the press. The concept of who constituted the enemy also differed greatly between the two.

Fourth, geographically the Gulf was vital for the strategic and economic requirements of Western powers dependent on Middle Eastern oil. This opened the Western powers up to accusations of profiteering and modern day imperialism. Kosovo, on the other hand, was seemingly economically irrelevant. However, it was a crisis in Europe's 'backyard' and a test for the 'moral' foreign policy agenda of New Labour. As a result of these differences the justifications for intervention forwarded by official and media channels had to be adjusted to reflect the circumstances.

Fifth, partly due to the geographical considerations, the Gulf War alliance was a United States-led coalition force. In contrast Kosovo marked the North Atlantic Treaty Organization's (hereafter NATO) first war. Balancing the strategic and national interests of a firmly established NATO against that of a more international, loosely based and temporary alliance meant propaganda had differing priorities but still employed similar techniques.

Finally, combat in the Gulf involved a sustained air campaign and a ground assault that echoed past traditional conceptions of war in which armies faced each other in massed formation.[2] Kosovo demonstrated that air power alone was able to defeat an enemy. This victory came about in spite of scepticism that success would be unachievable without a ground component intervening.

Despite the differences between the two conflicts and the newspapers that reported them, the five propaganda themes to be discussed in Chapter 5 were consistently reproduced and have been utilized both in previous and subsequent conflicts. It is this reoccurrence, despite the opportunity for diversity, which is the subject of this analysis.

Defining why these propaganda themes appear in the British press is harder to establish. The obvious target for criticism is the official and integrated military policy in place to manage the news emanating from the theatre of operations. A second consideration is political pressure or influence, exerted both through the supply of information and legal restrictions defining what editors are able to publish. On the part of the newspapers themselves they have editorial policies in effect that dictate the overall thrust of coverage. In addition to this the human element, the role of the individual journalist, is also capable of influencing the content of press coverage of war. There is nothing essentially new here. Possibly the biggest shift with the growing stature of mass media has been the development of the role of journalists. In television media especially they often attain levels akin to celebrity status.

This thesis will demonstrate that the press as a result of self-censorship and a meeting of interests utilizes the propaganda themes predominantly with the information providers, notably the military or the government. Such a meeting of interests is also not a new phenomenon during conflict. As the Second World War progressed the British government saw the need to shift their propaganda policy from one demanding sacrifices to be made, seemingly by the lower classes, to the concept of a 'People's War'. These shifts were reflected in the propaganda messages emanating from films made during the period, which were intended to generate profits and entertain. Both groups had different agendas but had compatible interests.[3]

Propaganda themes are reproduced not because the relationship between the state and the media is antagonistic and incompatible, but because they serve a common purpose. Two examples appear to negate this assertion. The much used phrase the 'Vietnam Syndrome' provoked a reminder of how negative media coverage allegedly lost the United States government its domestic and international public opinion and subsequently the war in Vietnam. The Falklands Conflict provided a counter-example of media coverage of war where technology, geography, political and military will united to restrict severely the free-flow of information. The Falklands example prompted a reassessment of relations between the media and state. But these two crises represent the extremes of the relationship between state and media. In the case of the Falklands state control was easier to conduct and subsequently the journalists could point to overt censorship to explain the existence of propaganda. However, the relationship is essentially more cooperative than these examples would suggest.

The propaganda methods employed create a conflict narrative to place the campaign into context and develop an identifiable rhythm and progress to the war, allowing the reader to 'follow' the events and identify with its combatants. This identification can be positive, in the form of association with allied forces, or negative in the depiction of a demonized enemy. These elements are advantageous to both the British Government and the military leaders. The British press, who benefit from increased circulation figures and hence increased profits, also shares the advantages. In the same way as the relationship between the electronic media and the press is sustainable, so too should media–state relations be seen as complementary rather than conflicting.

Chapter 1 begins with an examination of the evolution of propaganda theory. Discussion of a term so widely wielded as that of propaganda requires definition before commencing upon a project of analysis. The chapter seeks to identify some of the established commentators on propaganda and plot the development of these theories since the start of the twentieth century. The chapter is intended to highlight some of the distinctions held between those commentators and demonstrates where one's own interpretation lies. This chapter will then form the theoretical basis upon which the subsequent discussion will be based.

Chapter 2 considers the role of the journalist and questions whether the reporter and the media have become more important to the conduct and public perception of war. Here the press is examined within the wider context of the mass media and with consideration to the human elements that influence it. From the evolution of the British media, through to the war reporter, media influence on the public and government policy, up to the newspaper in the modern era, the chapter explores some of the elements that explain the shifting media–military–state relationship and its influence upon the general public. The chapter highlights a worrying acceptance on the part of some to report emotionally rather than objectively. While such an approach, if overt, can be admirable, the continuing support of intervention during contemporary conflict is a concerning trend and appears to suggest a mutually compatible framework for the reporting of war.

Chapter 3 begins with an introduction to the two conflicts providing the necessary understanding of the events that constituted the crises. The chapter will draw out the distinctions between the two crises. Notably the escalation towards war is included in this discussion, as opposed to only focusing on the conflict from the point when Western troops were called into action. The escalation provided an opportunity to study press coverage without the most obvious influences of military intervention and enforced media restrictions. If propaganda themes were present in a period when the needs of national security, military censorship or patriotic allegiance were absent, or at least reduced, then the reasons for their existence must be found elsewhere. The chapter thus considers what makes the Gulf War and Kosovo Conflict useful for the study and interpretation of propaganda during war with reference to the technological changes the two conflicts heralded. The assumption that the greater range of media sources available actually enhances public understanding is challenged. Instead the continuities with previous conflicts with regard to media–state and military–public relations remained in place.

The contrast between media restrictions imposed by the military and self-censorship on the part of the British press is then addressed. Self-censorship is most easily identifiable before the commitment of British forces and the implementation of the official military restrictions. To comprehend whether or not journalists are effectively gagged by military policy the restrictions under which they work must be evaluated. These restrictions have evolved into the current military–media policy, crystallized in the form of the Ministry of Defence's (hereafter MOD) *Green Book*. While this document is often referred to in previous discussions it has not been methodically deconstructed. Thus, this chapter seeks to understand the framework within which media reporting of conflict involving British forces works. Analysis of this text discloses that the overriding principle of military–media relations is still that of operational security over the public's right-to-know. What the *Green Book* reveals is a greater acceptance on the part of the military to address media issues in light of an enhanced perception of its influence. But more significant than this is the shift of responsibility for reporting news within official guidelines away from military personnel and on to the journalists. This has the effect of increasing rather than decreasing the influence of the military on media flow by committing journalists to a set of guidelines that they must interpret and remain within. Non-adherence to these principles leads to the withdrawal of accreditation and access to the MOD military briefings that so often dominate the news agenda. This reality is in contrast to the perception fostered by the armed forces that it is the media and not the MOD that determines the nature of war reporting.

After establishing an historical overview and the media restrictions that apply during conflicts involving British forces, Chapter 4 then considers the newspaper coverage of the crises both before and after identifiable starting dates. These starting points are taken to be the moments at which the events became identifiable as a crisis through heightened awareness and not solely the point at which the British government committed itself morally or militarily. Examination of a period outside the remit of the *Green Book* is essential to counter the argument that newspapers only echo official policy because of overt restrictions. In doing so this discussion is also seeking to redress the analysis of conflicts that only focus upon coverage during Western involvement. The analysis before the starting points reveals little propaganda rhetoric aimed towards either Saddam Hussein or Slobodan Milosevic suggesting no underlying presuppositions or at least no preconceptions worthy of a sustained campaign of critical diatribe. From the starting events the two conflicts presented different challenges to providing legitimacy for intervention, legitimacy that is essential for propaganda to be effective. Up to the commencement of hostilities the newspapers' views mirrored government policy in their uncertainty and lack of criticism. This would suggest a compatibility of views or an unwillingness to express opinions outside of the official agenda. This compatibility is then most evident in coverage of the actual hostilities involving Western forces.

Following this understanding of the nature of the conflicts, Chapter 5 defines the five propaganda themes consistent in British newspaper coverage of the Gulf War and Kosovo Conflict. The themes support the pro-interventionist argument and construct the framework within which the hostilities are favourably presented. The first of them, the enemy leader figure, consists of two elements, namely personalization and demonization. Criticism of the enemy leader figure consists of both a rational and irrational element, the two are contradictory assessments but each is intended to fulfil specific propaganda requirements. These negative connotations are repeatedly contrasted with the positive attributes of figures within those forces allied against the enemy, to increase the disparity between them, thus further legitimizing the conflict. Historical persons are also evoked as points of reference, comparing and contrasting individuals to establish likenesses which themselves carry preconceived connotations for public opinion.

Forming an extension of the first, the second theme concerns the portrayal of the enemy. This can be in the form of military leaders, a particular race or section of society or, in its most extreme manifestation, an entire nation's population. This theme shares many of the same characteristics with the previous topic, including the rational and irrational descriptions of the belligerents' behaviour. An integral component of this theme is the use of the atrocity story that again utilizes historical examples to demonize the enemy. Such demonization is especially useful for justifying war on humanitarian grounds.

The third theme regarding military threat again contains a contradictory element like the rational and irrational depictions in the previous themes. The enemy's military threat and capabilities are both enhanced and downplayed to suit the desired propaganda objectives. The reasons for this seemingly incompatible approach are explored and their benefit to the propagandist explained.

Fourth, Western governments make use of a perceived international threat posed by the enemy nation. The establishment of a danger to either other neighbouring countries or a Western domestic population demands of the populace that action must be taken. This is achieved through reference to the destabilization that may occur if there is no intervention. Contained within this theme, for example, is the threat of terrorism. Since this research was undertaken subsequent conflict has seen this terrorist threat and the wider theme of international jeopardy rise to the fore of justifications for intervention by Western societies.

The final theme deals with the use of technology in war coverage. Despite the many benefits to the reporter and the military in depicting the conflicts the focus on technology in war can lead to a sanitization of conflict and make explanation of mistakes less convincing. Technology can hinder editorial control and make the coverage less intelligible for the public.

Together these five themes constitute a propaganda model that is employed in two very distinct conflicts and across a range of different newspapers. There is also evidence presented that these themes are by no means exclusively employed in these two crises alone. The identification of these points is intended to provide a unique and clear model for the understanding of propaganda in the British press during contemporary conflicts.

Chapter 6 discusses views evident in the press that are not directly concerned with the pro-interventionist agenda. The influence of the press on shaping policy during conflict is questioned, as are models designed to measure this. The diversity of characters that constitute the anti-interventionist body is such that the relevance of any bi-polar models to define opinion is challenged. The chapter proceeds to discuss whether the press is obliged to promote peaceful diplomatic solutions over armed intervention and explores the depiction of peace initiatives in the process. While omission and criticism of non-interventionist opinion constitutes the more obvious form of support for war, the press coverage also reveals a number of subtler techniques that reinforce the dominant ideology. This approach can also skew the public perception of the attitudes to conflict held by some organizations or individuals. An example of this, discussed in the chapter, is the selective quotation of material published by humanitarian organizations such as Amnesty International and Human Rights Watch. These are organizations that are regularly critical of Western policies during conflict and peace. However, the selective interpretation of their reports means they can often be employed in a way that appears to demonstrate a compatibility of interests between themselves and Western governments.

Despite the dominance of the pro-war argument in the light of the subjugation of opposition opinion, certain events demand a re-evaluation of the justification for war. Incidents such as the bombing of a shelter in Baghdad causing civilian deaths or the attack against the Chinese Embassy during the Kosovo Conflict are examples where the dominant perception is challenged by the reality of events. How the press copes with these obstacles is thus evaluated. Finally, the chapter discusses some of the criticism that has arisen since the conflicts and its implications for future war reporting.

The book is intended to provide a balance between highlighting the differences of both conflicts and each of the five newspapers, while at the same time demonstrating a distinct continuity in propaganda techniques. Arriving at the best balance between these variables proved to be a challenging undertaking. For a student of history attempting to balance subject matter and methodology more akin to the many social scientists that have written on the subject was difficult yet rewarding.

Less satisfying was the response from members of the media. Perhaps surprisingly I was able to obtain some limited information from members of the MOD. This was possibly due to the enhanced understanding of their need to foster good public opinion. Whatever the reason they were relatively receptive to my approaches. As for the media little positive response was obtainable. This was disappointing, as I had to rely on the interviews gained by other academic writers in their publications and on the ever-increasing literature from celebrity journalists themselves. At least in this respect I was able to base my comments not only on my personal observations, but also from their own words, albeit from secondary material.

The book argues of a continuing propaganda existence in our media and more specifically in the printed media. It has sought to identify a facet of media that has been overshadowed by recent technological developments and is designed to help redress the balance of academic discussion into a contemporary context. Although the book has been out-dated by way of recent conflicts the propaganda themes have been evident in Afghanistan and Iraq once more. The evidence presented here and in the printed media reinforces the conclusion that the printed media are pro-interventionist and support this interventionist agenda through self-censorship and by the implementation of established propaganda themes.

1

THE THEORY OF PROPAGANDA

The analysis of propaganda in contemporary conflict cannot be successfully contemplated without an understanding of the debates surrounding the notion of what constitutes propaganda. Space does not permit a detailed evaluation of the merits or otherwise of the masses of literature concerning propaganda. However, it is possible to identify a number of the more prominent debates surrounding the concept of propaganda. Through the exploration of a cross-section of the commentators, it is feasible to extract a number of contentious issues and establish a sense of the evolution of the term since the turn of the twentieth century.[1] Finally, this process will enable a definition of propaganda to use as the theory upon which the subsequent findings are based.

The subject has been addressed by academics from a number of disciplines, traversing philosophy, psychology, sociology, politics and history, with an equally diverse number of writers. Partly because of this multiplicity of interests the classification of the term has presented writers with a number of quandaries. These enquiries have stimulated the search for a definition of propaganda capable of general and wide acceptance.[2] Divisions over the classification occur between those who argue the definitions are too all-encompassing or conversely that they are overtly narrow and as such fail to provide a suitably general term for universal usage. Commentators have also argued about the chronological period within which modern propaganda exists and have discussed the issue from personal value-laden assumptions, which influence their treatment of the topic. Such conjecture can arise from the political role of propaganda in either a democratic or a totalitarian regime, or from positive or negative attributes assigned to the term propaganda itself. These predetermined attitudes are difficult to remove entirely and any definition will undoubtedly reverberate with the cultural and political influences of the time, much as propaganda itself requires timely cultural significance to be effective. However, this should not deter one from making such statements, albeit with a recognition of these influences and limitations.

The study of propaganda in the twentieth century came to the fore in the aftermath of the First World War. The widespread employment of methods

11

to alter public opinion stimulated both interest in its usefulness and fears about its power to manipulate the public. During the conflict, rumours had abounded on both sides pertaining to the atrocities carried out by the other.[3] In an effort to understand these issues, writers have sought to dissect the incidences of propaganda and formulate definitions based upon the reasons and the results of these attempts at manipulation. For a phenomenon aimed largely at human emotion and interpreted via cultural stimuli and personal responses, the term propaganda has largely defied any single scientific definition.

For the American psychologist Harold D. Lasswell writing in the 1920s the definition was simply; '[p]ropaganda is the management of collective attitudes by the manipulation of significant symbols'.[4] This brief assertion itself highlights some of the difficulties inherent in providing a suitable definition. His use of the phrase 'collective attitudes' was, Lasswell explains, an attempt to portray an understanding that denoted uniformity without the implication of any physical accord. This can nominally be understood to mean public opinion, a shared attitude without the necessity of actual physical proximity. By 'significant symbols' Lasswell was referring to any number of relevant stimuli evoked to generate a reaction. These stimuli could include images, reference to historical prejudices, notions of racial superiority, indeed any number of verbal or visual symbols invoked to elicit a desired response. While his approach may initially appear too brief to be useful this definition and his further discussion of the issue actually summarizes many of the key issues required.

Lasswell's definition is brief but his wider discussion of the topic reveals the inadequacies of simply providing a definition of propaganda without explaining the context within which it is set. Lasswell proposed that the ever-present function of propaganda in society had become evident because of the social disorganization brought about by rapid technological changes.[5] He therefore saw the efficiency of propaganda being increased through the modernization of society, or as he phrased it by 'the complication of our material environment through the expansion of technology'.[6] His comments are telling for he enters into another of the debates prevalent in the discussion of propaganda. The story of the evolution of propaganda mirrors the technological changes encountered in society. While it is accepted that propaganda in one form or another has existed through much of human existence, some theorists have sought to draw a distinction between modern and older forms of propaganda. These discussions are returned to later in this chapter, but the argument centres on the concept that modern propaganda is made possible by contemporary methods of information dissemination in an industrialized country. Lasswell asserts this distinction in his definition of propaganda.

Harold Lasswell's approach to the study of propaganda is significant for another reason. Despite writing relatively recently after the First World

War and the exposure of many propaganda falsehoods, his definition avoids bearing any preconceived notions of either negative, or indeed positive, connotations. For many people the word 'propaganda' conjures up a negative image, suggesting underhand manipulation of public thought, or simply outright lies. After the propaganda abuses witnessed in the First World War the image of the concept was not improved.

In contrast to Lasswell, another psychologist Leonard W. Doob created a classification of propaganda that incorporated within it a degree of negative moral judgement. Initially this had not been the case. In a book by Doob first published in 1935 his main emphasis had been placed upon defining the difference between intentional and unintentional propaganda.[7] The statements were devoid of any moral judgement pertaining to the motives of the propagandist. However, in his definition initially published in 1948, Doob asserts that '[p]ropaganda can be called *the attempt to affect the personalities and to control the behaviour of individuals toward ends considered unscientific or of doubtful value in a society at a particular time*'.[8] His utilization of the expression 'unscientific or of doubtful value' reinforces the negative implications of propaganda by suggesting that the aims of the propagandist are in some way harmful or not useful. This approach appears to ignore the fact that propaganda can occur where both parties benefit. If the propagandist's cause coincides with the advancement of the whole or part of society, it cannot be wholeheartedly condemned as being of doubtful value. Doob's description falls short of presenting a neutral-value definition of propaganda, insisting that its use can only be detrimental to society. One can only speculate as to the reason for this shift in his opinion. He may simply have revised his theory in the light of further contemplation. Alternatively, the influence of the Second World War could have altered his perception of the uses and intentions of propaganda and its makers.

Leonard Doob's psychological interpretation went to great lengths to describe the factors that influence and construct human behaviour. In his assessment, Doob recognized that much of public opinion stems from what he called 'enduring public opinion' or behaviour and attitudes learnt through socialization.[9] In doing so, his definition recognizes the role of culture and society in providing the foundations for propaganda as well as the stimuli to be manipulated for the desired response. Doob is also appearing to draw a distinction between differing methods of influencing public opinion. Propaganda is one element of this and a distinctly negative element as far as his analysis is concerned. Yet, without a definition free from assumption regarding the positive or negative outcome of propaganda, it is not possible to commentate on the nature of it without immediately providing a suspect moral judgement of the propagandist and their motive. Propaganda is a way of altering public attitudes; it is a tool to be utilized but it is not inherently negative.

By the 1960s, the difficult balancing act of constructing comprehensive yet well-defined descriptions of propaganda was being tackled by the philosopher Jacques Ellul. In his book, entitled *Propaganda*, Ellul identifies the evolution of thinking concerning propaganda in the United States.[10] He outlines the theoretical movement from Lasswell's psychological interpretation, consistent with the intellectual emphasis from 1920 to 1933, to the focus upon the intention of the propagandist. Ellul's interpretation seeks to reject the idea of turning to the psychologist for any comprehension of the term propaganda. His interpretation widens the acceptable scope of how propaganda can be utilized. He asserts that there is no difference between the propaganda practised in the name of democracy or that on behalf of a dictatorship, stressing that propaganda as a concept is compatible with either system of government. By avoiding the association of propaganda with either form of government some of the negative connotations of association with dictatorial regimes are avoided. During a period in which the West was in ideological struggle with Communism in the East this development is significant. This approach is consistent with Ellul's overall definition of propaganda in avoiding the negative associations implicated in Doob's classification. Part of the stigma surrounding the phrase is thus removed and consequently broadens the acceptable range of what influences and processes can be termed as propaganda.

Part of the process of expanding the notion of propaganda, its influences, effects and employment is to consider not only the 'top down' movement of manipulation, but also the reverse. Ellul argues that the propagandee has a positive role to play in the process and can indeed derive some satisfaction from the efforts of the propagandist. In claiming this reciprocal relationship, the approach removes the image of the recipient of propaganda as an automatic victim. Additionally, in keeping with the concept of removing predetermined negative assumptions, the propaganda can be seen at times to be of benefit to all or a part of society.

Ellul does share some common ground with Lasswell concerning their respective understanding of propaganda. Through stressing the role of the mass society in making modern propaganda possible, the two commentators emphasize the importance of seeing contemporary propaganda as a separate manifestation from earlier forms of the concept. Their opinions represent a school of thought that believes the evolution of society into a mass society, with the additional advances in disseminating information rapidly and widely, has altered the composition of propaganda. The debate has often divided opinion. Another proponent of this theory, Amber Blanco White, stresses explicitly the differences between modern and early forms of propaganda.[11] The study concludes that modern political propaganda has existed in its current form since the turn of the century.[12] The dominant divergence identified here is the more rapid dissemination of information that has altered incalculably the scope and effect of propaganda.

Against this assumption, Professor E. H. Carr cites another possible reason for an increased use of modern propaganda.[13] Carr points to the broadening basis of politics, a shift to a mass electorate that makes influencing a larger number of people worthwhile.[14] His theory thus suggests that modern mass propaganda now has greater benefits than before. It is not just a case of appealing to a mass audience 'because we can' but also 'because it is worth doing'. Interestingly, Carr maintained at the start of the Second World War that the political power still lay in the hands of those inhabitants of and near cities.[15] He also asserts that these people were the most accessible to propaganda, something that contemporary technology and information dissemination is perhaps beginning to redress. Carr appears aware of the potential for this state of affairs to alter and leaves room for such changes within his ideological framework. He notes the fact that technological advances force a re-evaluation of power over opinion during crises and propagandists are likely to re-evaluate strategy based on the advancement of technology. This is in keeping with current developments as contemporary shifts to visual media and the Internet have forced a reconsideration of the relationship between propaganda and conflict, a trend likely to continue.[16] Mass society, mass media and shifts in technology each contribute to the structure of modern propaganda and the changes must be seen as part of an ongoing process. In this respect, any definition of propaganda must be equally fluid to apply despite changes in society, unless, that is, one draws distinctions between different forms of propaganda dependent upon the chronological timeframe.

There is a further variable to this early twentieth century discussion of modern propaganda, according to Professor F. C. Bartlett.[17] Another psychologist, Bartlett cites the increasingly effective contact between persons in society, a situation enhanced by a combination of a mass society and developments in mass communication. In addition, he mentions the rapid spread of popular education as a factor in determining how propaganda is disseminated.[18] Where educational levels are low the propagandist resorts to dramatic visual images to stir the emotions of the populace.[19] In his example, Bartlett cites the Russian regime as one that is used to utilizing propaganda in this way. In contemporary society, regardless of levels of education, the propagandist, entertainer and television provider resort to dramatic pictures to invoke support and sustain interest.

Returning to Ellul, his concern with the development of technology was only partially focused upon its impact on propaganda. The grander theoretical beliefs identifiable in his wider works focus upon the relationship of technology and society in the modern era.[20] He stresses that technology poses a threat to the freedoms of the social order. His theory pertaining to propaganda, moulded in the same vein, is just one element of this.

The definition offered by Ellul, though sharing some common ground with Lasswell and others, is a more inclusive approach to the topic. His theory is defined thus, '[p]ropaganda is a set of methods employed by an organized group that wants to bring about the active or passive participation in its actions of a mass of individuals, psychologically unified through psychological manipulations and incorporated in an organization'.[21] This definition contains the main elements deemed necessary by many commentators for a successful definition of propaganda. The description reflects the evolution of both thought and history in influencing the understanding of what constitutes propaganda and what effects it can have. Having moved away from the incorporation of any moral judgements the above definition describes a group seeking to influence opinion to solicit participation in its actions or ideas.

By using the word 'passive' Ellul allows the range of public response to include not only active supporters of the propagandist's aims, but also those people willing passively to accept events and not challenge them. This is an important distinction, for the propagandist does not necessarily have to inspire every recipient to physical or mental action, he or she can simply be satisfied with the quiet acquiescence of a passive populace who are unwilling to challenge their policies or ideas.

In discussions that are more recent, those seeking a clearer definition of propaganda have challenged Ellul's approach. The authors Gareth S. Jowett and Victoria O'Donnell claim the interpretation Ellul offers is too pervasive to be of any great use.[22] In contrast their definition attempts to restrict the boundaries of what constitutes propaganda and produce a more concise terminology. The single most important factor altered by them is the requirement of premeditation. The pair asserts that the actions of the propagandist must be deliberate and planned. In light of this the definition they put forward states that '[p]ropaganda is the deliberate and systematic attempt to shape perceptions, manipulate cognitions, and direct behaviour to achieve a response that furthers the desired intent of the propagandist'.[23] In this classification, Jowett and O'Donnell restrict the scope of what can be regarded as propaganda to only those effects that are designed. This removes much from the discussion concerning *ad hoc* or reactionary impulses that, especially during crises, cannot be foreseen by the propagandist.

The inclusion of this statement is not accidental. The authors stress explicitly that in their opinion propaganda must be intentional. The wider ramifications for this are great and divisive for the student of propaganda. The argument espoused in favour of their understanding reads thus:

> *Deliberate* is a strong word meaning wilful, intentional, and premeditated. It carries with it a sense of careful consideration of all possibilities. We use it because propaganda is carefully thought out ahead of time in order to select what will be the most effective strategy to promote an ideology and maintain an advantageous position.[24]

In adopting this approach, Jowett and O'Donnell's widely used definition does enable a more manageable evaluation of propaganda. Their emphasis upon the requirement for a 'carefully thought out ahead of time' approach limits the range of what is considered to be propaganda. By doing this the authors hope to distance themselves from the more inclusive yet harder to define concepts of propaganda, such as Ellul's. However, the above interpretation, in my opinion, is too narrow a definition. Propaganda cannot always be clearly planned out in advance. Circumstances may force the propagandist's hand. The definition also asserts that propaganda is utilized to 'maintain an advantageous position' implying propaganda by a regime or leader. This appears to exclude groups with no advantageous position, and those seeking power as well as those already holding it employ propaganda.

Jowett and O'Donnell are not alone in contemporary efforts to refine the definition of propaganda to achieve a simpler classification. Further evidence of these attempts comes in John M. Mackenzie's 1984 study of propaganda and the British Empire. His description preceded Jowett and O'Donnell's by an equally adamant stressing of the necessity for propaganda to contain an element of intent:

> Propaganda can be defined as the transmission of ideas and values from one person, or groups of persons, to another, with the specific intention of influencing the recipients' attitudes in such a way that the interests of its authors will be enhanced. Although it may be veiled, seeking to influence thoughts, beliefs and actions by suggestion, it must be conscious and deliberate.[25]

Both Mackenzie's, and Jowett and O'Donnell's definitions, narrow the acceptable range of what can be defined as propaganda. They explain the occurrence of propaganda in terms easier to grasp than the open-ended suggestions of Ellul. These reinterpretations of the theory are reassuring in the sense that an author or coordinator of the propaganda messages can be seen as the chief source. In essence, there is an instigator, culpable and definable.

However, to suggest propaganda policy is necessarily premeditated and conscious means ignoring aspects of propaganda that appear in the media and elsewhere. Both the opinions above were written after the Falklands Conflict where a combination of deliberate censorship or delaying of material, combined with a monopoly of both information transmittal and access to the battlefield, allowed a systematic propaganda policy to be developed by the British government. Tight control of information and the way in which the news was presented was able to exist because of unique technological and geographic restrictions. Yet other factors existed that are not as clearly definable as a consistent propaganda policy. Editorial policy could arguably be described as systematic only if one suggests complicity with the government propagandists. In addition, marketing and cultural influences affect the way in which news is depicted, along with the influences of individual journalists. To assume propaganda only occurs when there is a deliberate, conscious and planned effort, can either ignore these numerous variables or assume each of the various stages of the media chain is equally culpable for overall propaganda strategy. Historically, Nazi propaganda can be viewed as a systematic and carefully planned process, and thus supports the assertions of those requiring a systematic basis for propaganda. However, in contrast to this, as Bartlett has identified, one has the propaganda campaigns of Italy and Russia during the inter-war period.[26] These states employed what can recognizably be deemed propaganda, yet it was *ad hoc* and evolved from each new emergency. As propaganda is based upon cultural phenomena constructed through socialization, as Doob suggests, some elements of propaganda can appear unconsciously and unexpectedly, yet they can still reinforce the responses caused by deliberate stimulus and constitute no lesser a form of propaganda.

Although it can be argued that such systematic and premeditated propaganda exists, propaganda is often reactionary or not provided by a single, uniform source. Where a number of sources emit the same propaganda themes, or an institution or group has to react to an event, propaganda may not be conforming to a rigid predetermined structure. The occurrence of contradictory propaganda, malleable enough to adapt to the requirements of crises or other events, lends itself more to the concept of reactionary rather than formulaic processes. Thus, a more liberal and fluid definition of propaganda is necessary.

Some contemporary authors have proposed a more expansive understanding of propaganda. Philip M. Taylor, while pursuing an examination of only the deliberate forms of propaganda in his expansive study of its history, recognized 'that much propaganda is accidental or unconscious'.[27] Taylor's suggestion that propaganda does not need to be deliberate fits with Ellul's more encompassing definition. The classification permits unintentional propaganda that in retrospect can be seen to have advanced the propagandist's cause, despite the fact that this benefit may only be seen in hindsight.

Philip Taylor's definition does not conform or contrast wholeheartedly with earlier classifications. Lasswell and Ellul's insistence on the existence of a modern mass society may have led them to disagree with Taylor's concept of assessing propaganda from the ancient world to modernity. Indeed, an additional variable to consider in any definition of propaganda is the provision of a chronological framework within which the definition is intended to be relevant. Kevin Robins, Frank Webster and Michael Pickering argue that it was during the pre-silicon era and not with the introduction of microelectronics that the development of an integrated propaganda system was facilitated and in doing so reiterate the assumptions of Ellul and Lasswell.[28]

Aspects of propaganda dissemination have been helped by greater population density and the improvement of media technology. However, these advances in society also improve contact between people and potentially provide greater opportunities to come into contact with a diverse range of opinions and information resources. The study of propaganda should certainly show an awareness of the shifting structure of society and nature of culture but not restrict itself to any specifically rigid time period. Society and culture are relatively fluid and any assessment of propaganda needs also to be suitably malleable and relevant over any given period. Ellul and Lasswell's assertion regarding the necessity for a modern society is an interesting subject and one that requires further investigation.

Taylor is not alone in modern efforts to produce a more flexible concept of propaganda theory. In light of this need for a more open definition of propaganda, the description adopted by Oliver Thomson sought a more liberal characterization:

> The phrase 'manufacturing of consent' favoured by Walter Lippmann and Noam Chomsky captures almost all that is necessary, but to cover all eventualities let us settle for the definition of propaganda as: *the use of communication skills of all kinds to achieve attitudinal or behavioural changes among one group of people by another.*[29]

Thomson's classification includes the method of transmitting propaganda as well as the effects sought by the protagonist. It avoids either negative or positive connotations concerning the motive of the instigator. Furthermore, his method bypasses the question of whether propaganda must be intentional. The reference in Thomson's definition to Lippmann and Chomsky is deliberate because his assertion regarding the evolution of the theory of propaganda returns to Chomsky later in the book:[30]

> In the final decade of the twentieth century the academic fashion remained in the Chomsky pattern of being concerned about mass manipulation by the forces of the right, by the establishment and by capital. But equally there were signs of widespread massive destabilization due to the loss of credibility in authority itself.[31]

In an extension to the evolution of propaganda in a mass society, increasingly consumer and capital driven, contemporary discussions relate to influences exerted by political and financial leaders. Suspicion then becomes focused on Western leaders and global companies for orchestrating propaganda campaigns. These suspicions have increasingly become a popular as well as an academic fashion. Recent discussion in the light of 11 September 2001, and the invasions of Afghanistan and Iraq have re-ignited public interest in propaganda and scepticism pertaining to the motives of governments and politicians. Much of the debate concerns the United States (hereafter US) government yet complicity with their foreign policy and an alleged sharing of ideals unites Britain and the US. These connections mean that the discussion of propaganda in one usually concerns the other, if only by association. Far from being an academic phenomenon, the popular appreciation of propaganda is fed by literature of the anti-establishment genre. Such texts as Sheldon Rampton and John Stauber's *Weapons of Mass Deception* seek to highlight the propaganda used in modern war and expose the falsehoods behind official rhetoric.[32] The book is critical of the 'perception management' that accompanies conflict and the media reticence for failing to engage in a free exchange of opinions.

A further example of this genre is *The Five Biggest Lies Bush told us about Iraq*.[33] The authors seek to assert the lies, and they are secure in their use of this word, extolled by George W. Bush in order to justify intervention in Iraq. The authors argue that US foreign policy in the post-Cold War era has sought to shape the world to its benefit and that Iraq is the opening 'test case' for this guiding principle.[34]

The style of these books and their single-minded discussion of events reinforce the widely held negative connotations of propaganda use. However, at the same time as exposing official propaganda the books constitute a piece of propaganda literature by advancing the cause of those opposed to intervention. Arguably, this is a positive move to redress the balance of information. The authors justly believe an alternative opinion needs to be voiced. They may suggest their opinions are beneficial to society and they certainly have value in providing an alternate opinion so often missing from conflict coverage. However, the fact remains they are seeking to influence the opinion of another group in a manner that can be construed as propaganda. In light of this, one is left to question whether propaganda should always be classed as detrimental to the public good and be permanently assigned negative connotations. The end to which it is used distinguishes between positive and negative propaganda. Furthermore, propaganda cannot simply be seen as good or bad, the point remains that someone seeks to gain by its use and thus it is not entirely negative for society in its entirety.

It would be remiss, having analysed a sample of propaganda theories above, to offer no definition herein. The debate concerning modern or ancient propaganda seems an irrelevance if one is to adopt the position that some form of propaganda has existed for longer than the start of the twentieth century. Changes in technology have altered the capabilities and mechanisms of propaganda and will continue to do so. A definition of propaganda, in my opinion, should also allow for the cultural influences on society that engrain certain propagandist messages in each of us.

The efforts to manipulate public opinion can be regurgitated without the individual necessarily being consciously aware. Propaganda is a message and this may be predetermined for a propagandist's requirements, but it can be disseminated through numerous channels not all of which are equally culpable. The culpability arises when the message is not questioned and then passed on, or when there is evident complicity with the aims of the propagandist. Thus, propaganda can be both intentional and unintentional.

The diversity in the conduits of propaganda dissemination reflects a need for a multifaceted and flexible propaganda system. This system needs to be adaptable to the changing shifts in circumstances, especially during conflict when events are likely to alter drastically in short periods. Although systemized propaganda will continue to survive, not all propaganda will exist because of a predetermined structure.

Faced with such adaptability any singular definition of propaganda cannot reasonably expect to be all encompassing. Any definition must reflect this; propaganda techniques demand versatility as well as imagination and common sense. While no single classification can hope to remain without its critics, the following definition will suffice for the purposes of this thesis:

Propaganda is the conscious or unconscious attempt by the propagandist to advance their cause through the manipulation of the opinion, perception and behaviour of a targeted group.

The definition proposed here seeks to provide a suitably broad definition, yet will obviously prove too large in scope for those people who prefer a more limited classification. As discussed above, propaganda can be either conscious or otherwise. Where a middle party regurgitates propaganda disseminated from another source, such as the media, the accusation of conveying propaganda can still be levelled. This becomes even more apparent when commentators fail to analyse the information they put forward. Furthermore, both the information provider, for example military sources, and the disseminator may stand to gain from the propaganda. In this way, both groups seek to advance their cause.

By advancing their cause, the propagandist seeks to alter the opinion of the targeted group, such as the public at large, and their perception of an issue. The word behaviour is deliberately chosen to signify a range of reactions. The targeted group may indeed take positive action or quietly acquiesce and offer no resistance to the information with which they are confronted.

This definition alone, without context, would still leave many questions unanswered. It is important to identify who and what the *cause* of the propagandist is, how the *manipulation* is being conducted and through what channels, before assessing how the *behaviour* of the other group is affected in each example. It is also tempting to view such a definition in a linear and vertical fashion, with the state and its objectives at the top and the media providing the conduit for the *manipulation* of the public's *behaviour*. Such an approach is too restrictive as propaganda can occur on any number of levels and be carried out by any group.

Despite the numerous interpretations and statements, one must always bear in mind a single identifiable feature. It is the efforts of the propagandist to *advance their cause* by manipulating text, images, symbols and data which distinguishes the act from other forms of conveying information.

2

NEWSPAPERS, THE REPORTER AND THE WIDER CONTEXT

Introduction

After understanding the propaganda theory necessary to place this research into context, one must also define the role of the press within the grander elements of the media. Newspapers do not solely share a relationship with official sources in a sterile environment. Even during the relatively short period between the two conflicts considered herein changes have occurred that need to be evaluated in order to assess the significance of what is printed. This chapter seeks to incorporate the wider considerations of a media infrastructure that appears multifaceted yet produces clearly coherent propaganda themes. The research seeks to identify the relevance of newspapers in the modern era and by extension demonstrate the relevance to the student of propaganda in analysing such printed media.

Initially, this discussion examines the evolution of the media as an entity in Britain. This will involve a brief understanding of the historical relationship between technological advancement in society and the subsequent relevance for the evolution of a coherent national press in Britain. The development of a mass society has arguably fostered the environment within which contemporary propaganda is effective. As technological advances that facilitated the emergence of a national press came about, so too did the possibilities for propaganda dissemination increase. This relationship has developed into contemporary society where technology and propaganda continue to evolve.

Advancements in technology have generated a number of watersheds in subsequent conflicts, each building upon the foundations of the other. These watersheds relate to the development of weapons, the evolution of combat and international defence and the advances that facilitate the evolving nature in which each conflict is reported. Nevertheless, despite these changes the British press and the media as a whole remain reliant on the one consistent element of reporting conflict, the role of the war reporter. This factor further exacerbates the potential for news stories to be influenced by previously held moral assumptions; either because of immediate war propaganda or established prejudices and language embedded during years of national propaganda rhetoric.

In a consumer society increasingly demanding entertainment, even during news broadcasts, the celebrity journalist has risen to prominence. Not only do they represent national identity on the screen but also literature written post-conflict often purports to tell the real story. Not only does this increase the interrelationship between journalism and history, such publications also raise the question of why the real story was not reported at the time. The existence of such material also highlights the complexities behind news coverage and serves as evidence to an individual's alternative motivation for remaining in a war zone. This development is not inherently negative or even particularly new; however, when this is combined with a journalistic trend on the part of some to report in relation to personal moral codes, the influence of an individual reporter is potentially exacerbated. Movement towards a 'journalism of attachment' during conflict can effectively support official policies as well as running contrary to the propagandist's comparisons between a free Western democratic press and the biased reportage emanating from the despotic enemy's realm. The lines between objectivity and assimilation into the national cause can become distinctly clouded.

The chapter will then examine the relationship between the media, government policy and public opinion. The contrast between the Western depictions of the positive elements of democracy versus the negativity of totalitarianism is highlighted. Though an admirable component of the structure of society during peacetime, military commanders often continue to view a free media as a distinct disadvantage during conflict. In this respect, the battle for favourable public opinion is increasingly conscious of the need to generate positive media relations. The focus of conflict moves to the domestic sphere, a result of, and a factor in, the movement towards limited conflicts, where lowering the potential for Western casualties ranks alongside the implementation of effective policy to win a conflict.

Concern with the domestic sphere and the war for legitimacy is waged through the media against the backdrop of an international audience. As media becomes a worldwide commodity, the propaganda war and the process of diplomatic relations is conducted partially through media channels. In this respect, the Gulf War and Kosovo Conflict display continuity with previous conflicts in the twentieth century, where propaganda replaced conventional diplomacy..

Finally, the argument will seek to distinguish between the media as an entity and assess the relationship between the press and modern visual media. The assumption that movement towards modern visual media has negated the efficiency of the newspaper as a conduit for propaganda is challenged. Modern media has not become more diverse as a result of a greater number of outlets and round-the-clock news coverage. Instead, many of the advantages envisaged by such developments have benefited the press.

Overall, the press remains a vital component of the media chain and complements rather than rivals other media channels. For the propagandist, the newspaper remains a vital component in the battle for public opinion.

The evolution of mass media and war reportage

Newspapers evolved in line with historical and technological developments that aided the expansion and influence of the press. As with the evolution of war technology new methods have been sought to report upon and transmit news across the globe. However, such developments have not necessarily continued to facilitate the coverage and public reception of all media. Recently, new technology has questioned the ability of newspapers to provide relevant news and compete with popular television coverage. The development of media into a mass phenomenon has mainly come about due to technological advances. More immediate and visual forms of technology, which facilitate television and Internet news coverage, have seemingly diminished the relevance of newspapers in modern society.

The reality is somewhat different. The apparent levels of saturation coverage occurring in the media appear to demonstrate an enhanced understanding of world events. In contrast to this perception, the media remains event driven, relying on the spectacular, rather than the evolutionary, to provide news coverage. Because of this, news coverage continues to appear erratic. The media is also still reliant upon human activity, through the processes of news selection, interpretation and emotion. In these respects newspapers are not such an antiquated mode of news analysis as could possibly be argued.

Technological evolution initially supported the development of mass newspapers. The first modern newspapers began to appear in Britain during the 1830s and were achievable and desirable due to the evolution of technology and the development of mass society. Cheaper and more readily available paper paved the wave for slow hand-printing processes to be replaced by faster methods capable of satiating the demands of a growing domestic population. With the advent of the Fourdrinier machine, installed in London in 1803, and advances in the reliability of printing processes, large-scale printing became achievable.[1] This development was followed by the first practical powered printing press when in 1810 Fredrich Koenig combined steam power with the printing press, thus increasing the output capabilities further.[2] In this respect, the advancement of modern technology facilitated the publication of mass literature. These advancements were combined with the nineteenth-century expansion of the railway network, speeding up the distribution process and enabling the birth of a national press.

The establishment of mass media increased the opportunity for wider dissemination of facts; however, this societal change also aided the manipulation of mass public opinion. Commentators such as Lasswell and Ellul have argued that the changes to the structure of society into a mass society are essential for propaganda to exist.[3] Conversely, writers such as Taylor have sought to trace themes of propaganda back to much earlier ante-cedents.[4] The development of a mass society, informed by a cohesive, national press, has obvious ramifications for the development of national public opinion. Mass society provides a dual influence upon the concept of propaganda; increasing exposure to coherent and managed information while at the same time providing the illusion of greater choice and a variety of analysis. That is not to say that propaganda can only function in these environments; Taylor successfully describes a history of propaganda that precedes mass society. Despite these differences, the writings of Ellul and Lasswell retain relevance to the current understanding of propaganda in society.

As technology advanced during the late 1840s and early 1850s, the global electronic telegraph allowed for the creation of news agencies such as Reu-ters in 1851. Because of this news can begin to be understood in circum-stances in addition to single national perspectives. News may always have required stimulus and input in addition to traditional conceptions of the nation state, but the development of technology increased the scope of achievable newsgathering and dissemination.

The development of warfare cannot be understood without an under-standing of technological advances in weaponry. In the same respect, media and technology are intertwined. Propaganda, the media, conflict and society influence each other and cannot be viewed in isolation, in this respect an understanding of propaganda needs to adopt an interdisciplinary approach to be accurate. To support this assertion one only has to look at the breadth of commentators who have written upon elements of propaganda in the media, their number including those with backgrounds in the social sciences, media and cultural studies, politics and government, as well as history.

Despite advancements in technology, the media still relies on human inter-pretations of events. The advent of the mass circulation newspaper subse-quently saw the related development of the journalist, or more specifically in the context of this discussion, the war reporter.[5] The most widely cited starting point for the history of early British war reportage is the well-documented efforts of William Howard Russell during the Crimean War 1854–56. Russell was critical of the conduct of the British campaign in his pieces written for *The Times*. In response to this the then Commander-in-Chief, Sir William Codrington, issued a general order in February 1856 that forbade the publication of information deemed valuable to the enemy. Thus, as Philip Knightley has argued, the Crimean War can be seen as the origin of modern military censorship.[6] In essence, the Crimean War became the first media war and as such displays continuity with contem-porary efforts to emphasize the novel nature of each subsequent conflict in terms of military, technological or a combination of 'firsts'.

The Gulf War and the Kosovo Conflict perpetuated the established pre-dilection for the involvement of significant firsts in conflict. The First World War had seen the arrival of Total War, while the Second World War had heralded the arrival of the atomic bomb. Conflicts that are more contemporary have sustained this evolution. From the 1960s, the emergence of television meant a gradual eclipse of newspapers as the primary source of news for the majority of the population of Britain. The rise in instant tele-vision coverage and the influence of the Internet dominate contemporary discussions of the Gulf and Kosovo campaigns.

Media technology advances do not only affect the perception of conflict. Changes in the nature of warfare have also altered both the ability to cover war and the style in which it is reported. The First and Second World Wars presented a fight for national survival not evident in later twentieth-century conflicts involving British armed forces. The post-1945 Cold War era, whereby a bipolar ideological conflict defined the nature of hostilities, has been surpassed with the collapse of the Soviet Union. Even during the relatively short time span between the Gulf War and the Kosovo Conflict, it is evident that different military, political and ideological incen-tives for justifying entry into hostilities have formed. Furthermore, once conflict has begun its nature is also susceptible to change. The Gulf War eventually required a decisive ground offensive, a move initially deemed unimaginable in some early press reports. The Kosovo Conflict was fought from the air alone, shattering the widely held assumptions that the successful outcome of such conflicts was not militarily viable. To add further differen-tials, Kosovo operations were fought under NATO command unlike the US-led forces in the Gulf War. In these respects, the nature of a conflict introduces a further variable into the influences affecting media coverage of hostilities.

The character of conflict has shifted in focus away from massed military formations attempting to utilize tactical equilibrium to sustain international peace, as during the Cold War. Instead, British, and usually American, operations have predominantly begun to rely upon technological superiority to inflict defeat with the minimum of risk to Western forces. Such develop-ments affect the way in which conflict is presented to and accepted by an audience. In essence, as Michael Ignatieff argues, this movement has brought about the development of a concept of virtual war.[7] Western publics are shielded from the reality of hostilities by sanitized news coverage and by a sanitized version of combat in which only the enemy appears to suffer greatly. This suffering, however, is not portrayed in human terms compar-able with Western losses. The enemy is dehumanized through propaganda and the destruction deemed acceptable whereas public opinion constrains the acceptable number of Western casualties.

Modern technology enables the presentation of conflict in a computerized style, both distorting the reality of war and lending itself to presentation using visual media. With an increased military specialization and reliance on the high-tech, it is becoming harder for journalists to comprehend fully the military hardware being used. Difficulties in understanding the technology employed are compounded by media constraints that hinder the number of reporters permanently employed to cover specific areas, such as defence. Society then further compounds the gap between civilian and military comprehension as an absence of any formal military experience in many cases exacerbates this lack of military understanding. The problem of non-specialized knowledge of defence issues is best illustrated by the *Daily Mail*'s coverage of the Gulf War. Owing to visa difficulties, it was necessary to send Richard Kay, their Royal Correspondent, to cover the events in the Gulf.

The lack of an established worldwide network of reporters in distinct locations can in turn lead to accusations of erratic selection of newsworthy items. In an environment where media coverage appears to be operating at saturation level, there is a temptation to believe in the concept that coverage should be all encompassing. Yet, the existing contemporary academic and popular debates have stressed the commercial demands imposed on the press. Coverage of events often appears erratic, presenting the modern world as chaotic, without structure, and prone to sudden international flash-points. This is caused, according to Philip Taylor, by the media's random approach to selecting newsworthy items. Taylor explains:

> [O]ther people's war appear to erupt from nowhere on our television screens until the crisis subsides, and the media lose interest. The causes and consequences of those crises rarely command media attention. This leaves the impression of a chaotic and turbulent world when, in reality, there is an 'order' functioning in the invisible background of daily global life. But order is hardly newsworthy. It is the crises, the coups, the famines, the earthquakes, which make the headlines.[8]

Newspapers are event driven and cover conflict only as long as it remains an asset to the commercial and entertainment value of the media product. Events sell papers and keeping reporters on location to cover unfolding stories methodically wastes resources and fails to warrant column inches. This argument is not confined to newspapers and appears consistent with commentary concerning the wider media. As Nik Gowing of BBC World explains, 'the response of news organisations at all levels has become increasingly variable and unpredictable . . . a crisis in one part of the world can easily be viewed elsewhere as irrelevant'.[9] However, to suggest this is a new phenomenon is somewhat misleading. While it is necessary to stress the erratic appearance of news reportage one must not assume that this is a significantly new development. The piecemeal representation of events, filtered through editorial processes and the limitations of time and space, is merely the continuation of a traditional approach to journalism. The perception that this issue is greater in the modern era stems from the plethora of news sources available to the public. Greater coverage does not necessarily equate to broader or more in-depth appreciation of world events. When events do appear on the news agenda the surprise is exacerbated simply by the belief that news should be more comprehensive, rather than the actual reality of the nature of coverage.

The development of a mass society and coexisting advances in technology have seemingly shifted the balance of media power in favour of the visual and instant forms. Technology, initially an ally of the mass-produced national newspaper, now seemingly favours modern forms of information dissemination. However, it remains difficult to assess the content of newspaper coverage of crises without accepting the random elements that combine to force a news story into a newspaper. One must accept that the commercial and editorial constraints in place mean that news remains inherently selective and event driven. The necessity for news to be witnessed and interpreted by humans perpetuates traditional processes of news dissemination. While the contemporary mass media presents the facade of a comprehensive global information provider the reality of news content and the processes by which it is cultivated is little different to the early emergence of the press. In this respect, the newspaper appears to be little more disadvantaged than before. What becomes more relevant to the discussion of news dissemination is the role of the journalist whose profile can extend beyond traditional national borders as the media assumes global influence.

The war correspondent

The unpredictability of press coverage during conflict is sustained by the personal influence of reporters. In some respects, war reporters can influence the coverage, content, context and public perception of conflict. On other occasions, despite the efforts of individuals, the overriding perception of conflict is still dominated by the military leaders who conduct it and the editorial policies of the domestic media. The fact that this consideration is applicable to both written and visual media reduces some of the variations between the formats. The development of technology has failed to remove the occurrence of human error during conflicts in much the same way as it has failed to nullify the influence of individuals on news output. The war correspondent can not only affect the slant of coverage given to any particular news item, but can also become an intrinsic part of that coverage. Conflicts offer unique opportunities for reporters to impose themselves on a news story and the increasingly entertainment-orientated media has promoted the development of celebrity reporters. This situation challenges traditional benchmarks for independent and detached journalism. During conflict, national bias and personal opinion can often sour the objectivity of news coverage.

As already established, events make the news and even the commencement of an international crisis can prove to be non-newsworthy at times. The elongated diplomatic negotiations and troop build-ups provide little in the way of exciting news items and reporters often face the challenge of having to fill vital column inches. It is during this period that reporting may become particularly susceptible to personalization on the part of the correspondent in the field. The demand for entertaining news is great. This partially explains why technology often dominates early discussions of international crises as an entertaining alternative to the detailed evaluation of diplomatic wrangling. Espousing the various technological wonderments of military hardware will only be sustainable up to a point. During the Gulf War, a period of five months elapsed between Iraq's invasion of Kuwait and the commencement of Operation Desert Storm. Within this period and beyond, emotion, conjecture and opinion were increasingly demanded to satisfy the demands of a news hungry media. Alternatively, the story can fall from the news agenda, a move often adopted by tabloid newspapers. The event then explodes back onto the scene with each notable intervention and in doing so exacerbates the perception of events in chaotic terms.

The human storyteller is not only in evidence during crises or in their often-protracted escalation. The reporter as news story has even proceeded conflicts and extended into the history books, literally. Recently there have been numerous books written after the conflict attempting to expose the truth behind events.[10] This raises the issue about the motivation of reporters during conflict. While it might seem appropriate to assume the sole consideration of a reporter is their press obligations, this is not always the case. For example, John Simpson of the BBC explained why he decided to remain in enemy territory during the Gulf War:

> A variety of things kept me in Baghdad: a sense of duty; *the fact that I was writing a book*; the knowledge that if I left others would feel obliged to stay behind and do my job; curiosity. . . . I rather expected I was going to die, but equally I thought that if I survived I wouldn't be haunted by the feeling that I had let myself and others down.[11]

A significant consideration for his continued reporting of the conflict concerned his desire to write a book about events. Simpson's revelation illuminates the existence of external motives for journalists covering a conflict. These motives introduce a number of questions about the role of the war reporter. Having been based in Iraq during the Gulf War, he may have felt the need to explain events after conflict when the direct influence of enemy censorship was removed.

Nevertheless, one is left to question the extent to which untold stories exist because of a desire to produce such publications after an event, rather than reporting extensively during it. At what point can the omission of facts through the imposition of censorship traverse the divide into self-censorship in order to generate interesting debate after the crisis? The question is extremely difficult to answer without understanding the workings of an individual's mind. However, the fact, for whatever reason, that an untold story should be required must act as a warning against believing in the omnipresent media coverage of conflict.

A further human-related element of war reporting is the assimilation of Western correspondents with military forces. The war reporter operates within difficult circumstances that also influence the manner in which coverage is construed. Often the assimilation of the media with Western forces can influence their interpretation of events. Aware of this situation military leaders actively plan for the attachment of correspondents to the military. Individuals isolated with certain units or behind enemy lines cannot achieve a clear understanding of the wider context of events. Despite having a reporter on the scene, the collation of reports is undertaken on the domestic front and through the military channels that disseminate their own information. Thus, while first-hand reports may be available the wider perception of the conflict is moulded by editorial processes set in the Western countries, or, more worryingly, the agenda is dictated by the Western military forces.

In conflicts that are increasingly depicted in virtual terms, the war reporter remains part of the human face of conflict and individuals naturally react to events in a variety of ways. During this process, the war correspondent is in danger of becoming the event. The difficulty appears to be disassociating the personalized feelings generated from the circumstances. John Simpson draws attention to these complications although he was quick to dismiss any notion of personalizing events through the description of proceedings affecting him. He recalls one such occasion where his image threatened to dominate the news story during a broadcast back to the studio in London on the day he had accidentally broken his ribs:

> David Dimbleby, at the other end, asked me if there had been any casualties from the day's attacks. Irritably, I said that I had cracked a couple of ribs and was the only casualty I knew of. This was apparently taken in London to be a coded message meaning that I had been beaten up. I was deeply embarrassed. Having long disliked the journalist-as-hero school of reporting, I found myself a minor celebrity for something which hadn't taken place. An entire country's economic and military power was being dismantled, its people were dying, and I was broadcasting about a couple of cracked ribs. Each time they hurt I felt it was punishment for breaking the basic rule: don't make yourself a part of the story.[12]

Despite his protestations, Simpson's image dominates news items that he reports, becoming synonymous with the BBC's conflict analysis. His subsequent books have emphasized this depiction of himself as both a reporter of and component of news events. He is part of a growing number of celebrity journalists, many of whom have a number of publications to their name. The most recent crisis in Iraq saw the emergence of Rageh Omaar, BBC World correspondent, as the latest in this line of recognizable war reporters.

This development is not inherently a negative progression, much in the same way that propaganda does not necessarily produce negative outcomes. Where the criticism does appear justifiable is on the occasions where impartiality is rejected consciously. The objectivity of journalists cannot, if it ever has been, be taken for granted. Martin Bell, for example, promotes the idea that good 'journalism is the journalism of *attachment*. It is not only knowing, but also caring'.[13] This approach to journalism moves on from the necessity of having human beings to witness and interpret news. In its place, Bell's philosophy actively encourages war reporters or journalists as a whole to become emotionally attached to their news story. In doing this the possibility of objectivity being discarded in favour of an emotional response is heightened.

This desire to involve oneself emotionally in the story can be understood in terms of the chronological context of the statement. For instance, Kate Adie sees the development of this form of journalism because of historical evolution. In the same way as international tensions shift and technological developments alter the context with which war is presented, the development of journalism of attachment is also part of a process. Adie argues such journalistic fashions are the result of over fifty years of peace in the United Kingdom, during which time 'there has been a greater scope for a more sensitised attitude to tragedy and death'.[14] In this respect, reporting becomes more about what the reporter feels about the situation and introduces a moral value judgement into the news item. When the judgement is carried on a supposedly impartial channel such as the BBC, the comments are more damaging than the accepted political and editorial bias assumed of newspapers.

This situation appears contrary to the propaganda efforts of the Western powers to contrast the tolerant and objective principles of democracy against the restraints of totalitarian regimes. Sympathetic or empathetic journalism may be useful in some circumstances, such as stirring emotional sensibilities during intervention based upon humanitarian justifications. Overall, however, a loss of objectivity and impartiality undermines the West's desire during conflict to promote its liberal ideals. More specifically reporting that is not objective diminishes the moral high ground assumed by those championing the ascendancy of democratic rule. Philip Hammond emphasizes the difficulties and problems that are associated with this trend.

He notes the problem of journalists becoming the story, losing dispassion and reporting their emotional reaction to an event.[15]

When a reporter becomes involved in a story it can lead to a loss of objectivity and an immersion into the surroundings. The military use the process of assimilation to incorporate embedded journalists into the daily activities of the soldiers. In addition to producing a sense of empathy with the service men or women, the reporter's survival can become dependent upon their relationship with Western forces. As well as the more obvious effects of undermining objectivity the journalist may become caught up in the atmosphere in which they are working and lose sight of the domestic influences of their work. Attachment leads inevitably to detachment from the wider perspective of events and from the home nation.

This detachment can lead to a sense of losing contact with the domestic audience and editorial policies of the media back in the home nation. After reading a *Sun* newspaper article while reporting during the Gulf War for the *Daily Mail*, Richard Kay explains that half a dozen 'weeks or so had intensified the feeling of belonging to a special sort of family. Tales from Fleet Street suddenly began to seem a long way away'.[16] Kay's detachment may have been exacerbated by his unfamiliarity with war reporting, but he remained aware of his part in the immersion into events. Despite this realization, Kay dismisses the notion that assimilation within the military set-up presented any conflict of interest. Writing about his experiences in the Gulf War, Kay asserts that he offers no apologies 'for writing "my side". The idea of meeting out overtly evenhanded reporting is naïve in the extreme – we were part of the war effort. Presumably the Iraqis had their MRTs (Media Reporting Teams) too'.[17] Kay argues it is naïve to believe reporting during war can be impartial and uses a comparison with the Iraqi system of media to justify his assertion.[18] However, it is an anomaly to defend his style of reporting by introducing the example of Iraqi MRTs. Comparison with the Iraqi media contradicts Western assumptions of the credible superiority of the free press. Freedom was, after all, a justification for intervention in the war itself, a war that the majority of British press opinion supported. However, what Kay is emphasizing is the human element of war reporting, the inability or lack of desire amongst journalists to detach themselves from their environment, upon which, after all, their lives may depend.

Kay is not alone in his attitude towards the responsibility of journalists during war. Max Hastings, writing about his life covering conflicts, insists it is wrong to reject censorship. His comments concerning the Falklands War focus upon the question of national security. He doubts the abilities of journalists to decide for themselves what information is safe to be published. His attitude is summed up clearly, arguing that whatever 'the follies of censorship in the Falklands, and there were plenty, none of the sensible journalists on the islands doubted its necessity'.[19] In this respect, Hastings accepts the idiosyncrasies inherent in the censorship system. In light of contemporary conflicts the Falklands presented greater challenges to the war reporter than has been witnessed since, not least because of the military's sole control over the means of communication from the Task Force to mainland Britain. However, despite this he is willing to excuse the censorship policy as a whole. He then utilizes a method favoured by propagandists when dismissing the opinions of those opposed to intervention. Hastings suggests the necessity of these rules is not doubted by sensible people.

Max Hastings' opinions on the Falklands War are based on the dominant assumption that censorship is required to safeguard military lives. Any assimilation with the British forces is part of this process and a willing acceptance of the military knowing what best constitutes a threat to security. During the Gulf War, his rejection of journalists' opinions that continually slated the military commanders appears to be less reliant upon the strictures of military security. Instead he remained unconvinced of the need to display objectivity because of his personal conviction that Saddam Hussein was an 'evil man'.[20] His willingness openly to admit this conviction based upon personal opinion could reflect the move towards the validity of Bell's form of journalism of attachment.[21] Hastings is clear about his reasons for supporting the conflict and supporting British troops, but the question remains whether other coverage is tainted by personal motives without the writer declaring this openly. Whether right or wrong the fundamental distinction remains, while it could be readily assumed that Iraqi information would be tainted by national policy, through the existence of their totalitarian regime and the repeated assertions of Western policymakers, could it readily be assumed that Western coverage was slanted by national pride?

Interpretation of the above discussion should not be taken as an assertion that all news coverage is affected in this manner. The degree to which acceptance of association with the military is tolerated is not a foregone conclusion and it is subject to change. It is not my objective to assert that Western media coverage of conflict systematically panders to official policy although greater even-handedness when describing influences upon media output would be welcome. Just as with any historical interpretation an understanding of change as well as continuity must be appreciated. The willingness of reporters to participate and cooperate with the military forces alters on judgements often made by the individual reporters. Hammond, for example, has argued that a willingness or otherwise to depend upon the military is related to the degree of scepticism with which those authorities are viewed in the conflict concerned. He utilizes the following examples of the 1990–91 Gulf War and the 1992–95 Bosnian War to substantiate this hypothesis:

> You know that journalists complained about the pool arrangements in the Gulf, in some cases risking life and limb to escape Western military 'minders'; whereas in Bosnia reporters called on the UN

military to provide just such a pool system. Why is this? I think it's because in the Gulf at least some reporters viewed the Western military with mistrust; whereas in Bosnia they often felt they were on the same team.[22]

The difference between these attitudes towards military intervention could be explained partially by the peacekeeping nature of military duties in the Bosnian War. The conflict appeared to consist of a definable enemy and the Western forces were viewed favourably in light of their non-belligerent basis for intervention. The above example also demonstrates the influence of a human moral value judgement about the credibility of intervention even before reporting has begun. It is evident that the influences under which the reporter files his or her news story need to be comprehended. This comes not only in the form of MOD guidelines and official censorship, but also in the less definable realms of day-to-day interaction between reporters, the military and their sources of information. Perhaps the best way of overcoming allegations of cooperation with authorities in return for safe passage would be simply to make clear to the public the conditions under which a report was produced.

While it is assumed that enemy media under state control are censored it must also be made clear that allied reporting has unseen influences. Geoff Meade, TV-AM's chief reporter during the Gulf War, has pointed out media management 'is subtler under the Allies, but only a little less effective. We had to work within the rules, for to refuse to abide by them would invite withdrawal of credentials and a ticket home'.[23] The authorities that journalists often have to live with are also major, if not the main, sources of their information. That the military provided the security and ground rules as well as the briefings and utilization of these media channels often caused a degree of despair. As Peter Goff and Barbara Trionfi have explained in their book regarding the Kosovo Conflict, the reporters 'covering the NATO briefings felt an escalating sense of frustration and irritation that the events were primarily platforms to disseminate sound-bites and NATO propaganda aimed at consolidating the alliance'.[24] It is difficult to comprehend the restrictions and difficulties encountered by human beings during the reporting of conflict. Human elements undoubtedly influence the output of media and the restrictions of war and the demands of a hungry media machine compound these difficulties. However, while reporters may have been exasperated by the propagandized output of the NATO media machine, the British press was largely uncritical of the process at the time of conflict. If the above feelings were widespread, the reaction against it as seen in the media content is minimal. The propaganda may have been received with frustration, but it was reproduced without allusion to this irritation.

If such mistakes are to be avoided in the future, positive action needs to be pursued. A simple and straightforward approach would be to adopt the same information warnings afforded to the enemy to Western correspondents during conflicts. In times of war, reports from hostile nations often carry a disclaimer notifying the viewer or even reader to the influence of censorship on the report. In addition to explicit reference there has to be a growing willingness voluntarily to provide the Western public with an understanding of the restrictions incurred during conflicts. To achieve coherence Alex Thomson of Channel Four recommends that the media have 'a responsibility to tell viewers the basis upon which they're getting their news and I think all news programmes failed to do that during the operation of the pool system'.[25] Matthew Kieran of the University of Leeds stresses that 'journalists are under an obligation to make clear in what way they are interpreting the event concerned'.[26] In his approach, Kieran recognizes that reporting is essentially value-laden but asserts that the journalist must be aware that their interpretation could be wrong. These sentiments can be applicable to both visual and printed media. In openly admitting the fallibility of coverage the media would be able to substantiate many of the arguments that are often revealed post-conflict, namely the interference of censorship, voluntary or otherwise, on their reports.

Patrick Bishop and John Witherow's book, *The Winter War*, explains precisely the type of conditions under which they had to report during the Falklands War:

> For the hacks it had been a communications war: a constant struggle to get stories back to London. The Navy would have preferred a private encounter with Argentina with the occasional release in London to say South Georgia or the Falklands had been retaken. Reporting British losses was always fraught with difficulties and dispatches would arrive on newsdesks with gaps and words crossed out. On land we were preoccupied with survival, building 'bivvies', cooking 'scran' and taking cover during air raids. We became in effect historical reporters, reporting what had happened and avoiding speculation about what would. Some reports were so delayed, however, they became little more than footnotes to history. We had been warned, though. At the outset we were told there was a conflict of interests. Our job was to disseminate news, the ministry's was to suppress it. It was an axiom which proved all too accurate.[27]

Such influence would dominate any interpretation of events during a conflict, combining the personal experience with the established bureaucracy to influence the relevance and content of a story. However, unless it is the requirement of the media to sustain the government's policy unwaveringly surely it is not against the national interest to reveal these influences upon the press.

Notwithstanding the right to refrain from providing the enemy with information of military value, allowing the public to draw their own conclusions rather than presenting the article as the whole truth would facilitate the depiction of a free and democratic society, desired by propagandists. As Bishop and Witherow have pointed out it has been left to the history books to attempt to reveal 'the true story', and while conditions conspire to limit the understanding and ability to report the whole story during conflict, through little fault of their own, the reporter surely has a duty to highlight these limitations on their interpretation of events. In doing so, they would provide insight into the influence of both the authorities and personality on war reporting.

Public opinion, the media and government policy

The evolution of modern media and the role of the correspondent have not only changed the way in which wars are covered, but have also influenced the manner in which conflict is conducted. To complete the understanding of the relationships between the media, the nation-state and the public one must also consider not only how the establishment influences public opinion but also how it has to adapt to it. In keeping with the understanding of interrelationships between parties, it would be a mistake to ignore such influences. So far, the relationship between the relevant groups has been portrayed in a linear fashion working from the top down. It is now necessary to consider the relationship in reverse and contemplate the influence of public opinion and modern media on government policy.

The Gulf War has arguably provided a watershed in the relationship between these three elements of society. Philip Taylor identifies the commencement of hostilities against Iraq as the starting point for the modern considerations of the government–media–public relationship. Taylor proposes that the Gulf War was the 'first major international conflict fought against the background of accessible global telecommunications and domestic video-recorders, and might thus prove a watershed in the way states publicly conduct their relations with one another'.[28] His comments raise the concept that modern media can influence not only domestic audiences but also international diplomacy. As the media technology advances so the military and government attitudes towards it necessarily have to alter. The Western fears of a 'Vietnam Syndrome' exacerbate the perceived danger the media potentially have in shaping public opinion, both civilian and military, at home and abroad.[29] Thus, the fight for positive public opinion moves into the international arena. This echoes the attempts by governments to demonstrate international cooperation for military intervention, though it is not always achieved. Media influence is inextricably linked to military objectives and, as such, its influence upon the government and armed forces needs to be considered.

While there remains debate concerning the effectiveness of peace journalism to influence government policy, there is a degree of consensus regarding the press and other media's importance to political and military planners. Reporters' presence 'in theatre' has come to be seen as a stabilizing force, mediating potential military excesses. John Simpson, in reference to the Gulf War, has argued that the 'fact that there were Western news correspondents in Baghdad should have made the Americans more wary about causing civilian casualties. Their continued presence should ensure that a similar mistake isn't made again'.[30] His remarks came in the aftermath of the bombing by Western forces of the Amiriyah shelter in Baghdad, which led to a significant number of civilian casualties.[31] The event was employed by objectors to intervention to demonstrate both the inhumanity of the campaign and the fallibility of so-called precision bombing. While undoubtedly such events can be used to highlight potential faults in the Western military strategy, they do not necessarily give any indication of media influence upon that policy.

Increasingly, the perception generated by heightened media and political debate is that of media policy occupying a position as a major planning consideration. Media handling has become officially ingrained in military procedures, cementing the consideration as a factor within wider strategic variables. The official attitude adopted by the MOD is as follows:

> Public support for any military operation must be rooted in an accurate understanding of events and their background. Reports of events can be broadcast virtually as they happen; therefore the media operations maxim is to release as much accurate information as possible as quickly as possible, subject only to operational security and the safety of British and allied lives. This requires close co-operation with the media at home and in theatre. Moreover, the ready access of personnel on operations to extensive media coverage of the conflict or crisis means that it is more important than ever to ensure that our own forces are properly informed of events. Media operations also need to persuade third parties that the action being taken is right and justifiable and to counter malicious or ill-informed reporting in the theatre of operations.[32]

In the above text, the media are depicted as being responsible for a number of key issues. Policy is designed to reduce any potential negative influences the media may have on both domestic morale and military morale. Furthermore, the media are seen to be at the forefront in reinforcing the legitimacy of military goals both domestically and in the international arena.

On a more intimate scale, the media occupied the thoughts of both military personnel and commanders. General Sir Peter de la Billiere revealed that a 'major burden which senior commanders of western contingents faced was the need to cultivate Press and television'.[33] Within this comment are not only the obvious considerations of media policy, but also the insinuation that Western military leaders were, by nature of the free and independent British press, at a disadvantage to despotic regimes with state-controlled media. This attitude is in contrast to the perception cultivated by Western propaganda eschewing the benefits of a free and democratic society. The quandary is indicative of the moral dilemmas often faced during conflicts. For example, during the Second World War the British government and the public at large faced a re-evaluation of their own moral standards. The public and military alike were forced to question whether one should abandon some gentlemanly concepts of traditional British national character in order to safeguard democracy. Evidence of such dilemmas can be found in sources of national culture. A notable example of this is the 1943 Michael Powell and Emeric Pressburger film *The Life and Death of Colonel Blimp*, initially banned by the British government for its sensitive subject matter.[34]

While the same threat to national survival was not present during the Gulf War, some of the same challenges were faced. General de la Billiere admits that as the countdown to war began the British military 'adopted a more Draconian attitude, and created five compact Media Reporting Teams (MRTs) and left it to individual editors to decide who should be included'.[35] Thus, on the one hand such an assertion can suggest that the military, while cracking down in light of imminent hostilities, were refusing to meddle with the press' decisions on who should occupy the places within the pools. However, a more cynical view could assert that the military sought to weaken the position of the media further by way of divide and conquer, creating internal media disagreement rather than facing uniform condemnation from a unified press. This second analysis would appear to be the most accurate in light of de la Billiere's own assertion that this policy was the more draconian. The statement made is that open and democratic media are a disadvantage to a democratic society during war. The existence of such institutions, though, is necessary to sustain the domestic and international legitimacy for intervention against unrepresentative and despotic regimes. Herein lie the difficulties of operating a free media policy while conducting conflict. The answer to the problems posed in this case appears to be the fragmenting of unified media by way of divide and rule.

Whether arguing in favour of, or against, the current media policies, the existence of an increased need to consider the effects of media policy appears unquestionable. The significance of assessing the nature of the influences has increased in the priority list of Western leaders. United States former

Chairman of the Joint Chiefs of Staff, General John Shalikashvili, explains one such dilemma faced by US military commanders:

> Maybe there's some good in the fact that commanders know there is going to be live coverage, and they will work their tails off to ensure there isn't a debacle. The bad aspect is . . . they're going to become timid because they know mistakes happen. They know the more active you are, proactive you are, the more mistakes are probably going to happen. And because none of us wants to become the subject of ridicule, we will grow up as a group of leaders who will prefer to be timid, because they don't want to be second guessed back here.[36]

Military considerations are directly occupied with the influence of public opinion upon policy making. The media are seen as the fundamental conduit for the presentation of positive policy procedures. What becomes important, therefore, is not only the influence of the media on military and political opinion, but also its effect on public opinion. The nervousness of contemporary Western leaders is understandable, military and political survival occupies the thoughts of those in command. The media offer a spy-hole through which to view conflict and shape the public's perception of the hostilities, as one study revealed:

> For the vast majority of our respondents, however, the war was a distant event, personally as well as geographically, to which they responded with support, but also in many cases with anxiety. Their responses were mediated by various social and cultural influences, but above all by the mass media of communication.[37]

The media were the channel through which not only was news provided, but also a structure within which news could be understood. Here, the propaganda techniques evident in the British press reaffirm existing ideas and introduce opinion regarding the conflicts both subtly and blatantly, consciously and unconsciously.

This opens up the role of the media beyond the simple understanding of influence upon public morale. It highlights a shift in the nature of conflict, if not a new phenomenon then at least an increased awareness and importance. As Michael Ignatieff has commented the 'presence of cameras in the field of operations does more than exert a constraint on military actions. It changes the focus of hostilities from the enemies' fielded forces to the civilian opinion at home which sustains the will to fight'.[38] Ignatieff is asserting that the emphasis of war has shifted from the battlefield to the home front; such emphasis on the home front is more reminiscent of historical discussions concerning total war rather than contemporary limited campaigns where

40

the Western sacrifices faced during the First and Second World Wars are no longer tolerable. This extension of obligations from the traditional military role has become increasingly exacerbated in light of both new technologies allowing for the swifter dissemination of news and with technological advances in weaponry. The Gulf War and Kosovo Conflict saw overwhelming technological advantage, if not numerical, held by the Allies, especially with regards to air power. As the likelihood of a swift and easy victory increases, so paradoxically, unquestioning public support falls. The need to justify the level of force required rises as the threat to the nation or military is reduced. Thus, the question of public support, especially before hostilities have commenced, becomes the seemingly dominant battle. These considerations also have wider implications with regards to the importance of positive international media policy. In effect, the media become part not only of the domestic policy-making process, but a key element of international diplomacy.

The media are increasingly becoming a global commodity and their influence upon international policy is significant. As argued earlier in the chapter the role of the individual reporter or newscaster forms a considerable factor in the composition of news coverage. With this in mind the influence of the media upon official foreign policy and the increased geographical reach of the information providers subsequently elevate the status of reporters and newscasters. Patrick Bishop of the *Daily Telegraph* has raised the issue in regards to the Gulf War:

> TV anchormen had come to occupy an important place in the long distance diplomacy being conducted between the regime and the rest of the world. The propagandists of the Ministry believed that the mere repetition of their version of events would eventually swing world opinion against a military intervention. Tariq Aziz had made the offer of an open-ended dialogue with Washington in an interview with the ABC Nightline host Ted Koppel, but had been turned down. Now the Iraqis were attempting to reach the foreign public over their leaders' heads by broadcasting direct to the citizenry.[39]

What is most significant about this development is the individual influence of journalists. The authority of international communications as an institution is not a unique development, identifiable post-Gulf War. Once more, to disassociate these considerations from the longer history of propaganda policy would be a mistake. Similar considerations arose during the Second World War as Taylor has identified:

> More-over, the continued development of the communications revolution had, since the advent of sound cinema and radio, provided

41

a direct link between government and those they governed, and between the government of one nation and the people of another. Propaganda was in this respect the alternative to diplomacy.[40]

The fight for public support has not only reached the domestic front but an international struggle for legitimacy. Growth in the number of media outlets available increases the opportunity to reach larger audiences, although whether or not those audiences choose to listen is another concern. However, greater coverage does not necessarily equate into greater breadth of opinion.

By conveying messages through the press, governments perpetuate specific propaganda aims supportive of their wider political policies. Greater reliance on visual media and the increased scope of information diffusion enhances the capacity for propaganda dissemination. If the media policy generally follows the pro-interventionist agenda, established by the government, the process can be viewed as beneficial to the propagandists' cause. The influence of the media also has a secondary advantage; by transmitting their message widely, the authorities sidestep traditional channels of both communication and policy processes. Speaking directly to the population gives the appearance of closing the gap between governments and the governed. In reality, this method reduces the number of dissenting voices by diminishing the influence of the elected legislature. For example, Parliament was denied the opportunity to vote on the desirability of NATO involvement in the former Yugoslavia. This is in keeping with the twentieth-century shift of power increasingly into the hands of the executive.

The net outcome of these processes means the media, once again, become the focus of debate. While this is justified to the press and public on the home front, attempts by hostile nations to reach the population of another are viewed with deep suspicion, and reporters facilitating this are branded unpatriotic. As with the simultaneous utilization of the rational and irrational approaches to the perception of the enemy, the duplicitous approach adopted over media policy reveals the hypocrisy of propaganda, while its acceptance reveals its success.

Newspapers in the modern era

The majority of contemporary academic and popular discussion regarding the positive and negative uses of the media during contemporary conflict revolves around the dominance of television coverage. A number of books by commentators such as Philip Taylor and John MacArthur have concentrated on the newer formats for the presentation of conflicts to the public.[41] As the conflicts discussed herein perpetuate the desire to describe each conflict in terms of significant 'firsts', so too have commentators attempted to analyse the conflicts through examining contemporary conduits of media dissemination. It is worth taking time to distinguish between wider under-standings of media policy and contrast these with the role of the newspaper in contemporary society; questioning whether the printed media still have a role to play. As will be discussed, some writers have argued that this is no longer the case. On the surface, it would appear that newspapers are irre-concilably disadvantaged when compared with the modern competition. However, whether this is either correct or desirable are two considerations open to question.

Dr Stephen Badsey, a senior lecturer in the Department of War Studies at the Royal Military Academy Sandhurst, represents the school of opinion that has become dismissive of the role newspapers can play in providing war coverage. In 1992 he asserted that:

> Nevertheless, it is undeniable that the replacement of newspapers by television as the dominant news medium has radically changed the way in which wars are reported. In a world of instant communica-tions, newspapers produced once a day cannot hope to compete, and since the 1960s they have visibly reverted to their original function either as overt political broadsheets or as popular entertainment.[42]

Badsey's view, one that he was to reiterate four years later, emphasizes the anachronistic method of producing daily newspapers that, apart from the revisions of certain editions, are almost instantly out of date by the time of distribution.[43] The challenge of television has seemingly won the battle for dominance over public opinion through its immediacy and ability to cover events rapidly and with continual revisions. In addition to this, the strength of television as a medium of news dissemination is, it can be argued, also the ability to show the public events on the screen rather than through words or still images. However, these arguments do little to address the issue of analysis and while providing immediacy and stimulating visuals, television news does not compete with analysis provided by the printed media.

Another school of thought utilizes many of the same arguments raised in favour of television coverage, against the same medium. Often this criticism can be found within the pages of newspapers, but more surprisingly, criti-cism comes also from the ranks of those who perpetuate the popularity of instant news and celebrity journalism.

In reference to Badsey's argument, the evolution of technology has not left the newspaper as far behind as some would argue. Each of the five national newspapers analysed in this study has on-line editions. These digital versions are regularly updated allowing a regular visitor to follow the news as often and as easily as a regular television viewer does. The Internet also has global reach allowing the dissemination of these views and propaganda to cross international borders. In this respect, the printed media have kept pace with the type of technological watersheds during the conflicts covered herein. Kosovo, after all, was the first conflict fought during the Internet era.

The insinuation that newspapers have reverted to a previous function of political bias or as entertainment should not be taken out of context. The media as a whole, in Western, commercialized nations, pander to the demands of popular consumerism. Concerns about what a public will stomach rank highly in the competitive television market also. Kate Adie has described how these demands have altered the considerations of those producing television:

> [A]s British television in the new century begins to turn itself into an entertainment-dominated medium, consigning serious programmes to late nights or specialist channels, news programmes are pressured into changing their style. Style in itself becomes a dominant argument, coupled with anxiety that the audience should not be offended or upset too much by eccentric-looking individuals, lest the ratings suffer.[44]

The combination of Adie's and Badsey's observations demonstrates a shift in the overall demands society places upon the media. It would be wrong to single out the printed media as a unique component of a wider shift of public demands upon news and increasingly, entertainment providers. The secondary argument of newspapers' outdated provision of news is countered by the existence of web editions; furthermore, the advantages of rapid news dissemination are not necessarily wholeheartedly accepted.

It is undeniable that the changing technological environment of society has affected the media and international concepts of understanding contemporary diplomacy. Not only can these changes be identified since the development of mass society, the challenges of two world conflicts or even in the subsequent peace of the latter, the shifts have occurred in much more recent times. This is a development Philip Taylor has sought to explain:

> The world has changed so rapidly since the end of the Cold War that everyone, including the media, is still grappling with modes of behaviour appropriate to the new 'order'. There is no simple Cold War-type framework for analysing *events* any longer. And when you have 24 hours of airtime to fill that leaves a lot of time for speculation, talking heads, and erroneous or incomplete facts about what that order may be. Live television may be exciting, and it may appear to be more 'real', but the news still has to be entertaining if it is to keep the attention span of its audience. Complexity can be a turn-off for many people.[45]

The changes in technology have altered perception massively. These developments are evident not only for the historian looking at the Second World War, the Falklands or the Cold War era in comparison with contemporary conflict, but also between the Gulf War and Kosovo Conflict. News broadcasts in Kosovo were real-time whereas most dispatches during the Gulf War had still taken between ten and twelve hours to get to air. During the Balkan crisis, the Internet was used to bombard enemy's computer systems as a form of cyber weapon and portray alternate perspectives to the dominant messages carried in the mainstream media. During the campaign against Milosevic the Internet was, Taylor argues, the Serbian people's only form of retaliation.[46]

Taylor's conclusions also reveal that the technological revelations that are occurring do not necessarily favour the medium of modern visual and instant media. The new technological developments generate an ever-expanding media vacuum that needs to be filled. This in turn places fresh demands on news reporters to hold the attention of the public. Printed media are attacked for their inability to respond promptly to events and to remain relevant in a fast shifting media world. Yet, one of the biggest deficiencies of televised news would appear to be its immediacy. One commentator has suggested:

> Technology, too, seems to be against the journalist. The impact of transmission technologies that might have been thought to herald the dawn of a new era of media coverage can in practice form a powerful constraint. The lack of time to reflect, check, and contextualise is bound to push journalists evermore towards the accepted wisdom of their elite sources.[47]

This argument states that the incessant demand for news inhibits traditional journalistic behaviour and promotes dependence on readily available, but official, sources, such as the military or the government. Despite the concerns of some military commentators regarding the ability of the media to hinder or affect military planning, the advancement of technology can actually encumber the journalists. Without the time for cross-referencing and soliciting alternate opinions, the demand for news pressurizes the reporter into accepting the validity of those with their own agendas. Combined with an apparent array of media sources, generating the illusion of choice and alternate opinions, the demands of time restraints and the need to develop a story around images can force reliance on a relatively narrow range of swiftly available sources. Instead of acting as a brake upon the propaganda activities of political and military policymakers, the advancement of technology could aid the dissemination of propaganda. In this respect, the propagandists can hope to infiltrate a wide range of media sources through the swift and widespread dissemination of information.

If later the information is found to contain errors or omissions, the subsequent publication of these findings will receive less critical analysis once time has elapsed.

The case for the advantages of modern visual media is not as attractive as first insinuated. Those within this modern media have also arrived at this realization. Martin Bell, in his reflections on his time as a reporter, defines the difference between the marked improvement in the quantity of media coverage against any advantages this may have generated in terms of improving understanding and journalistic standards. Bell states that there are indeed 'many arguments for a rolling and continuous news service, but quality of reporting is not one of them. More means worse. The multiplication of deadlines takes us away from the real world, and drives us back into our offices and edit rooms'.[48] In this environment, the desire to get something to air eclipses the need to get something relevant on air. Not only is news needed rapidly after the event, updates require reporters, perhaps in a remote area or without all the necessary equipment to file on location, to report regularly to their editors. This is to the detriment of sustained investigations carried out at a pace geared towards the daily publication of news.

In the example of the Iraqi incursion into Khafji, one commentator believes the printed media held a distinct advantage over television sources.[49] David Mould argues that early television coverage of the event was unreliable and at times bordered on speculation.[50] In Mould's opinion, this was due to the pressures of deadlines and live coverage, which contributed to the difficulty of reporters to make sense of the situation. In contrast, print journalists' deadlines were less frequent allowing for a smaller quantity of material but with the benefit of greater consideration.

In addition to the above quality versus quantity debate, Bell has highlighted further distinctions between the two forms that challenge the assumption of visual media dominance. In relation to the amount of material available and the need to obtain pictures, print journalists are, in the opinion of Martin Bell, at a distinct advantage over their television rivals. During the Bosnian conflict, for example, he points to the flexibility of print journalists as being a benefit:

> The information blockade was something of a professional crisis for the few war reporters still in business in Bosnia at the end of the war's third year. It was less of a problem for the print people whose simpler logistics and ways of working I had never envied more. Not only did they carry no tripods, but because they lived on big words alone they could still glean those words, even in times of restricted access, from the United Nations, from the few liaison officers still working in Pale, from diplomats and relief agencies, and from Bosnian government sources of varying credibility. And if all else failed, they could apply the knuckle to the forehead

in the time-honoured manner of foreign correspondents the world over, and think their thoughts out loud. The resulting 'think-piece' or 'analysis' would be at least a passable substitute for the missing front-line dispatch.[51]

Once again, his words diminish the perceived advantage of television over the older forms of written media. While criticism can be levelled at the introduction of commentary pieces in lieu of facts, the nature of the British press, with the assumed political bias and avoidance of neutrality, in effect legitimizes this approach to reporting. Conversely, on the occasions when opinion in the press is limited and in support of the official interventionist argument, the criticisms of pandering to propagandist rhetoric actually increase. The British press enjoys a degree of flexibility in the means in which it reports news. If the resort is often to individual opinion or comment pieces, for these to echo government interventionist policies points to either the success of the propaganda campaign waged by the leadership, or a compatibility of aims in pursuing war. Despite the ability to produce wide-ranging opinions the overall policies of the press generally produce, as Roy Greenslade has noted, narrow, black and white arguments.[52] The opinions are compounded by the utilization of what Greenslade terms 'self-fulfilling polls' of opinion.[53] Opinion polls reproduced in the press do little to gauge public reaction to events and instead diminish complex issues into compacted, virtually irrelevant and often misleading, opinion polls.

While the press fails to produce comprehensive debates over issues, television has continued to receive criticism relating to the quality of its coverage. Martin Bell was not alone in reaching the conclusion; other television media figures have issued similar warnings about the efficiency of visual media to report conflict accurately. This shift suggests a sustainable lifespan and relevancy for the press in the reporting of future conflict. Another of these commentators is Kate Adie. She has stated that although television 'with its element of sensationally up-to-date information and its predilection for exciting pictures, favours war', this is not necessarily indicative of any real quality in that coverage.[54] Instead, one of the leading personalities of visual war reporting argues the medium is:

neither comprehensive nor incisive; it lacks detail; it lacks reflection; it lacks a context; it has problems of access; it has problems of verification of material. It tends to sensation but it stops well short of the full horrors: a major problem to those of us who report from war zones.[55]

She claims the realization that television filtered the true horrors of what she was trying to convey led to her becoming 'immensely frustrated'.[56] Adie sees the limitations of television as a medium for war reportage, and the printed media addresses some of these limits, although other problems are not unique to either medium. Furthermore, she raises the point that reporters and the television are two separate entities. One may attempt to get a whole story out, but the limitations, imposed and self-imposed, of television often leave the whole story untold.

Perhaps less surprising criticism of the limits of television reporting has come from the press. A *Daily Telegraph* article succinctly stated that 'as so often with television, it is not the scale of the horror that shapes the coverage, but the nature and quantity of available visual material . . . Television is a marvellous medium of impression, a hopeless medium of analysis'.[57] In effect, the newspaper was repeating Adie's reservations. With wide criticism coming from within, one is left to wonder why such issues have been left unaddressed. One explanation forwarded is that the movement towards speculation and reliance upon official sources has been driven by economic considerations as much as anything else. In the case of American television coverage, it has been argued that the goals of both the CNN and ABC news channels and the government were being served at the same time:

> Television news, particularly when reporting foreign events, oper-
> ated in a closed system, reinforcing its own presuppositions and
> frames. 'we will fight/we will win' became a common sense enigmatic
> code for television news and was supported by speculations and
> scenarios. It simultaneously served the economic interests of media
> organizations that needed to captivate viewers and the political
> goals of a government that desired public support for military inter-
> vention. Finally, this enigma provided an interpretative frame that
> suggested news viewers be politically passive but emotionally
> active, responding to events in the Gulf as spectators.[58]

It is debatable to what degree these observations can be, or should be, transferred to the British media coverage of the Gulf War. Nevertheless, this argument resonates with the explanations raised in this discussion for the correlation between propaganda requirements and newspaper content. Whether it is newspapers or television, the need is for all media outlets to be interesting, entertaining and ultimately to sustain viewers or readers.

The lack of analysis and interpretation, in favour of images and instant, breaking news, leaves a gap in the ideological framework of news reportage, which, it seems, the printed media are ideally suited to filling. In respect of this, perhaps it is inappropriate to view the television versus press debate as one with a victor. Instead, the press and visual media complement each other. The printed newspaper is prone to many, if not more, propagandistic rants. The press falls short of providing the degree of immediacy that television can provide. However, the statement is only in part true; the widespread establishment of on-line versions of newspapers bridges the gap between the traditional printed media and the contemporary visual sources.

When analysing the propaganda content of the British press it is imperative to understand the importance of the newspaper in British society. If, as some have argued, it is an outdated form of media, totally eclipsed by television coverage of war, there is little point in highlighting its propaganda content as the audience would be insignificant. However, this is not the case and while people continue to read newspapers, the influence on opinions regarding conflict will remain a relevant debate. Despite the depiction of the Gulf War as the first live conflict, a study carried out during the campaign deduced that national 'newspaper readers were generally more satisfied with the paper's level of informativeness (probably because they could choose a more differentiated product)'.[59] The same report also concluded that 'newspapers, although generally unable to compete with television in terms of immediacy and instant communication of war, were nevertheless able to offer much more ideologically complete interpretations of events and stronger advocacy of particular positions'.[60] While the public is satisfied with and willing to utilize the British press, it will remain an important conduit for state and military propaganda.

Conclusion

This chapter has sought to examine newspapers within a wider context of the media and to examine the role of the war reporting in influencing coverage. These elements form vital components of a media system that complements, rather than competes, to provide news. Much contemporary discussion has placed a greater emphasis on the role of newer, visual and instant forms of news dissemination, some going so far as to suggest the newspaper's role is a diminishing one. While viewing figures may have eclipsed readership levels, the printed media continue to participate in the construction of public perception of world and national events. Furthermore, the British press continues to act as a conduit for conflict propaganda.

The evolution of media is an ongoing process, as is society and technology at large. The mass circulation national daily newspapers initially developed from such advancements. However, despite these changes the media is still reliant on consistent elements of news reporting, most significantly the role of the war reporter. News continues to be evaluated and described by individuals and, in the same way, it continues to be consumed by the public. News must conform to the commercial requirements of the broadcasters or newspaper proprietors and produce entertaining items. As a result, despite the plethora of news outlets available, newsworthy items such as the development of international disputes can go unnoticed if they are deemed unattractive to the audience.

The selection of news during international crises must also conform to these requirements. During periods of protracted negotiations, the tabloid press often drops the crises from the pages until such point when a newsworthy event occurs. This has the effect of continuing the perception of world events as chaotic and erratic. When the media continue interest in the unfolding events, or even during conflict, the demand for copy of any description is paramount. It is often the war correspondent's job to fill this void with comment pieces.

As crises develop the war reporter can become a focal point for news coverage. In this sense, a society that demands entertainment also sustains a market for celebrity journalism. This, in itself, is not necessarily a negative occurrence. However, the British military actively seek to assimilate news reporters within their ranks to secure the maximum exposure to their version of events and provoke a degree of empathy. This has combined with a relatively recent trend for some journalists openly to adopt an emotional attachment to their news reporting and in doing so reject traditional concepts of objectivity. This trend, if it develops, could actually begin to undermine the propaganda aims of the government and military policymakers. The supposed objectivity of the press and media at large in Western democracies is yet another component in the weaponry of pro-interventionists to level against their totalitarian enemies. The concept of a journalism of attachment may not inherently equate to a support of government policies, but has so far tended to favour intervention, notably on humanitarian grounds. While propagandists would enjoy the support, they will be wary of openly compromising the objectivity of journalism in order to achieve this and, thus, undermine their own claims to moral legitimacy.

Propagandists' attempts to influence the media mean that an appreciation of how negative press can affect their campaign has risen. With the battle for public opinion subsuming the need to restrict Western casualties, the relationship between tactical policy decisions and the reaction of public opinion must not be underrated. The, now worldwide, media has the ability to seriously hamper the public relations objectives of pro-interventionist campaigns.

The opportunities for exploiting the media, as well as the need to ensure positive representation, have also grown. The plethora of media outlets provides the facade of a free and opinionated infrastructure. Yet, by restricting the source of information released into the system the military during conflict can in fact enable their message to dominate news coverage. Diplomacy is carried out worldwide through the media during conflict and one's own domestic elected bodies can be sidestepped. The debate about the desirability and legitimacy for intervention can be taken directly to the public and international community through this variety of media.

As part of this powerful media system, the British press remains a strong component. Attributes afforded to instant visual media, such as instant coverage, have actually led to widespread reservations, even amongst television war reporters themselves. Rapid deadlines force journalists increasingly to rely on elite sources of information, enhancing the propagandist's message in the process. The visual format may lend itself to covering war, but it does little to enhance the public's understanding. Newspapers with on-line editions provide comparable up-to-date revisions of their stories and worldwide access. As such, they continue to participate in the wider battle for public opinion.

3

WAR AND THE *GREEN BOOK*

Introduction

A definition of propaganda and an understanding of its evolution as a theory
are defunct without reference to specific events. In order to assess the continuity of propaganda as a mechanism for the mass persuasion of public
opinion during war it is necessary to study both the events during which it
is utilized and the means by which the messages are transmitted. Background
understanding of the conflicts is necessary for two reasons. The press, media
in general and governments justified their right to intervene through utilizing
history. History also offered the opportunity for the press to construct conflict narratives, to set out the role of belligerents in the conflicts and provide
a timeframe easily identifiable to the public and one that demonstrated a
forward motion of plot development. This attempt to pre-date conflicts, in
order to create depth in the narrative, is often at odds with the actual coverage of conflict that tends to explain daily events in terms of short-term
catalysts.

The chapter will examine the backgrounds to the Gulf War and Kosovo
Conflict in order to highlight their significance to the changing nature of
media technology and its influence on policy and public opinion. Each conflict presented separate challenges for the propagandist in legitimizing intervention to the public. In addition to the necessity to take into account
developments in media transmission, allowing potentially swifter and uncensored information to be relayed, the nature of the conflicts required a shifting emphasis to be placed upon the justifications for war. However, despite
the development of technology, the media, it will be argued, did not enjoy
greater powers of restraint on government actions. Instead, the growth of
news coverage offered a window of opportunity for the propagandist to
exploit.

After establishing the broad historical outline of the two crises, the
chapter will proceed to explore the specific media restrictions that the
MOD utilize in an effort to control the flow of news during conflict. Once
the media restrictions are understood, it will then be possible in subsequent

chapters to measure these restrictions against the reality of war coverage. Comprehensive analysis of the *Green Book* will demonstrate the existence of a censorship system that, in theory at least, covers the length of the media chain from correspondent to the home front. The examination will reveal a four-layered system of military control over the media and demonstrate how the methods employed have shifted responsibility for reporting 'responsibly' away from the military and onto the journalists. In addition to this shift of emphasis, the section will also reveal the consistencies in attitudes towards media–military relations, which exist despite the differing natures of the two confrontations.

Historical background: the Gulf War

For many reporters and indeed politicians of the day, the Gulf War began in August 1990 with the Iraqi invasion of Kuwait. With the benefit of hindsight, historians have attempted to pre-date the causes of this conflict to establish lengthier precedents. Dilip Hiro in his book *Desert Shield to Desert Storm. The Second Gulf War* argues that the Persian Gulf War's roots can be traced back to 1961.[1] On 19 June 1961, Edward Heath informed the House of Commons that the Anglo–Kuwaiti Treaty of 1899 had been superseded by a concord of close friendship. This concord included a defence provision for Kuwait to call upon Great Britain in the event of invasion. Just six days after this announcement the then Iraqi leader, Abdul Karim Kassem, insisted Kuwait become incorporated into the Basra province.[2] This, Dilip Hiro believes, was the start of the 'Second Kuwaiti Crisis'.

Such attempts to pre-date events were also employed by the British press in an effort to provide some limited context. The provision of such historical perspective is employed to aid the creation of a war narrative; the history used reinforces the newspaper's stance on the conflict. The selective use of historical 'evidence' can, for example, aid the identification of an enemy, justify intervention or apportion blame. The narrative of war is useful for the media and the policymaker alike; the defining of the enemy, juxtaposed with one's own position, creates legitimacy and moral ascendancy. The evolution of the narrative provides an ongoing story that drives the progress of events onwards giving the impression at least of the advancement of one's cause. Historical context plays a significant role in providing the grounding for this narrative.

Newspapers, however, tend to undermine and contradict the efforts made to provide deeper historical context. The press often displays the number of days a conflict has been running that coincides with an immediate, identifiable event, such as an invasion, rather than historical precursors. This shows a concern for the immediate over the historical and can distort the understanding of broader historical context. It is a tendency that can also affect historical analysis of events. For example, while Dilip Hiro attempts to pre-date the start of the 'Second Kuwaiti Crisis', he contradictorily uses the 16 January 1991, in Appendix I a chronology of events, to define the instigation of the Second Gulf War. This dismisses the notion that the conflict began as Iraq invaded Kuwait. Rather the commencement of the US-led coalition air strikes against Iraq is the starting point.

British media coverage of the events in Iraq and Kuwait began in earnest in the period leading up to and after the Iraqi invasion of Kuwait. This means an analysis of propaganda in the British press should accept the start of the conflict as the onset of hostilities rather than the commencement of an allied military offensive against Iraq. The propaganda campaign began before the allied military campaign, and it is the period used to construct their consensus regarding war.

For a more relevant understanding of the causes leading to the 1990–91 Gulf War, it is necessary to consider Iraq's involvement in the 1980–88 war with Iran. During this period, Iraq became heavily indebted to many of her Arab neighbours, including Kuwait. Iraq insisted she was fighting a war on behalf of the Arab world with Saddam Hussein promoting himself as the champion of a pan-Arab cause. This was a position that he was to cultivate and perpetuate throughout the Kuwaiti crisis in an attempt to foster Arab support and weaken the alliance. After the war with Iran, Iraq faced stiff debt repayments in the face of what was claimed to be a deflated oil price.[3] Iraq blamed oversupply by members of the Organization of the Petroleum Exporting Countries (hereafter OPEC), for the low barrel price. This failure to maintain the price of oil was seen and declared as a form of war against Iraq. Thus, on 15 July 1990 Tariq Aziz, the Iraqi Foreign Minister, complained to the Arab League that the oversupply of oil had forced the barrel price down to between $11 and $13. This was significantly below the OPEC reference point of $18 per barrel. This, Iraq proclaimed, was costing her economy around one billion dollars per annum in lost oil revenue.

It was in light of these issues and historical border disputes that Iraq invaded Kuwait on 2 August 1990. A culmination of posturing and supposed sabre-rattling brought the Iraqi army to invade and comprehensively overrun Kuwait. We can identify this point as the start of the Gulf War. The coverage of the issue as a crisis begins with the invasion of Kuwait and not only when an Allied offensive begins. Initially, Iraq and Saddam Hussein faced little more than international condemnation. On 2 August 1990, the United Nations (hereafter UN) passed Resolution 660 condemning Iraq's actions and calling for a ceasefire and troop withdrawal.[4] However, after the failure of the Iraqis to respond to these demands the UN passed a further resolution four days later. UN Resolution 661 reaffirmed the requirements of 660 and imposed economic sanctions. The sanctions covered all materials except 'supplies intended strictly for medical purposes, and, in humanitarian circumstances, foodstuffs'.[5] The resolution also insisted that no state 'recognise any regime set up by the occupying power'.[6] Thus, when Iraq announced the merging of Kuwait within its borders on 8 August UN Resolution 662 declared the annexation 'null and void'.[7] As it became clear that increased pressure was required, the UN sanctioned the use of any 'such measures commensurate to the specific circumstances . . . to halt all inward and outward maritime shipping'.[8]

Further UN resolutions responded to Iraqi action towards foreign nationals.[9] In retaliation to the UN embargo, Saddam Hussein called for the internment of many of the 8000 Western and Japanese citizens present in Kuwait; essentially imprisoning those nationals whose countries were participating in the embargo. Iraqi responses also extended to 'acts of violence against diplomatic missions and their personnel in Kuwait'.[10] Instead of compliance with requests to refrain from such activities, hostages were taken to undisclosed destinations to act as human shields and as propaganda tools in Hussein's television messages to the West.

In addition to UN initiatives, numerous peace plans were forwarded throughout the period leading up to the commencement of Allied hostilities. King Hussein of Jordan revealed plans for an Iraqi withdrawal from Kuwait and for the United States to move out of Saudi Arabia. This proposal was accepted by Iraq but rejected out-of-hand by Saudi officials and Kuwait. Then, on 1 September 1990, Libya promoted its own seven-point peace initiative, again rejected by Saudi Arabia and Kuwait.[11] However, despite such ongoing diplomatic manoeuvring toward a peaceful settlement allied military intervention appeared increasingly likely, especially as President George H. W. Bush decided, at the end of October, to increase the number of United States troops in the Gulf to over 400,000. This coincided with an ever-expanding rhetorical battle between Iraq and her would-be adversaries. The aggressive posturing by both sides was confirmed by UN Resolution 678, which called upon Iraq to implement fully all previous 11 resolutions relating to it and authorizing 'all necessary means to uphold and implement Resolution 660 (1990) and all subsequent relevant resolutions and to restore international peace and security in the area'.[12]

Under the provisions of the UN resolutions, without Iraqi compliance and with the failure of peace initiatives, the allied forces commenced offensive operations. When Operation Desert Shield ended and Operation Desert Storm[13] began on the 16 January 1991, it was estimated the alliance had gathered around 680,000 troops to face a reported 545,000 Iraqi troops in Kuwait.[14] The air offensive lasted until 24 February at which point Operation Desert Sabre began. With supreme air power, the ground war was a swift success. By 27 February, Iraq had announced the withdrawal of its forces from Kuwait. The allied offensive had lasted just 42 days.

The technical advances, which helped to make the military victory so swift and comprehensive, were seemingly complemented by the technical support enjoyed by those reporting it. The Gulf War was, and indeed still is, hailed as the first 'live' war. As Philip Taylor has noted the 'Gulf War, then, was the first major international conflict fought against the background of accessible global telecommunications and domestic video-recorders, and might thus prove a watershed in the way states publicly conduct their relations with one another'.[15] During this period the British public and indeed a worldwide audience, it has been assumed, were able to tune in, turn on and read about every facet of the Iraqi invasion, the weaponry, and the air strikes and, eventually, the decisive ground battle. The saturation coverage of the unfolding events via a plethora of media outlets certainly gave the media consumer the appearance of choice through a multiplicity of information resources. In this atmosphere of apparent overwhelming media scrutiny, it would be possible to believe the restrictions imposed upon the media during the Falklands War were no longer applicable or feasible.[16] However, despite this appearance news broadcasting was still subject to restraints on timing and information was still often released at times beneficial for the military or governments involved.

With apparently greater choice available, one might have assumed that the coverage of the Gulf War would be more accurate, competitive or thorough. Greater competition could have fuelled considerable pressure on the authorities to 'get their facts right'. Furthermore, with instant access to events beamed 'live' to news desks, delay and censorship could be reduced at a stroke. This, however, was not to be the case. Despite the technological advances made since the Falklands War, similar arguments regarding the media and military relations persisted, most notably the question of the public's right to know versus the military's demands for operational security.

While failing to alter the media–military relations comprehensively, the abundance of media sources at least ignited and held the public interest. During the conflict 85 per cent of the British population declared they watched television news regularly and 54 per cent read a daily national newspaper regularly.[17] These figures only give an indication of the depth of understanding of those media consumers and they do not consider pre-war levels, however, they do offer evidence of a substantial degree of public awareness of international affairs. Evidence like this has led some observers to conclude that the breadth and quantity of media sources available to the British public meant the government had to temper its actions. Others have argued that perhaps more than ever before, the omnipresent media forced those in power in the 'free world' to measure their actions against the opinions of those they ruled.[18] This view assumes that coverage was independent of government intervention and as such posed a potential threat to the government's monopoly of information regarding the war, a view that can be countered.

The heightened interest in foreign affairs acted not as a restraint upon government action but instead offered a tantalizing window of opportunity for the propagandist. If a cooperative propaganda policy could be disseminated through existing, legitimate channels, any government action could hope to enjoy a higher degree of public acceptance. Furthermore, the British government and her allies were well aware that the eyes and ears of the world were upon the internationally transmitted cable networks and their national newspapers. As such, the media became a formal sounding ground of policy for consumption both at home and abroad. In this sense, the Gulf War would lend itself to the title of historical watershed concerning how states communicate and interact with each other.

Historical background: the Kosovo Conflict

The conflict in Kosovo differed greatly to that in the Gulf. Not only was the crisis in Europe's own backyard, but also the spark that induced worldwide concern was far less definitive than that of the Gulf. The Kosovo Conflict had little in the way of a discernable starting point. There is no 'tidy' invasion date by which reporters and the public can 'set their watch'. This confuses the West's ability to understand the issues in terms of traditional narrative structures.

Historically, the Serbs trace their claims to Kosovo back to 1389 when the Ottomans defeated the Serbs during the battle of Kosovo Polje and where Prinze Lazar was martyred. The myth that has developed from this battle has become a central event in Serbian history, leading many Serbs to feel Kosovo has a special link to them.[19] Kosovar Albanians, on the other hand, believe they are the original inhabitants and constitute somewhere in the region of between 80 to 90 per cent of the population in Kosovo.

Kosovo was partitioned between Serbia and Montenegro in 1913 and then incorporated as part of Yugoslavia after the First World War. In 1974, a revised constitution granted Kosovo autonomy. However, from 1989 the Albanian population of the region began to experience degrees of repression from Serbia. In 1990, three years after Slobodan Milosevic had risen to power, the autonomy granted to Kosovo in 1974 was revoked. Initial opposition to this repression was peaceful. The Albanian leader, Ibrahim Rugova, maintained a non-violent objection to the Serbian intervention. It was widely believed by Kosovans that their case would eventually be noticed by outside powers. Indeed, there was an expectation that after the 1995 Dayton Accords were agreed the Kosovan situation would also be addressed.[20] However, this proved not to be the case and Rugova's peaceful method, which yielded few results, became discredited. Increasingly, the growing Kosovo Liberation Army (hereafter KLA) came to symbolize opposition to Serbian domination.

Throughout 1998, the crisis emerged into the international foreground. During February and March, the Serbian authorities mounted an operation in the Drenica region of central Kosovo. This assault on a KLA stronghold resulted in the death of around 80 people in the first of the atrocities to mar

Kosovo in this period.[21] According to Michael Ignatieff this episode marked the end of non-violent opposition, thus, the final discrediting of Rugova's chosen path.[22] Initially, the UN response was to demand a cessation of hostile activities and impose an arms embargo on Yugoslavia that included Kosovo.[23] Despite the implementation of this, the fighting escalated and by September 1998, the UN estimated around 230,000 persons had been displaced due to the hostilities.[24] It was not until NATO issued orders for air strikes on 13 October that Milosevic eventually acceded to demands. Under the threat of aerial bombardment, Milosevic allowed the deployment of an unarmed Verification Mission, which was directed by the Organization for Security and Cooperation in Europe (hereafter OSCE). The objective of these monitors was, quite simply, to make sure the Yugoslav Army stayed in its barracks and the KLA kept to the hills. A NATO aerial verification force supplemented this while the UN added its weight by sanctioning both endeavours.[25]

The situation was not to stabilize indefinitely and on 15 January 1999, Serbian forces entered Racak and killed 45 civilians under the pretext of searching for KLA members and arms. The spark required to rekindle public indignation and rally the international community into action appeared to have materialized. The UN condemned what it conclusively described as a 'massacre' and placed the blame firmly on Yugoslav forces.[26] On 31 January 1999, NATO authorized the use of air strikes if the Serbs failed to agree a peaceful settlement. The talks, which were held at Rambouillet, France, failed and NATO commenced offensive air operations on 24 March 1999.[27]

Unlike the Gulf War the air campaign in Kosovo was sufficient to induce a Serbian capitulation without a single NATO casualty. Milosevic agreed to G8 proposals for an end to hostilities on 3 June and Serbian forces began to withdraw from Kosovo on 10 June.[28] This withdrawal was marked by a suspension of the bombing campaign by NATO.

Arguably, the toughest challenge faced by the allies during the conflict was that posed by the battle for public opinion. NATO came under significant pressure because of its refusal to fly low-level missions, thereby enhancing target recognition and improving accuracy. In an effort to avoid undue risks to aircrews, NATO planes continued to fly medium-level missions. Such an option inevitably led to mistakes, the most reported of which were the destruction of a civilian train passing over a bridge on 12 April and the much-publicized attack on the Chinese Embassy in Belgrade on 7 May. The latter prompted NATO to call upon the services of New Labour's Alastair Campbell, Downing Street's head of media, in an effort to reorganize the conduct of its information campaign.

Such mistakes called into question NATO's justification for its campaign and the ultimate objectives of the mission. The Gulf War had provided a relatively easy justification for military intervention. The invasion of one sovereign state by another seemed to offer an unquestionable justification for international action. The dubious nature of Kuwait's existing leadership could be ignored and the West's desire to safeguard oil supplies relegated to a mere sideshow when faced with such 'unprovoked' aggression. However, the Gulf was a conflict in which NATO had avoided involvement. At the time of the Gulf War, according to Chris Bennett editor of *NATO Review*, NATO was not concerned with issues outside of the Euro-Atlantic area.[29] Furthermore, he suggests, NATO was so concentrated on collective defence that the organization was incapable of conducting the type of operation necessary.

Kosovo posed a more complex problem for coordinators of NATO policy and, in contrast to the Middle Eastern situation, it was felt all other possible avenues of policy had been exhausted. In light of previous atrocities in Croatia, Bosnia and Herzegovina, Bennett suggests the stability of the entire Southern Balkans region was at risk. This led the 19 NATO members to surmise that the risk of inaction far outweighed the cost of intervention.

In Britain, support for intervention appeared bolstered by the leading political party's attitude to non-domestic affairs. In 1997, New Labour had laid out its vision for what was described as an 'ethical foreign policy'. The Labour manifesto of that year, entitled *Britain Deserves Better*, stated:

> Labour wants Britain to be respected in the world for the integrity with which it conducts its foreign relations. We will make the protection and promotion of human rights a central part of our foreign policy. We will work for the creation of a permanent international criminal court to investigate genocide, war crimes and crimes against humanity.[30]

In a re-emphasis of these ideals, Foreign Secretary Robin Cook unveiled his New Mission Statement for the Foreign and Commonwealth Office that incorporated four goals of foreign policy, the fourth of which insisted 'foreign policy must have an ethical dimension'.[31] Kosovo provided an opportunity to test this new ethical ideology, as the alleged genocide in the region appeared to dovetail conveniently with their moral objectives. The plight of Albanian refugees and the reports of ethnic cleansing could have been enough to spur intervention.

On this occasion, the proposed enemy was no Middle Eastern, Arab dictator with values alien to those of Western communities. Instead, Kosovo involved distinctly European affairs and an internal conflict. Until recently the United States and Great Britain had regarded the KLA as a terrorist organization; in 1998 Robert Gelbard, President Clinton's special envoy to the Balkans, had asserted that the KLA 'is, without any questions, a terrorist group'.[32] An Amnesty International report published in the same year commented that both the Serbs and the KLA were guilty of human rights abuses.[33] Furthermore, the United Nations had also condemned the 'acts of terrorism by the Kosovo Liberation Army'.[34] These assertions affected the situation in two ways. In the first instance, it made any Western intervention, which may appear to favour the KLA, indefensible in light of attitudes towards terrorism. Second, from this declaration the Serbs could draw some justification in pursuing an aggressive policy in order to alleviate a domestic threat to national security. At 'best', the conflict could be seen as a civil war. In this sense, compared with Iraq and the Kuwaiti crisis, the West's justification for military action was on a less than solid legal foundation from the outset.

As has already been noted the 'question about war and peace in the context of the use of force is always concerned with the issue of legitimacy, on which the characterization of actions like military intervention depends'.[35] As the Kosovo crisis did not conform to standard notions of legitimacy, as the Iraqi invasion of Kuwait had, the war was instead 'sold' to domestic and international audiences in the context of post-Cold War ideals of humanitarian concerns. United Nations Secretary-General, Dr Javier Solana stressed that the 'objective [of intervention] is to prevent more human suffering and more repression and violence against the civilian population of Kosovo . . . NATO is united behind this course of action'.[36] This statement, released on NATO's website, reaffirmed the connection between the military actions of the alliance and the humanitarian concerns and objectives of the wider international community. Tony Blair declared in Parliament that the repression of the Kosovar Albanians ensured that the country had an 'obligation' to act.[37] New Labour attempted to frame the justification for the conflict within the notion of an ethical foreign policy that necessitated action. However, intervention on these grounds is difficult to justify and Blair failed to secure unanimous support.

A number of MPs from the Campaign Group, which included Tony Benn, Tam Dalyell and George Galloway, opposed NATO's intervention. Tony Benn argued in Parliament that the action 'whatever the legality or morality of the war that has been launched against Yugoslavia, the bombing has gravely worsened the refugee crisis'.[38] Notably, Benn asserts the action is a war while dismissing the relevance of its legality. Tam Dalyell questioned whether the Serbian people could be 'bombed into submission'; he was not only questioning the legitimacy of intervention, but also the methods by which that intervention was pursued.[39] Yet, despite criticism the dominant message remained that of the pro-interventionists. As critics such as Noam Chomsky have pointed out since the conflict, intervention on moral grounds has gained legitimacy.[40] Not only do such justifications appear to allow intervention in the affairs of other countries, but they also help to shape the public's perceptions of those actions. As Philip Hammond has argued, the West adopted the moral high ground and this is reflected in the depiction of their soldiers as peacekeepers, or aid workers; significantly portrayed in non-military circumstances.[41]

Kosovo did present a different problem and this rested on the nature of the ethnicity of the conflict. Some observers noted the troubled history of the Balkans and pointed to the ethnically motivated violence as reason for non-intervention. Such views clouded the war narrative structure that demanded a clearly identifiable enemy. This was specifically pertinent in the case of Kosovo where the enemy was vilified on humanitarian grounds. However, as Noel Malcolm has discussed, this argument is less clear-cut than initially supposed.[42] He acknowledges a substantial degree of separation between the Serb and Albanian populations. Linguistically they are separated and religiously they are split between Eastern Orthodox on the part of the Serbs and Muslim. But, he argues, evidence of a continuing simmering ethnic hatred is less than convincing. Malcolm suggests that although the Albanians are politically mobilized there is no history of mobilization along religious grounds with any recognizable Islamic political movement. This makes it difficult to prove the existence of a systematic plan of ethnic cleansing in the absence of distinct ethnic friction. Not until a spark, such as Racak, could the necessity of involvement be proved. Even then, allied intervention would continue to proceed on a precarious footing.

Because of the delicate position the Western powers found themselves in, the air campaign started cautiously. It was assumed a few days 'light' bombing would offer sufficient diplomatic room for Milosevic to back down and do so in a manner allowing him to save face. This assumption proved to be a woefully optimistic evaluation of the situation. An awareness of the delicacy of public opinion, not helped by the vague definition and explanation of allied objectives, meant allied offensive air strikes were initially tentative. It was not until the end of March 1999 that General Wesley Clark, Supreme Allied Commander Europe (hereafter SACEUR), received authorization to go after a broad range of targets.

The tentative nature of the military initiative reflected to some degree the acceptance of the role of public opinion during the conflict. Undoubtedly a swifter conclusion to hostilities could have been reached by the full implementation of air power available to the allied forces. The destruction of power supplies, civilian facilities and infrastructure would have forced an earlier capitulation. However, as the Gulf War had shown, public opinion had its role to play. As Michael Ignatieff explains, the 'presence of cameras in the field of operations does more than exert a constraint on military actions. It changes the focus of hostilities from the enemy's fielded forces to the civilian opinion at home which sustains the will to fight'.[43] The tactical battle for Kosovo could seemingly only be lost on the domestic front. Just as in the Gulf War and subsequent conflicts, the tactical advantage gained by full-scale military deployment was dissipated by public relations concerns. Once again, this was especially relevant in the case of Kosovo where the war was being fought in the name of humanitarian concerns. A more aggressive policy could have ruined NATO's justifications for intervention on moral and humanitarian grounds. As a result, military action came second to the desire to maintain national and international support for intervention. A reasonable and clinical assault was required to maintain not only the strategic alliance, but also public harmony and support.

In another respect Kosovo presented a further challenge to the policymakers. If the Gulf War was branded the first 'live' war, Kosovo has its own claim to exclusivity. The conflict took place during the Internet age and this offered fresh challenges in the fight for domestic public opinion. The Internet offered a haven for dissenting voices, a forum for non-mainstream opinion, and an ideological challenge to state-influenced traditional media. Those people seeking news on the Internet were often those people looking for alternative opinions. While Serbia found it difficult to disseminate information and propagandistic messages through traditional media the new technology of the Internet age made information more difficult to monopolize. Philip Taylor goes so far as to suggest that, for the Serbs, the Internet was perhaps their only weapon of retaliation.[44] Enrico Brivio supports the view by arguing that compared with Desert Storm, the Allied Forces in Kosovo had to deal with an enemy far more skilful and efficient in the use of modern communication media.[45] The advancement of mobile communication systems and the Internet potentially provided not only journalists with more opportunities to transmit uncensored views, but also facilitated transmission of information by the belligerent nations.

Despite the addition of new technology to the armoury of those seeking news outside of the traditional media facilities, questions remain about the effectiveness of the Internet. Indeed, as mentioned, the new technology could provide a haven for dissension and a voice for those who may otherwise be excluded from participation in the media chain. Yet, the extent to which this can affect public opinion remains uncertain. Those seeking information from the Internet are often people already seeking a more radical or alternative argument. As such the influence upon public opinion can be seen as limited. Preaching to the converted the Internet would reinforce rather than transform public opinion. Alternatively, if the Internet is utilized by opinion formers, such as journalists, the influence of this digital medium could result in a disproportionate exposure of such views. Either way, the role of traditional media, such as the printed press and television, remained the foremost battleground in the fight for shaping public opinion.

The *Green Book*

History is only one element in understanding propaganda during war. In any discussion of the role of the media in conflict it is necessary to understand the circumstances under which the information presented finds its way into the public domain. Most discussion of the restrictions the media face during war focuses on that imposed by the governments or military of the nation concerned. Secondary literature often analyses the factors that contributed to shaping the daily stories disseminated by the press and other media. Media sources often cite the restrictions placed upon them as a defence against accusations that they became a mouthpiece for the government or military message. These are relevant discussions and will be considered below. However, it is also necessary to examine to what extent the press exercise self-censorship during conflict.

Noam Chomsky comments when 'the guns are firing, even if only in one direction, the media close ranks and become a cheering section for the home team, sums up the traditional arguments regarding media censorship during conflict. Overwhelmingly, that is what happened in the Gulf conflict'.[46] Although ostensibly discussing the media in the United States, this criticism can also be levelled at the media in Great Britain. The involvement of the 'home team', however, means that media restrictions have usually been implemented and as such, the media can use the argument of external restrictions in an attempt to deflect some criticism. If the British press were reiterating a domestic military or political view in their coverage of the Gulf War and Kosovo, one may be able to justify their actions to some extent under the restrictions of war. However, when establishing the context of conflict, before British forces are called into action, the press is not confined by such restrictions.

The MOD has established a media policy for the treatment and facilitation of information during crises. The policy has evolved and remains available for consultation throughout peace and war and thus becomes a point of reference for journalists and editors. It has also established what is and what is not acceptable for the press to report and in what context. Allegations that it shapes the daily news stories are upheld even during peace. Newspapers follow certain propagandistic traits throughout conflict, which is the basis for discussion in this text. However, to suggest this is solely the result of enforced restrictions is incorrect. The basis for how conflict is reported is firmly established in the initial phases of a crisis. In the cases studied here, this is before British military involvement. It is a period when a well-established conflict narrative is instigated. However, it is important then, in the study of propaganda during war, to establish how censorship has evolved, what restrictions are in place and to consider to what degree newspapers conform to this during and outside of the context of war.

A coherent media policy for the conduct of both the media and military during crises is, according to Stephen Badsey, of relatively recent importance. Badsey claims that before 1990 the planners of British military activity had regarded the influence of the media as a peripheral issue, something that is no longer possible in contemporary conflict.[47] This assertion initially appears to ignore earlier conflicts where the role of the media was questioned. It seems plausible to cite the Falklands Conflict of 1982 between Great Britain and Argentina as the commencement of a perceived need to develop a media policy. It was during this conflict that the basis for contemporary media policy was forged and an update was certainly due. As Robert Harris has noted, upon application to join the British Task Force the 'correspondents filled in accreditation papers so old that they contained passages in Arabic, relics of the Suez adventure twenty-six years before'.[48] The dated nature of these forms mirrored the antiquated assumption upon which the military–media relations were based. It was widely assumed the objectives of the media and the military were incompatible; that the 'essence of successful warfare is secrecy. The essence of successful journalism is publicity'.[49]

The Falklands War was an anomaly concerning media relations. The remoteness of the islands, some 8000 miles away from Britain, handed the initiative to the military coordinators. Images and text could be delayed and transmitted at intervals suited to media–military plans, with the average story arriving back in Britain two days after initially being written. The lack of footage available saw the reinvention of the war artist and this exacerbated the perception of the conflict in terms of a traditional form of imperialist adventure. With the development of modern technology, achieving such a monopoly over the dissemination of information would be far more difficult in the future. However, contemporary media policy resonates with many of the same concerns and influences encountered during the Falklands campaign.

The Gulf War was to provide a fresh test for media management. The requirement of journalists to travel with the Task Force during the Falklands had eliminated most scope for diversity in war coverage. The only conflicting stories were emanating from Argentina as no foreign news correspondents were allowed to travel with the fleet. This meant no journalists were able to travel independently such as had been the case during the Vietnam War. The idea of incorporating the media in this way evolved into the system employed in the Gulf. The media policy, adopted in unison with United States' forces, involved, as Philip Taylor describes, a 'three strand system'.[50] Briefly, this meant Saudi Arabia hosted a Joint Information Bureau in Dhahran and daily press briefings in Riyadh. The third strand was the pool system that had been a necessity during the Falklands and was now seen as the desired method in future conflict. Media policy was addressed and absorbed into the military structure in order to regulate it. The pool system consisted of Media Reporting Teams (hereafter MRTs) that were formed and supervised by MOD public relations officers (hereafter PROs). The limited number of these places, around 200, meant that copy generated by them was shared amongst all news organizations that required it. This, therefore, restricted the scope of media sources, especially as no places were made available for reporters from countries other than Britain, France and the United States. Field censors reviewed the text that was then sent to the Forward Transmission Units (hereafter FTUs), which had access to the direct satellite links to London. This, in theory, was the structure and organization of media representation associated with the military. However, it did not cover the existence of satellite phones that allowed some independent transmission of information. As a result, journalists who attempted to work outside this structure, known as 'unilaterals', were to cause some additional problems for the military.

By the time of the Kosovo Conflict the evolution of media policy had crystallized into its current form, the MOD *Green Book*.[51] As the foreword suggests:

> In short, the handbook sets out what editors can expect from the Ministry of Defence and what the MOD seeks from the media. It is the result of a dialogue between the MOD and the media which began after the Falklands Conflict and which takes account of the lessons learnt in the Gulf War and other operations.[52]

The document provided the media policy during the Kosovo Conflict and recently was invoked during the conflicts in Afghanistan and Iraq. It is an attempt to clarify media–military relations during crises, but succeeds only in clearly defining the ambiguity. The text establishes a legal framework, a contract for media representatives to sign. In return for access to the nation's military representatives, the journalists become tied to a document that hands all of the initiative to the armed forces. It is deliberately vague with interpretation performed by the military themselves.

The overriding tenet of the *Green Book* is the protection of operational security. Falklands War policy constructed upon the foundation of irreconcilable media–military objectives has not been escaped, merely recognized and addressed. Just as the Falklands War's media policy referred to the conflict of interest the new text reiterates a similar message in updated terms. The *Green Book* states that when 'it is necessary to impose security vetting, the MOD will [seek] the co-operation of editors in achieving a system which is fair and even handed and which is applied only in the interest of national or operational security, to safeguard UK or Allied operations or lives'.[53] The overriding principle of operational security over public right to know persists. This demonstrates a consistency in media policy that has withstood technological change. In fact, the *Green Book* bears a remarkable similarity to the instructions issued to Falklands correspondents. The policy established during the Falklands was set out by Sir Frank Cooper and is worth noting at length for an effective comparison with the *Green Book*. The directive stated:

Officers and crews of ships with embarked correspondents should be reminded of the standard rules for dealing with the press and are to be specifically briefed to avoid discussing with them or in their hearing the following:

a   Speculation about possible future action.
b   Plans for operations.
c   Readiness state details about individual units' operational capability, movements and deployment.
d   Details about military techniques and tactics.
e   Logistic details.
f   Intelligence about Argentine forces.
g   Equipment capabilities and defects.
h   Communications.[54]

Despite the numerous changes in technology in the intervening years the current regulations are notably similar:

12. Restrictions on Reporting. Correspondents must accept that, in the conditions under which they will be operating, the appropriate operational commander has the right to restrict what operational information can be reported and when. Correspondents will be advised on current restrictions (which will differ from operation to operation) by the nominated PR officer, acting on behalf of the senior commander. Subjects that correspondents may not be allowed to include in copy, or radio or television reports without specific approval may include at least some of the following:

a   Composition of the force and the locations of ships, units and aircraft.
b   Details of military movements.
c   Operational orders.
d   Plans or intentions.
e   Casualties.
f   Organisations.
g   Place names.
h   Tactics, details of defensive positions, camouflage methods, weapon capabilities or deployments.
i   Names or numbers of ships, units or aircraft.
j   Names of individual servicemen.

13. Control of the Release of Information. In the interest of the security of the force and of the individual, correspondents must accept that, on certain occasions, they will be required to submit

all written material, voice items intended for radio or television, films or video recordings produced for associated scripts or voice accompaniments and still photographs for before transmission.[55]

The contemporary regulations continue along similar lines to those in place during the Falklands, but with some additions. Perhaps the most striking alteration is the shift of emphasis in responsibility. The Falklands directive is aimed primarily at officers and crew serving on ships carrying journalists, and as such, the restrictions apply to what a reporter should or should not be exposed. The emphasis denigrates the position of journalists, relegating them effectively to the level of a spy whose mere exposure to sensitive information would result in front page news. When one reconsiders the military leadership's view of the incompatibility of media–military objectives, this attitude appears inevitable.

The shift in emphasis adopted by the *Green Book* reflects the acceptance of the role of media during conflict and its growing influence. The restrictions are issued to journalists, for journalists to conform to. It states the conditions under which they will be expected to operate and the likely censorship they will have to endure. By doing this the MOD shifts the burden of responsibility from themselves onto the media. While appearing to move with contemporary developments this change, in fact, further reduces the media's room to operate. A signed declaration of the acceptance of these guidelines, upon application for accreditation, reinforces the legality of the arrangement and subjects those who have accepted to military law. Therefore, as Badsey suggested, before 1990 the issue of media relations was one of peripheral concern to the military and an item for which they took responsibility. Despite the similarity in the areas of concern about media reportage and the subsequent debates about the Falklands and media policy, the issue is not truly addressed until after this conflict. As such, the Gulf War can be seen as a turning point in military–media relations in Britain. The acknowledgement of the importance of modern media in contemporary conflict has manifested itself in an attempt to remove the military's burden of responsibility and place it at the feet of those reporting the war.

The complete dominance of the military over the media, theoretically at least, is demonstrated consistently throughout the document and extends from the front-line war correspondent to the domestic, home front, media. In four distinct ways, the *Green Book* constructs a framework of censorship extending from the location of British armed forces to the front pages of newspapers. First, the military machine disassociates itself from the provision of equipment to transmit news items back to Britain. The regulations commit some effort to be made by the military by claiming that '[s]pecialist PR staff will be dispatched to the theatre of operations with the first troop deployments to assist with the provision of media facilities at British and Allied headquarters and with units in the field'.[56] It is true that during the

Gulf War the media was supplied with transmission facilities by the armed forces, but the speed at which this service was provided was a form of censorship in itself. What the media censorship framework establishes is the removal of responsibility, again, from the military to the media. In other words, when it is beneficial for the military, transmission facilities can be provided. The disclaimer reads:

> Correspondents will also be expected to provide their own communications and transmission equipment. If absolutely necessary, assistance with communications may be given using military or MOD-controlled civil facilities. However, since the actual act of transmission could endanger an operation, or the safety of a unit under some circumstances, the use of both military and correspondent's own equipment will be at the discretion of commanders. Charges will be raised for the use of Service equipment.[57]

Thus, this section removes the obligation for the military to provide media facilities. In doing so, the passage takes into account the development of satellite technology that permits journalists to transmit data independently. This point is reiterated with reference to the Front Line Media Pools (hereafter FLMPs):

> The success of the FLMPs and any other front-line facilities, for both the media and the MOD, will depend on the rapid processing of material from the theatre to news offices. However, the movement and transmission of news material in an operational area will be fraught with difficulties and at times the act of transmission itself could jeopardise an operation or endanger a unit. Therefore, the carriage of media material, and its transmission, will be subject both [to] the safety of military personnel and to operational and security requirements.[58]

This covers the military for delay as well as denial of transmission, a tactic that proved useful during the Falklands Conflict. Once again, the justification for this is included under the umbrella term of operational security. While it is not disputed that operational security is a legitimate necessity for controlling aspects of data transmission, the reason could be subject to abuse if continually cited for the military's disregarding of its media obligations.

Second, the restrictions on front-line war correspondents are extended to all accredited journalists. In the case of the Gulf War, this meant all journalists receiving information from the operational updates in Saudi Arabia. The text above refers to correspondents, or more specifically war correspondents, which have separate obligations due to their attachment to front-line forces. It is explained to them that:

> The purpose of security vetting material produced by our war correspondents attached to units is to ensure only that no information is inadvertently made public which might be of benefit to an enemy, or would endanger an operation, or the lives of British or allied Servicemen or civilians.[59]

This is a specific reference to war correspondents with the front-line troops and seems to make them a unique example. The differentiation between types of journalists and their responsibilities is further reiterated in the main text:

> In time of conflict, accredited correspondents attached to front-line UK Forces will be designated as **'war correspondents'** and issued with authority documents. They will be encouraged to wear distinguishing 'media' insignia while working with the units in the field. They will not be permitted to carry arms.[60]

However, despite this emphasis of distinction between the types of journalist, the situation is not unique to those assigned only to front-line field units. Registered correspondents, or non-accredited media, are provided with briefings, interviews, limited communications and transport facilities to accompany units to the field. Concerning these provisions it is stated:

> All media representatives accepting these special facilities, will be required to agree to abide by the **'GROUND RULES for CORRESPONDENTS'** (see annex A) and to submit all material for security vetting if required. Breach of the Ground Rules may result in facilities being withdrawn.[61]

The condition of submitting copy for security vetting is extended to all accredited journalists and others utilizing the MOD facilities and not simply to those designated as war correspondents. Any source wishing to use MOD facilities is subject, first to security vetting via the application process and second through possible military censorship, further enhancing the military's grip on the flow of information.

Third, the restrictions imposed on journalists reduce the number and variety of sources available for reporting the events. By tying in all correspondents with accreditation the military establish conformity of output to some degree, all text can be assessed against certain criteria. The number of sources is further reduced with the implementation of the pool system itself. In theory the implementation of a pooling system is not automatic:

Wherever possible, all other facilities given by the MOD and British Forces will be granted to all media representatives. However, for security and practical reasons, on occasions – especially in the theatre of operations – numbers may have to be limited. In such cases, the MOD will endeavour to provide as many places as possible, allocated under a pooling system, so that the media as a whole can be represented.[62]

In effect, 'pooling arrangements will apply whenever demand exceeds capacity on a facility'.[63] It would be safe to assume that in most international crises, for which these restrictions are designed, demand is likely to exceed capacity. The interests generated by the mobilization and intervention of home forces will indubitably generate public interest. In reality, therefore, the pooling system will be implemented during military conflict involving British forces.

The fact that the censorship system limits the number of sources available to the media is denied in the *Green Book*. Contrary to the reality established above the guidelines claim that '[b]y making a wide range and number of facilities available and by adopting the pooling system, both in the UK and in theatre, it is hoped that editors will be represented fairly and will gain a complete overall picture of events from a variety of sources'.[64] However, to claim the interpretation comes from a variety of sources is absurd. The sources are strictly limited by the military and funnelled through military channels to be dispersed through media organizations. The multitude of media outlets vying for commercial market-space on the domestic front are in fact virtually sourced, if not *by* the military, then at least *through* the military. It reduces not only the quantity of material but also the variety of interpretation, which now has to be superimposed onto other journalists' text out of its original context. In addition to this, the mechanics of the pool system further reduces the opportunity for a variety of journalistic opinion by restricting rotation in the FLMPs:

> The MOD does not intend to impose compulsory rotation of FLMPs except possibly where operations continue over a protracted period. Indeed, once attached to a FLMP, it may be operationally difficult for a correspondent to leave. FLMPs have been shown to be more effective and less of an operational risk once correspondents have become familiar in working with their assigned units in operational conditions and a degree of mutual trust has been established. Therefore, FLMP members normally will be rotated only in the event of accident, or fatigue, or at the request of editors. If for any reason, a correspondent were to leave a FLMP, the place would be offered to another from the same media category – not necessarily from the same newspaper or broadcasting company

but on a 'next-on-the-list' basis. Any general change-over of correspondents would be made by the MOD in consultation with
media organisations.[65]

It may be that rotating a reporter in some situations is impractical, but
retaining a particular correspondent with a particular unit has its advantages
for the military. In addition to training a correspondent in such a way that
they are not a military liability, assimilation also promotes an increased likelihood of a positive portrayal of life with the fighting unit. Because 'members
of FLMPs will live and work alongside the troops, sharing their food,
accommodation and basic domestic chores' they become dependent upon
the military and as such assimilated within it.[66] One is less likely to criticize
certain facets of its duties once part of the close-quarters running of a unit.
Instead, criticism is likely to be of only the day-to-day difficulties of administration, living conditions and equipment, which in itself evokes sympathy for
the soldiers. This microcosm of access afforded to the press denies a sense of
presenting a larger, more diverse understanding of the issues.

The pool system, therefore, restricts the number of 'witnesses' to military
action and assimilates those assigned to them. By restricting rotation, the
overall numbers are kept to a minimum and the system imposes limits to
what the individuals actually bear witness. In such an environment, it would
be impossible for a single reporter to gain an overall perspective of events.
The scenes they are privileged to witness are likely to be stage-managed
and constructed to give a certain desired perspective. These restricted reports
are then funnelled through the military censorship to be digested for mass
consumption by the rest of the media. The rest of the media, including
those not assigned places, are usually the smaller, regional and non-
mainstream press. Such a system does not facilitate information gathering
from a variety of sources and a multiplicity of opinion.

Some attempts have been made to operate outside these boundaries and
report news in a manner independent of military restriction. During the
Gulf War, the much-vaunted 'unilaterals' sought to research events by operating on their own initiative. However, for those who attempt to seek alternative ways of gleaning information outside these 'legitimate' boundaries,
the *Green Book* contains a thinly veiled warning:

> Media representatives who gain access to operational areas, other
> than under the auspices of MOD or Allied PR staffs, should appre-
> ciate that they do so at their own risk and that neither the MOD nor
> Allied staffs can be held responsible for their safety or assistance.
> Journalists who choose to act independently should also appreciate
> that, if their presence or actions are considered to pose a threat to
> operational security, however inadvertently, they may be liable to
> removal along with other civilians.[67]

In short, the official media channels quickly begin to take the appearance of the only media channels acceptable to the military leadership. As the Gulf War demonstrated, some unilateral action was attempted, but these regulations are designed to keep such action to a minimum.

Fourth, and finally, the *Green Book* manages to make provisions for what is reported directly to the home audience. In addition to indirect censorship via military manipulation of the individual reporters, the conditions imposed make direct reference to what newspapers should actually print. Editors are reminded that:

> On the home front, editors should be aware that analysis of events and capabilities by well-informed specialists, such as academics, or retired officers and officials, could be of assistance to an enemy. They are requested, therefore, to take special care when inviting speculation from such experts.[68]

One point to note is the employment of the term 'home front' instils a degree of nostalgia, reminiscent of the First and Second World Wars. The idiom insinuates the existence of a battlefront 'back home', one that needs to be fought and won. More overtly, editors starved of information, with the exclusion of that permitted by the military, are now asked to refrain from speculating about probable events and issues. With a protracted build-up to any conflict, this would be virtually impossible to dispense with. Diplomatic wrangling combined with military preparations can take a significant period of time, time in which little or nothing is happening militarily. During this stage, it is necessary to fill a news void caused not only by inaction but also by military secrecy. It seems implausible that the combined strategic guesswork of editors and experts is likely to provide any substantial information that an enemy could not ascertain for themselves. Furthermore, if a plethora of possibilities were formulated and expounded it would exacerbate the enemy's confusion.

At this point, however, the restrictions show some exception to the strict utilization of information concerning the conflict. While it is inadvisable for those on the domestic sphere to second-guess the practical implementation of intervention it can at times be of benefit to one's own military objectives:

> Wherever possible, the PR staff and commanders in London and in the theatre of operations, will attempt to explain the reasons why information cannot be given, or must be delayed. They will not attempt to deceive journalists or use them deliberately and unwittingly in furthering deception plans, although there will, of course, be occasions where operations are mounted to deceive the enemy when their true purpose will not be disclosed.[69]

In essence, the military reserve the right to utilize the press and media in general to transmit propaganda ploys to deceive the enemy. The above passage appears to contradict itself, initially reassuring the media that they will not be 'deliberately' deceived, yet conceding that there will 'be occasions where operations are mounted to deceive the enemy when their true purpose will not be disclosed'. The passage is open for interpretation; its vagueness lends itself to the justification of incidents whereby deception is used to deceive both the enemy and the press.

These four elements: control of information transmission, subjugation of all accredited journalists to military restriction, the restriction of access to sources and interference with domestic output, are combined into one, legally binding document to which editors and journalists have to subscribe in order to gain access to the British military. Without such access, opportunities to report from the battlefield are considerably more dangerous and journalists risk being detained or removed by Western forces. Admittance would also be denied to the MOD's briefings and the absence of coverage from these media events would place a journalist or news organization at a disadvantage to rivals, as well as leaving them open to accusations of producing unpatriotic and biased news. Thus, the *Green Book* offers the blueprint for what is potentially an extremely strict form of censorship. If this is in operation, it begs the question why has there not been more resistance to it.

Conclusion

Both conflicts required the press and governments to utilize history for a number of reasons. Reference to past events from Iraq and Kosovo placed the crises into context; this can become clouded during the evolution of the crises. However, the press often exacerbate the uncertainty regarding the precedents of war by framing events within an immediate timeframe. The necessity to frame events explains another use of history by the press, the creation of a war narrative. This method defines the circumstances for war, identifies the belligerents and aids the advancement of the war narrative.

The establishment of an identifiable starting point for any conflict, a requisite of the war narrative, also has implications for legitimizing intervention in a crisis. The Gulf War lent itself to a relatively straightforward justification for action. Aided by UN backing and given the legitimacy of a wide-ranging coalition, British and American policymakers could point to the Iraqi invasion of Kuwait as the simple excuse for intervening, despite opponents' attempts to highlight the strategic and economic benefits of these nations acting. Kosovo had a less clearly defined starting point as well as indistinct belligerents and, as a result, this made the construction of a war narrative more difficult. However, a shift in emphasis concerning the form of legitimacy employed meant these hurdles could be overcome. Whether these justifications would have sufficed if ground forces and subsequent allied casualties had been encountered remains open to debate.

The much-vaunted definition of the two crises in terms of the media technology available at the time has less influence on the conduct of the conflicts than may at first be assumed. Despite reference to the first 'live' war, or conflict in the Internet age, the influence of technology has not brought with it a greater public understanding of events or critical coverage of political decisions. Although the development of technology and the experience of the Falklands meant that recognition of the existence of the media was necessary, this failed to seriously affect the conduct of war. Instead, an overhaul of the media restrictions produced a multilayered blanket of media restrictions that, theoretically at least, stifled the media's ability to report the crises comprehensively.

One must stress the term theoretically when analysing the nature of military media restrictions. Philip Taylor has emphasized how little the British military interfered with journalists' copy. For example, he cites BBC reporter Kate Adie commenting that 'few military personnel – if any – were hostile to open reporting; most thought it democratically correct to have the media alongside'.[70] However, if the framework exists, the fact that few reports were censored suggests the boundaries were not tested. The establishment of a narrative structure began in both cases before the commitment of British forces to aggressive military action. As such, the press were not restricted by the requirements of the *Green Book*. However, despite this the coverage of events still conforms to the desired framing of events to support calls for intervention. This suggests a realignment of the media versus military relationship. Not realignment in favour of either one or the other, but a compatibility of objectives that sees the propagandist and the commercial newspapers construct mutually beneficial war narratives.

4

UNCENSORED NEWS, CRITICAL DEBATE?

Introduction

The previous chapter established the potential for the military to dominate news dissemination through the implementation of the *Green Book*. With this degree of restriction achievable, it appears feasible to concur with the assertion that 'in the nation-state of late capitalism information management is inherently totalitarian'.[1] However, debate surrounding the influences of and influences upon the media is varied. This leaves open the question pertaining to the media's influence, a debate that rises to prominence during conflict. It is also not appropriate merely to discuss the influence of the media or politicians as singular entities.

One can argue that the executive has usurped the power of the legislature and that visual media dominate the flow of information. Peter Riddell of *The Times*, for example, argued that the dominant forum for political discussion is now the broadcasting studio as opposed to Parliament.[2] While Riddell drew a distinction between visual and printed media, asserting the balance of power favoured broadcasting, Professor Jeremy Tunstall of City University London, stated that newspapers in fact retain a dominant level of political influence:

> In Western democracies, much of the potential political and partisan power of television has been deliberately neutered in line with consensual public interest. Newspapers, however, exercise a continuing prerogative both to bias the news and to slant comment. It is newspapers, not television, which go for the politician's jugular.[3]

It is debatable which opinion retains most credibility. The theory of a totalitarian media system is one that would sit uncomfortably with both political and military leaders. In conflict against dictatorial regimes, the 'free' press in Britain is championed as another facet of the superior, democratic nature of society. However, this does not necessarily correlate into a press willing to attack the political system.

Dr Piers Robinson of Liverpool University addressed this dilemma in an article on the existence of the 'CNN effect'.[4] The model developed by Robinson asserted that the media would have influence if the government policy were uncertain. In this instance, the media coverage would be extensive and critical. Conversely, the media would enjoy no influence when the government line was certain, in these circumstances the media coverage would be in line with official policy. Although this model was developed in relation to US media during Bosnia 1995 and Kosovo 1999, media influence is often discussed in relation to 'Western democracies' rather than individual nation-states. It is therefore useful to test this hypothesis against British press coverage.

The notion that the media can be dominated by the totalitarian nature of information technology and assert little influence over government when policy is clearly defined seems more credible during the involvement of British forces in conflict, especially after analysis of the *Green Book*. However, in the absence of official media restrictions and a non-defined government policy the period before the commencement of hostilities on the part of British forces should be a time when varied opinion is present in the press.

This chapter will examine the creation of the war narrative in the press that complemented the pro-interventionist argument in both crises. However, the period to be examined will be that before the commencement of hostile military activities by British forces, and hence seemingly unrestrained by the *Green Book*.

The initial periods of conflict establish much of the tone and rhetoric to be employed by editors throughout the crisis, a narrative that will shape the public's understanding of the events. A thematic examination allows comparison of both the narratives and propaganda themes employed and comparison between newspaper sources. This analysis will establish both the structure and utilization of propagandistic themes by the newspapers in the periods preceding hostile British military activity. For the Gulf War a period of July through to August 1990 will be examined. This allows for some analysis of coverage surrounding Iraq in the run-up to the invasion of Kuwait. For Kosovo there is no clear 'invasion' date so the period January 1999, the time of the Racak massacre, through to March, when NATO launched air strikes, will be used.

The chapter will argue that despite the opportunity to report events before the decision for military action had been declared, the bulk of coverage and editorial stance created the foundations for the war narrative and utilized propaganda to create legitimacy for intervention. While the themes may be developed, expanded or altered during a crisis, the initial phases of media attention construct a basis from which any understanding of future events is grounded. This challenges the assumption that newspapers became the propagandistic mouthpiece of government during conflict solely because of the external restrictions placed upon them.

The chapter will begin with an analysis of news before the crises and examine how the foundations for pro-interventionist propaganda were laid. The chapter will move on to examine how the press, to place their stories into context, selectively utilizes historical background. Finally, the efforts to legitimize future intervention will be considered. The two conflicts, with widely varying natures, demonstrate the behaviour of the press regardless of the circumstances. The comparison of the Gulf and Kosovo crises will demonstrate the continuity of style of coverage and propagandistic methods employed during contemporary conflict. It will be argued that newspaper coverage of neither conflict followed the assumptions forwarded by Robinson regarding television coverage of conflict. Instead, despite the lack of official military censorship and an as yet undefined political policy the newspapers continued to mirror the official political agenda; a policy that was to continue during the conflicts.

News before the crises

The MOD's main argument for the existence of media restrictions is security; as such, they are applicable from the commitment of British troops. However, newspaper coverage begins before the involvement of British forces and hence allegedly free from overt censorship. For example, the press briefings provided by NATO during the Kosovo Conflict did not begin until the 25 March 1999, whereas the issue experienced heightened media awareness from January 1999.

Before the Iraqi invasion of Kuwait, newspaper coverage of Iraq and Iraqi leader Saddam Hussein was notable for its absence of the more visible excesses of propagandistic rhetoric. This raises questions regarding the level of vitriol afforded to Hussein and Iraq during the conflict. The presentation of the enemy was significantly different to its portrayal relatively close to the onset of hostilities. To demonstrate the absence of propagandistic language during this period one can utilize the case of the release of British nurse Daphne Parish. The event marked a clear link between the two nations and involved aggression on the part of Iraq towards a British citizen. The example of this news story allows for a comparison of attitudes in the press towards Iraq before the onset of hostilities with those after. Less hostile reporting of Saddam Hussein and Iraq during this event undermines the degree of hostility towards and personalization of the conflict to Saddam Hussein that appears less than a month later.

Daphne Parish was arrested along with *Observer* journalist Farzad Bazoft who had been accused of spying and subsequently executed. Parish was later released for her part in allegedly abetting Bazoft. *The Times* carried the story of her release on the 17 July 1990, noting her freedom was made possible by the intervention of President Kaunda of Zambia. However, rather than presenting the story as an opportunity to criticize the Iraqi regime, the case was portrayed as an opportunity for reconciliation between the two countries. *The Times* led with a quote from Foreign Office spokesman William Waldegrave taken from a BBC Radio 4 interview stating:

> Although the president [Kaunda of Zambia] knew of the problem we had with Iraq over this, he goes back a long way with Saddam Hussein. I hope it means our relations, which are always liable to be [a] bit bumpy with Iraq, for historical reasons, are aimed in the right direction again. We would like to have good tactical and normal relations with Iraq.[5]

The Guardian adopted the same tone and quoted the above passage.[6] *The Daily Telegraph* paraphrased identical sentiments by suggesting that 'Western diplomats in Baghdad believed the freeing of Mrs. Parish, 53, reflects willingness by the Iraqi government to begin improving relations with Britain and the west after the crisis over the execution of Bazoft'.[7] The broadsheets reflected to some degree the belief or desire that these events marked the opportunity for improved relations between the countries. *The Times* further promoted the mood of optimism by asserting that the release was a publicity stunt aimed at drawing attention to Saddam Hussein's efforts to introduce a new constitution to the country. This constitution, the newspaper proposed, would encourage the set up of new political parties in opposition and create a free press and broadcasting network.[8] Even when reporting President Kaunda's criticisms of Britain, where he blamed rhetorical attacks on Hussein by Britain for Bazoft's death, the report reiterated words of reconciliation. Citing Peter Hinchcliffe, British High Commissioner to Zambia, the article stated 'I hope we can start a new chapter in the long relations between Britain and Iraq'.[9]

It would be wrong to utilize these comments as unified, optimistic analysis of events by the broadsheets; notably, the positive comments come from government officials and diplomats. *The Guardian*, for its part, remained relatively silent on the significance of the event. *The Times* coverage appears to support the optimistic interpretation of Parish's release. Significantly, though *The Daily Telegraph* took a firm editorial line. The paper attacked Iraq openly, stating that 'President Hussein's ruthless pursuit of military power poses a major threat to the peace of the Middle East, beside which the release of a single British citizen pales into insignificance'.[10] There is a clear distinction between the editorial attitudes of *The Times* and *Telegraph* towards Iraq, with *The Guardian* taking a more neutral stance. While the *Telegraph* sought to insert a degree of scepticism, the coverage of each newspaper reiterated the thoughts of official sources and reflected the tone of optimism.

Missing from the reports is any form of overt propaganda rhetoric and vitriol that during the conflict were to become a regular occurrence. This demonstrates no predisposed antagonism or strong editorial position on Iraq and Saddam Hussein. In fact, the press was willing to reiterate optimistic assertions presented by official sources. Only the *Telegraph*'s editorial hints at a degree of scepticism. This event therefore suggests a willingness on the part of the broadsheets to adopt the official British line over relations with Iraq. As such, the change in coverage when Iraq invaded Kuwait mirrored the change in attitude presented by official sources.

Tabloid coverage of Daphne Parish's release adopted a similar stance to that of the broadsheets. The newspapers once again reiterated William Waldegrave's words and displayed an editorial stance that was complementary to official attitudes concerning Iraq. Neither the *Sun* nor *Mirror* took the opportunity to condemn Saddam Hussein with the type of rhetoric that was utilized during the conflict. Clearly noticeable during this period is the dearth of coverage afforded to the issue by the tabloid press. Iraq was not a major concern and Saddam Hussein's regime was not under personal attack. The situations required a spark or turning point to both fuel and justify the escalation of propagandistic rhetoric.

The change in attitude towards Iraq began as Saddam Hussein started to openly challenge his Arab neighbours who had helped finance the war against Iran. *The Times'* coverage was strangely contradictory, it reported Saddam's claim to the Kuwaiti island of Bubiyan and referred to the over-production of oil by fellow OPEC members. The newspaper warned:

> An Iraqi invasion of the large but virtually uninhabited island now might plunge the Gulf Arabs, all of whom are treaty-bound to Kuwait in the Gulf Co-operation Council, into a war. So fearsome is the Iraqi president's reputation for unpredictability that such an outcome is regarded in some of the regional capitals as a virtual certainty.[11]

The following day *The Times* noted Iraq's anger towards Kuwait over the alleged plundering of the Rumalia oilfield and called this development an 'unexpected deterioration between former allies'. However, later in the same article the correspondent, Hazhir Teimourian, suggested:

> Indeed, a new aggressive stance by Iraq was predicted soon after the end of the Gulf War . . . At the very least, it was expected that he would use the threat or the actuality of military intervention against Kuwait and Saudi Arabia to avoid repayment of his estimated war debt of $45 billion to the two countries.[12]

The newspaper had difficulty in deciding whether or not the deterioration in relations was unexpected. *The Times'* uncertainty about the outcome of these developments was to be repeated throughout the rest of July. Reports

79

often presented conflicting views on the same day. For example, along with other articles related to the issue, the 26 July 1990 edition carried two pieces on the same page, one insisting 'Experts believe Iraq will stop short of invasion', while another claimed 'Saddam rhetoric "may lead to war"'.[13]

The editorial ambiguity surrounding the events and the probable resolution produced a more conciliatory attitude towards Iraq. In light of the willingness of the broadsheets to reiterate, and apparently support the conciliatory interpretation of Daphne Parish's release, this approach appears consistent. *The Times* was not alone in this policy with *The Guardian* suggesting that, 'there is a distinct note of sympathy – outside the Gulf – for Iraq's rhetoric about the abuse of Arab oil riches'.[14] The newspaper went on to predict that 'President Saddam Hussein is unlikely to court international sanctions with a big military strike, but he may be preparing a limited attack on the Kuwaiti oil fields in the disputed border region'.[15] These predictions were further watered down the following day as the newspaper reported an Iraqi withdrawal from the border. The *Telegraph* followed the precedent established by the other two broadsheets. Indeed a pattern of indecision is prevalent up to around the 27 July 1990 with frequent and conflicting reports appearing to explain the unfolding events. Generally, the actions of Iraq during this period were seen as sabre-rattling in order to achieve Iraqi demands concerning oil rights and prices. Because of this uncertainty, the rhetoric of the newspapers is relatively conservative and reflects an unclear and hesitant editorial line.

The tabloids managed to avoid contradicting themselves on a daily basis, as the broadsheets had, by ignoring the issue. After the release of Daphne Parish both *The Sun* and *Daily Mirror* remained relatively quiet on the issue until the 26/27 July when Iraqi troop build-ups became harder to ignore. The *Daily Mirror* conservatively complained that Saddam Hussein was employing 'bully boy' tactics, while *The Sun* declined largely to comment.[16] Thus, while the broadsheets provided a running commentary of events with a degree of criticism the tabloids were, perhaps surprisingly, more refrained. Less unforeseen is the severity and rapidity with which the attitudes of the tabloids change after the invasion. This highlights the need for a defining moment to shape press attitudes to an event. Newspapers were unwilling to commit to a clear stance over the issue until the legitimacy of their arguments could be easily sustained.

The turning point for coverage of the Kosovo Conflict was more indistinct than that provided by the Iraqi invasion of Kuwait. Overt Iraqi aggression coupled with blatant flagrancy of international law drew a firm line underneath previous attitudes to events in the Gulf and supplied a clearly identifiable starting date from which the narrative could be plotted. The Kosovo Conflict had a more ambiguous and protracted start, however, the massacre at Racak became the defining moment for the resumption of the Kosovo crisis.

The Kosovo Conflict was deemed to be the re-ignition of the failed October 1998 peace where Slobodan Milosevic had avoided NATO air strikes. Because of this newspaper coverage and public understanding of the situation in Kosovo was tainted by relatively fresh memories of the previous year's events. As such, there is no clear event, such as the release of Daphne Parish, to measure pre-crisis attitudes to Milosevic and Serbia. However, as the Iraqi invasion of Kuwait was to provide the onset of a new crisis, so the massacre at Racak provided the benchmark for new coverage of the Kosovo Conflict. It is from these points that it is possible to verify the germination of propaganda rhetoric that was to be employed during both events, before the full military participation of Britain and thus, before the full implementation of MOD media restrictions.

Creating historical context

The establishment of an identifiable starting point is essential for understanding the necessity for and aims of propaganda rhetoric. Before the war, the newspapers' uncertainty reflected official attitudes. The starting points identified above provide the periods from which hostilities commence. Yet this period is still before the full commitment of British forces to hostile actions and the press coverage cannot be seen as considerably affected by military censorship. Despite this, the newspapers began to construct a pro-interventionist argument that facilitated and promoted the official opinion. The war narrative, which is utilized to explain events and justify intervention, thus began before the involvement of British forces.

From the instigation of the crises, as defined above, the press attempted to provide historical context to explain the events to their readers. The history provided to readers helped to mould attitudes towards conflict. The selective employment of dates, omission or inclusion of historical facts, can determine attitudes and reactions to press coverage during the conflict itself. Thus, an understanding of the context the crises were placed in is essential for understanding the construction of consensus the press wished to pursue.

By the time Iraq invaded Kuwait the history surrounding the crisis had already been spelt out. The broadsheets had given periodic updates of the events and a regular reader would have established the combined themes of war debts stemming from the war with Iran as well as the debates over the sovereignty of the Bubiyan Island and the price of oil. *The Times* attempted further to establish the roots of the conflict by providing the following brief historical outline. 'In 1961, soon after the Anglo-Kuwaiti agreement of 1899 was terminated by mutual consent, General Kassem, the unstable ruler of Iraq, claimed sovereignty over the whole of Kuwait and threatened to occupy it'.[17] In this respect, both the tabloids and broadsheets developed a similar attitude to explaining the context of events. The invasion provided enough reason for intervention without the need for detailed analysis of the events running up to it.

Kosovo, on the other hand, required some explanation by the press after the Racak massacre was reported. *The Guardian* reminded readers that:

> About 2,000 people have been killed in the year-long conflict and at one point last year up to 300,000 were forced from their homes during a Serb offensive aimed at crushing popular support for the KLA.
>
> The monitors were deployed as part of a last-minute deal in October in which the Yugoslav leader, Slobodan Milosevic, agreed to pull back some of his troops from Kosovo to avoid a Nato air bombardment.
>
> The monitors, or 'verifiers', have a mandate to check the Serb troop withdrawals and vague instructions to prepare Kosovo for possible elections. But they have quickly found themselves pulled into a peacekeeping role without any force to back them up.[18]

However, notwithstanding the insinuation of Milosevic's ignition of the current crisis *The Guardian* hesitated from apportioning blame solely to the Serbs. In a more cautious tone, the newspaper noted that:

> Despite the sudden crisis there should have been no surprise at this development, though optimists had thought it might be delayed until an expected spring offensive by the Kosovo Liberation Army.
>
> Under the Holbrooke agreement, which ended a Serb offensive under the threat of Nato air strikes, Serb security forces were supposed to be reduced or withdrawn to barracks and the OSCE monitors were to 'verify' a ceasefire with the ethnic Albanian guerrillas.
>
> The aim was to use the 'credible threat' of force to provide a breathing space for US diplomacy to negotiate an interim political settlement giving Kosovo the broad autonomy it had before 1989.
>
> But events on the ground have moved faster than negotiations. The KLA has been resupplied with weapons smuggled across the border from Albania and has reoccupied villages vacated by Serb security forces.
>
> 'It's all too easy for the KLA to provoke the Serbs, and the Serbs always over-react by taking reprisals and killing civilians,' a well-placed official said. 'This brings back Nato and serves KLA purposes.'[19]

An editorial in *The Times* lamented that the flawed peace settlement of October 1998 had 'as predicted, come apart'.[20] In the same article *The*

Times' editorial policy recognized that the aim of the KLA was cynically to instigate a Racak-style massacre to unleash Western military support, yet, the newspaper insisted that the massacres must not be allowed to continue. *The Daily Telegraph*'s editorial also concluded that Racak had 'blown away the fiction that a shaky ceasefire was in place'.[21] In this respect, Racak is firmly established as a watershed for the events in Kosovo. By defining it in this way, asserting the uniqueness of the incident, a distinction is made with past events that justify a change in policy.

The Sun demonstrated another way in which the historical context was created. The newspaper followed a question and answer formula to establish the context of events. Under the headline 'Kosovo: What is going on?' the article explained:

Q. Why does it matter so much to the Serbs?
A. In 1389 a Serbian army tried to defend their homeland of Kosovo but were crushed by Turkish invaders. Serbia collapsed and since then the Serbs have regarded Kosovo as their heartland and vow never to let it become independent.

Q. What brought about the present problems?
A. In 1989 Milosevic stripped Kosovo of its autonomy. In February 1990 he sent troops, tanks, fighter jets and more than 2,000 police to put down resistance to the Serbs. In July 1990 he made Kosovo a Serb-run police state.

Q. How did the Kosovans fight back?
A. They set up underground schools and universities and started their own parliament. Attacks by the rag-tag Kosovo Liberation Army on Serb police were followed by a string of atrocities. Last week 45 Kosovans were tortured and murdered in the village of Racak, prompting international outrage.[22]

This simple distillation of historical events was laden with a predisposition favouring Kosovar Albanians and as such justified intervention on their behalf. Reference to 1389 and the proclaimed Serbian vow to 'never let it become independent' insinuated a degree of inflexibility, almost unreasonable obstinacy. This attitude manifested itself in the imposition of a 'police state', comparable with preconceived notions of dictatorial rule and intolerance. Finally, the Kosovan fight back is initially framed in terms of peaceful resistance in the form of schools and democracy. Even reference to the KLA placed heavy emphasis on its 'rag-tag' and hence underdog status, in contrast to the atrocities committed by Serbian forces.

Newspapers during both conflicts commented on the historical background and presented a weight of evidence to insinuate Serbian culpability.

However, there is a fundamental difference between the contexts of the Gulf and Kosovo crises. The historical pretext of the Gulf War was virtually irrelevant, despite some consideration of Iraqi claims before the invasion of Kuwait, the very act of outright hostility meant little justification was required to explain a position opposed to Saddam Hussein. Kosovo, on the other hand, had no clear 'bad-guy' and this affected the newspapers' attempts to legitimize the conflict and Britain's involvement in it.

Creating legitimacy for intervention

Once a clear starting point for hostilities has been established and placed within necessary, but often contrived, historical context, the efforts to legitimize official policy commence. In order for suitable propaganda rhetoric to be employed during a conflict, there can be little room for uncertainty pertaining to the legitimacy of intervening. Establishing the legality of government actions is a necessity if favourable news coverage is to be achieved. Establishing this legitimacy of action as early as possible is also advantageous. The two conflicts provide different examples of challenges in establishing this authority. Proving the legitimate right to intervene is an essential prerequisite for other propaganda tools, such as, personalization of the conflict, public approval of objectives and establishing an overall acceptance of the need for, and desirability of, intervention. The media restrictions considered in the previous chapter address military issues but, as has been mentioned, during this period the press is free to express opinions. However, despite the differences between the two conflicts the attempt to establish these pretexts is evident in both.

Providing legitimacy for military intervention involves proving the infallibility of one's own position and developing a clear and identifiable enemy. The Gulf War provided an apparently simple task for the British government and military and consequently for the press as well. An uncomplicated story offers a better framework within which to develop the narrative, but by accepting this rather simplistic narrative, the press reinforces the message emanating from official sources. Furthermore, the oil interests of Britain provided a recognizable threat to everyday life in this country; as such, the opinion of the public was easier to form.

Initially, the broadsheets condemned the invasion but ruled out possible intervention by Western forces, explaining that economic sanctions were the only credible answer. *The Times* reported the invasion as 'Iraq's naked villainy', stating that the 'Iraqi invasion angers both East and West'.[23] *The Guardian*'s front page proclaimed 'Superpowers unite on Iraq,'[24] while similarly *The Daily Telegraph* announced 'Superpowers unite against Iraq'.[25] The initial emphasis of these articles was directed at fostering the notion of unanimous international condemnation. Fostering and sustaining such ideas of unanimity would become vital in sustaining public opinion both domestically and internationally in favour of military intervention. *The Times* summed up this attitude towards the invasion by commenting that the 'international outrage made it likely that economic and diplomatic moves against Iraq would be approved quickly'.[26] It was an attitude that Margaret Thatcher sought to generate and the repetition in the press of her words 'I can't remember a time when the world was so strongly together against an action as now' added weight to the line adopted.[27] With regard to the right of the United States to intervene, *The Times* carried an article that suggested unlike 'Vietnam, this is a clear-cut case of aggression, comparable to Pearl Harbour'.[28]

The most notable voice of dissension from *The Times* came on their letters page and warned not against intervention but rather the role of the press during the impending crisis. A letter from Admiral of the Fleet Lord Fieldhouse (Former Commander of the British Forces in the Falklands) read '[t]he freedom of the press – indeed of all the news media – during crisis such as that which the world has recently entered carries far greater responsibilities than those of keeping the public informed'.[29] He went on to attack the media's second-guessing of possible military action saying it was liable to damage the coalition's cause, a view clearly in line with the MOD's current media guidelines. Furthermore, his letter suggested that during the Second World War the press were wholeheartedly behind the government, but by the Falklands valuable lessons had been forgotten. This was a clear demonstration of the expectancy that still prevailed among at least some military personnel that the media regard informing the public as a subordinate requirement to safeguarding military security.

There was some, albeit limited, criticism of the British government and her would-be allies. *The Guardian* voiced some doubts about how Saddam Hussein had been allowed to develop into such a threat militarily and claimed that the 'invasion of Kuwait may force Saddam's one-time friends to face up to a monster that is partly of their own making'.[30] The newspaper pointed accusingly at France, the Soviet Union and China as the main suppliers of his military hardware. Yet, such remarks were vastly outweighed by the consistent prose supporting the overriding message of international solidarity and the right of intervention. These themes were to form the benchmarks of later propaganda rhetoric.

The invasion of Kuwait raised few quandaries for the editorial policy of the tabloid press and released an onslaught of propaganda techniques. The *Daily Mirror* exclaimed 'Run for your life!' and continued inside with a comment piece call to 'Halt this monster now'.[31] The newspaper launched into an attack of Saddam Hussein that intrinsically involved personalization and demonization of Saddam to explain both the events and the reasons for the invasion. These issues, which will be analysed in more depth in the next chapter, demonstrate how inseparable propaganda themes were from the explanation of action.

The Sun attempted to adopt an alternative perspective on the invasion, but again this was aimed at the domestic audience to provoke maximum emotive response to the events. The front page warned '20p. Petrol Prices set to Soar as the Baghdad Beast Seizes Kuwait', and proclaimed that 'He's got the Oil World in His Hands'.[32] The severity of the situation was masked partially by *The Sun*'s optimistic prediction that the crisis was set to boost the economy as companies such as BP and Shell benefited from higher oil prices. However, the second of the headlines infers Hussein's attempt to play God with the world's resources, a dangerous and powerful threat to Western society.

The coverage was highly personalized and instantly aggressive. The invasion marked a sudden shift in attitude and this shift was exacerbated by a previous lack of coverage. The tabloid's process of legitimizing opposition to Saddam Hussein came less through the establishment of international solidarity, but instead through personalizing the conflict as Saddam against the world.

The Kosovo Conflict once more provided a different challenge to the constructers of consensus. Kosovo did not involve two sovereign nations but lurked within the muddied legal water of an internal conflict. The Kosovar Albanians could not be presented to the public as distinct victims of external aggression. Indeed, the newspapers initially seemed to harbour some reservations as to which side to back, if either. It was only once the Albanians had signed their side of a peace agreement that Slobodan Milosevic could be presented as the sole obstruction to a diplomatic settlement.

The acceptance of these circumstances led to a feeling that, as one enemy could not be identified, intervention may possibly be unwise or impossible. An advocate of this policy was Patrick Bishop writing for *The Daily Telegraph*:

> The stage is set then, for a long, ugly and complex conflict, which it will be increasingly difficult to present as a struggle between good and evil. The absence of clearly identifiable villains and victims lessens the attraction of the Kosovo story for the electronic media, which in turn will diminish pressure on American and European politicians to do something about it. That will come as a relief to them. Nobody who matters has any desire to intervene seriously in Kosovo.
>
> Short of deploying Nato troops to protect the civilian population – which would effectively mean declaring war on Serbia and backing an independent Kosovo – there is nothing now for the outside world to do. Our role will be restricted to trying to provide humanitarian aid to the victims, observing the carnage and bewailing, once again, our inability to stop it.[33]

Bishop's comments are laden with presumptions and assertions. He is dismissive of any alternatives to the crisis apart from his own, claiming '[n]obody who matters has any desire to intervene'. Bishop also presents the crisis in a polarized manner; asserting NATO deployment of troops would automatically 'mean declaring war on Serbia and backing an independent Kosovo'. As the press had struggled to define a clear enemy and as the KLA had previously been branded a terrorist organization, intervention under the terms put forward by Bishop would be unacceptable. While attempting to insinuate the story would be unattractive to the electronic media owing to unidentifiable enemies or allies, Bishop is reinforcing this perception for his own newspaper.

In contrast to the *Telegraph* on the same day *The Times* was bemoaning the government's inability to push through positive action by claiming '[w]ords at Westminster are not the harbingers of action but the alternatives to action. The more violently the British Foreign Secretary attacks President Milosevic, the less likely the British army is to invade Kosovo'.[34] Whereas *The Daily Telegraph* was promoting inaction *The Times* was attacking it. *The Times* also recognized that the Albanians were partially culpable, especially for not seizing their chances to ostracize Milosevic during the peace negotiations. However, its editorial concluded that Europe must not allow 'massacres in their midst and refugees on their doorsteps'.[35]

The Times did include some articles expressing reservations regarding intervention and warned that 'every bombastic intervention makes things worse. But to make them worse only to make us feel better is the height of immorality'.[36] This uncertainty of attitude led the newspaper to conclude that there was nothing in the United Nations Charter to give the United States and Great Britain the authority to attack Serbia; in doing so *The Times*' policy mirrored that of the *Telegraph*. These discussions in the press were echoes of the dilemmas facing policymakers and reflected international uncertainty about the best course of action to pursue. As *The Times* reported:

> One concern expressed by Nato diplomats over the week-end was that the alliance should not be seen to be biased against Mr Milosevic and in support of the Kosovo Liberation Army.
>
> To that end, the North Atlantic Council is expected to call for urgent studies by the military planners into the possibility of sending ground troops to Albania to monitor arms smuggling into Kosovo.[37]

Once the initiative had been taken to involve British troops the newspaper's editorial line opted to support the cause, yet the traditionally conservative newspaper still found an opportunity to be critical of Tony Blair's handling of the situation:

The Government is right to have taken this lead. But Tony Blair needs urgently to explain why it is right for Britain, a middling power, to be so heavily engaged in the cause of wider peace. This question will be asked even if he persuades the country that Kosovo cannot safely be left to burn. He must convince anxious citizens that British troops will be there to serve the cause of European peace, not to fly the flag in support of his ambitions to demonstrate Britain's 'leadership in Europe'. He must guard against future accusations that the British people, whose support for this country's high military profile is a national strength, were in this case not given the full reasons for putting troops in harm's way. The people of this country understand well that a trading nation with global interests must be prepared to deploy its forces where international stability is threatened. But informed assent is the indispensable basis of public support.[38]

A certain amount of confusion surrounded the events, confusion that was not present in the Gulf crisis after the invasion of Kuwait. With the government appearing indecisive and uncertain as to British objectives, *The Times* failed to develop a coherent policy. The massacre at Racak had been enough to generate interest but not to crystallize opinion as to what should be done about it. In fact, *The Times* cast further doubt over Racak by printing:

> The reality of what happened at Racak is still shrouded by claim and counter-claim. What is known is that four Serb policemen were killed outside the village in a Kosovo Liberation Army (KLA) ambush. Subsequently at least 40 ethnic Albanian men from the village were shot in a dawn attack by the Serbs. The Serbs say that all the dead were KLA guerrillas killed in action. The Albanians say they were all civilians killed after capture.[39]

It appears that without a clearly defined policy, or rather a clearly identifiable enemy, *The Times* and *Daily Telegraph* failed to develop a coherent policy, either advocating or not, intervention in Kosovo. It was a problem *The Guardian* faced and for which it provided only vague answers:

> [E]vents press on with their own logic toward three possible outcomes. There could be general war in Kosovo, followed by a withdrawal of the Western monitors and the end of any attempt to control the situation.
>
> Secondly, there could be a partial confrontation with Milosevic which would end in him accepting that a substantial armed force had to enter Kosovo to interpose itself between Serbs and Kosovars

while a political settlement was worked out. That settlement would have to be either independence or something very close to it.

Thirdly, there could be a full scale confrontation with Milosevic, involving air action and Nato ground forces entering Kosovo even if there was Serbian opposition. The first outcome would be disastrous. The second would be difficult, and involve onerous new commitments, but it would be the preferable option. The third would be dangerous business indeed, but it might at some point have to be contemplated.[40]

Intervention on humanitarian grounds was now promoted as a way of overcoming traditional obstacles to intervention when faced with unconventional conflict. The broadsheets struggled to come to terms with these developments and this led to a rather muddled message up to the commencement of NATO hostilities against Serbia. The foundation for propaganda concerning NATO's rights and necessity in intervening in Kosovo was based on ill-defined justifications.

The tabloids largely circumvented the potential pitfall of contradiction by ignoring the legitimacy question. Coverage of events was, understandably, less extensive than in the broadsheets. However, one article by journalist Paul Routledge in the *Daily Mirror* did reflect the concerns presented by the broadsheets, namely that:

> This is not a black-and-white issue. It is not the plucky little Kosovars (who should be known by their right name of Shiptars or Albanians) versus the bullies of Belgrade.
>
> It is a battle of armed separatists versus the government of the country in which they live. If we were to invade Kosovo, it would be like giving the Russians the right to intervene militarily in Scotland, should independence activists take up arms there.[41]

However, Paul Routledge's was an isolated voice; his analysis of events ignored the issue of genocide. In contrast, the editorial comment of the newspaper insisted that action be taken to 'Stamp out the Butcher of Kosovo'.[42] In general, the coverage that existed tended to focus on the threat of air strikes and details of troop deployments and military hardware to be employed by the allies. Far less attention was given to discussion about the political wrongs and rights regarding intervention. Even with coverage of the Racak massacre the news was dominated by the NATO threat of bombing rather than the details and circumstances surrounding the horrific events.[43] Once the decision had been taken to intervene militarily, the tabloids were quick to register their support and rallied around the cause with the demonization and personalization of Milosevic. Despite Routledge's assertion that Britain should remain out of the conflict as the 'Serbs have been fighting the Albanians for centuries. They will still be scrapping when Tony Blair is pushing up the daisies',[44] the overriding quantity of news regarding Kosovo in both the *Sun* and *Mirror* confirmed the antipathy towards Milosevic and in doing so supported the interventionist argument.

Conclusion

The analysis of news outside the normally accepted parameters of the two crises demonstrates the views of the newspapers free from direct military censorship. If one assumes Robinson's model could apply to the British press, we should be able to demonstrate the existence of extensive and critical debate.[45] During the Gulf War, the justification for intervention appeared relatively clear-cut. There was little antagonism aimed towards Saddam Hussein before the invasion of Iraq, as the case of Daphne Parish demonstrates. Once Iraq invaded Kuwait the government policy was relatively set against Iraq and as such the press generally fell in line behind government policy. In this respect the behaviour of the press during the initial stages of the Gulf crisis would appear to support Robinson's theory. Coverage of Kosovo challenges this assumption. Government policy was ill defined in contrast to the Gulf crisis. The commencement of hostilities was protracted and the belligerents more difficult to define. Whereas Robinson's model would predict extensive and critical coverage the British press and their editorial policies mirrored the government uncertainty.

Tunstall has argued that the press rather than the television news had the ability to attack politicians, yet this does not appear to be substantiated in this period.[46] Once a clear policy line had been established, the press generally acquiesced to the pro-interventionist stance. These conclusions undermine the argument that the press conforms to the military or political line because of overt pressure or censorship. In a period where diversity of opinion was possible, the newspapers' editorials mirrored the official policy, even when this was undetermined. A pattern that was expanded as the conflicts escalated.

5

THE FIVE THEMES OF CONFLICT
PROPAGANDA

Introduction

Although conflicts involving British armed forces have altered significantly regarding scale, duration, location and period, the press reportage has displayed consistent propaganda themes. These themes can be broken down into five elements, leader figure, the portrayal of the enemy, military threat, threat to international stability and technological warfare. The propaganda themes addressed here are those that support British government policy, which in the case of both the Gulf War and Kosovo Conflict were pro-intervention. In the next chapter alternative opinions and sources of information, outside of the mainstream channels, will be examined. However, the pro-intervention propaganda dominated British press coverage of both crises.

The five propaganda themes transcend the variables between the conflicts, with the dominance of each element shifting in relation to the specific propaganda requirements of the crisis. Both the Gulf War and Kosovo Conflict occurred in the post-Cold War era but shared propaganda requirements and messages with earlier conflicts. The changes to international politics, which have occurred since the collapse of the former Soviet Union, affect the relative importance of each theme. The identification and analysis of these patterns of propaganda techniques allows a greater understanding of how conflict is presented to the public, why it is constructed in this way and ultimately enables one to hypothesize about coverage of future crises.

There are a number of important questions to address when considering the implications of propaganda content in British press coverage of the Gulf War and Kosovo. One such issue should be the consideration of for whom was the propaganda useful. The question of what influences the press leads onto the consideration of whether the themes are merely a subconscious regurgitation of official information channels, or an active attempt to construct a clear conflict narrative to shape public perception of war. On a broader level, we return to the question of the relevance of the British press in the modern instant media age. Television has been used as a conduit for diplomatic manoeuvring; if the same can be said of the press then the influence of propaganda should be measured internationally. Finally, it is necessary to identify the changing emphasis placed upon the different themes as the malleable five-strand model shifts the emphasis afforded to each theme subject to the circumstances of justifying intervention in the conflict.

The themes are not confined to the Gulf War and Kosovo Conflict alone and are intended to demonstrate continuity with British coverage of previous and subsequent crises. The selection of two post-Cold War interventions will highlight how the changing international balance of power has shifted altering the political and military considerations for legitimating war to sustain a positive public opinion. The use of press coverage, instead of incorporating other media channels, is intended to redress some of the academic focus on war coverage that has tended to denigrate the influence of newspapers on public opinion.

Theme one: the portrayal of the leader figure

One of the most striking elements of propaganda techniques utilized during conflict is the role of the leader figure. The cultivation of a particular public attitude towards the enemy leader is a desired war aim for political and military planners and constitutes a vital component of the war narrative. The identification of the enemy leadership provides a focal point towards which the war effort can be targeted. Once the leader is identified, the character and perception of that individual can be cultivated and presented to the public to support the policy aims of government.

When portraying the role of the opponent's leader figure the propaganda takes two forms. First, the war or crisis is specifically personalized with the enemy leader so that the introduction of their name becomes synonymous with the conflict. Second, the individual, once directly associated with the conflict, is demonized, provoking negative connotations through the invoking of their name. The two aspects complement each other and provide a necessary framework for constructing a positive public attitude towards involvement in international crises.

Political and military spokesmen consistently use this dual approach to reinforce key propaganda messages. These are systematically reproduced in the press, often without critical analysis and as such are complicit with the aim of focusing the cause and continuation of a conflict onto an individual. In addition to this, newspapers perpetuate the approach independently as part of the process of constructing an identifiable narrative structure for the reader. Of the five themes, the role of the leader figure is the most consistently employed technique during both conflicts and across the range of newspapers.

Personalization

The personalization of any conflict with the enemy's leader figure serves key strategic and diplomatic requirements. From an early period in any crisis the leader figure is identified and the process of personalization begins. Leonard Doob acknowledges this effect through his discussion of what he refers to as 'displacement'.[1] To summarize, Doob hypothesizes that the perception an individual has of belonging to a larger group legitimizes actions against a scapegoat. The media facilitate the perception of that unity despite the individual's displacement from the larger group. This leads Doob to conclude that in the event of 'war the displacement of aggression upon the enemy is effectively promoted by propaganda among people who are widely separated'.[2] It is the very essence of the group mentality that Jacques Ellul argues is necessary for successful propaganda to exist:

> A mass society is a society with considerable population density in which local structures and organizations are weak, currents of opinion are strongly felt, men are grouped into large and influential collectives, the individual is part of these collectives, and a certain psychological unity exists.[3]

The identification of an enemy leader as the instigator of a conflict effectively focuses the attention of the masses away from government policy and onto the desired target. The media are a necessary component in facilitating the perception that a larger group shares the individual's feelings toward the enemy leader and in doing so introduces a feeling of legitimacy. The government must therefore focus its propaganda themes towards the manipulation of what Lasswell entitles 'collective attitudes'.[4]

Once the association between the enemy leader and the conflict is established the invocation of the individual's name, in this case Saddam Hussein or Slobodan Milosevic, becomes synonymous with the hostilities. By associating the leader so intimately with the crisis, the policymakers focus public attention directly onto an individual. Reference to the leader figure is possible in many circumstances, for example during the Kosovo Conflict the Deputy Chief of the Defence Staff, Air Marshall Sir John Day, utilized Milosevic's role in the hostilities to explain difficulties encountered by NATO planes due to adverse weather conditions. While conceding that late March was not the ideal time to initiate an air campaign Sir John Day stressed in a press briefing that NATO 'certainly had no choice in the start date, which was driven entirely by Milosevic's decision to begin the brutal repression of Kosovar Albanians'.[5] This example both detracts from criticism of NATO's military planning and succeeds in returning the issue back once again to Milosevic's culpability for events. Compounded by references to 'Milosevic's war machine', 'Milosevic's military' and 'President Milosevic's military capabilities' the MOD briefings reiterated the connection between Milosevic and the conflict.[6] The press then reiterates these connections.

Personalization also has the additional result of deflecting the potential criticism that Western aggression is directed against an entire country or ethnic group. The propaganda is intended to limit the conflict to a specific individual and the specific national apparatus that sustains their power. By doing this international support can be cultivated and moral legitimacy obtained by the avoidance of directly threatening civilians. As the intended desire of conflict, if not the openly stated objective, is often to depose the existing leader figure, personalization prevents the wholesale alienation of all sections of the opponent's public. After all, they may have the ability to remove the leader through their own efforts. The political and diplomatic aims in utilizing the personalization technique occur in the press as well. Here, the leader figure assists the development of a narrative structure built up during the crisis. The leader figure plays a starring role in identifying the opponent and constitutes a consistent symbol in the evolving war narrative.

Propaganda during conflict seeks to associate the enemy leader directly with both the outbreak of the hostilities and its continuation. The effect is to shift the emphasis away from allied decision-makers and onto the opponent. In doing this the Western powers can be cast as the conscientious diplomats and reluctant belligerents, while the enemy is portrayed as the antagonist. There are numerous examples throughout both conflicts and across the range of newspapers of this happening. *The Sun* and *Daily Mirror* may provide some of the more memorable references, notably *The Sun*'s use of 'Slobba' in reference to Slobodan Milosevic, but evidence is also available in the broadsheets.[7] In both conflicts, despite the differences of circumstance between the two, the same propaganda theme is utilized. During the Gulf War *The Times* explained the start of the allied air offensive in terms designed to focus the blame for the hostilities onto Saddam Hussein. The following section of a *Times* editorial illustrates the utilization of this technique to assert the necessity of beginning an air campaign:

> Such action has been inevitable not just by the passing of the United Nations deadline on Tuesday night but also by the utter intransigence of the Iraqi leader, President Saddam Hussein. Those who have reasonably pleaded for a continued search for peace over the past five months have been left with no shred of evidence to base a case for further procrastination. The allied leaders were justified in ending the suspense, agonising though it was to do so.[8]

The paragraph above typifies press reports from both conflicts and contains a number of important propagandistic elements. The piece describes the inevitability of conflict, insinuating that war and, more importantly in this case, a ground war is unpreventable. Because of this inevitability, the author is dismissive of alternative views and asserts their backing for the current policy. The United Nations is mentioned, strengthening the impression of an international united front against Iraq. Referral to the quantity of support from other nations implies a unified, democratic and international opinion against a single, isolated, individual. Despite the fact that the allies instigated the air campaign, Hussein's intransigence is portrayed as necessitating the action. The allies are seen to have reasonably pursued peace over a considerable period and been induced, reluctantly, to employ a military solution. This form of article absolves the allies from blame and suggests the continuation of the conflict lies solely in the hands of the enemy's leader.

The above editorial in *The Times* was consistent with their policy on Saddam's role in bringing about the hostilities. Before the United Nations deadline for Iraq's withdrawal from Kuwait had expired, the newspaper reminded readers that the war was not about to begin. Instead, the editorial reiterated that hostilities had begun five months previously when Iraq had 'brutally annexed Kuwait'.[9] The report placed the current conflict within the continuing narrative, rather than suggesting this was the beginning of a new event, in doing this the war was re-associated with Iraq and Saddam. By producing this type of report, the newspapers were echoing Western leaders. *The Daily Telegraph* obligingly reproduced an extract from a speech by President George Bush that emphasized Saddam Hussein's role in 'plundering a tiny nation' as if having done so single-handedly.[10] In using the referral to Saddam as the reason for allied aggression, the coverage was perpetuating a well used and necessary propaganda theme.

The same messages were depicted during the Kosovo Conflict with reference to Slobodan Milosevic. *The Guardian* accused Milosevic of a 'kamikazee stand-off with the West over Kosovo'.[11] Here, once again, Milosevic is isolated while the employment of the term 'West' alludes to a communal position against him and on the war he has brought about. Therefore, when the air strikes are conducted they are against 'president Slobodan Milosevic's power base' personalizing the focus of air attacks.[12] This approach also serves the additional virtue of emphasizing the distinction between a conflict geared specifically towards Milosevic and his political and military apparatus, as opposed to the Serbian people as a whole.

The personalization of the conflict with the enemy leader figure also forms a vital part of the newspaper's explanation for supporting a particular course of action. Here, there are divergences between the newspapers as to what the desired war aims should be and how they should be achieved. Because of these differences, the role of the leader figure is employed varyingly. For example, during the initial stages of the Gulf War *The Times* forwarded a restrained opinion on dealing with Iraq's, or more usually Saddam's, invasion of Kuwait.[13] The newspaper stressed that it was not the intention of the United States or Great Britain to topple Saddam. In light of this under-standing of policy, the editorial opinion suggested a limited response, with clearly defined objectives and effected under the authority of the United Nations. The article highlighted the need for international authority to legit-imate any future action, again drawing a distinction between international cooperation and the solitary actions of Saddam. In keeping with a diplo-matic and democratic approach to tackling Saddam's invasion *The Times* pushed for a recall of Parliament.[14] By emphasizing that democratic debate of the crisis should be encouraged, the newspaper is also introducing, possibly subconsciously, a contrast between the measured and democratic decision-making process of Great Britain against the dictatorial regime of Saddam Hussein and his rash foray into Kuwait.

Despite the early moderation of *The Times*, the coverage continued to reflect the contrast between international democratic outrage against Saddam's selfish and irrational incursion into Kuwait. The initial reaction of *The Guardian* was different and, as such, the role of Saddam Hussein altered accordingly. For *The Guardian* not only Saddam was to blame for the current crisis. The newspaper was also critical of Saddam's previous sponsors which included Western, democratic governments. Therefore, while describing Saddam as 'a monster' he was 'partly of their own making'.[15] The personalization still exists, with Saddam the central 'monstrous' figure, but blame is apportioned to the Western governments who had turned a blind eye to, or indeed actively supported, his regime.

To highlight this position *The Guardian* emphasized reactions to Hussein's human rights record. One article cited the censure of Beijing compared with only verbal criticism of Iraq despite an annual report from the State Depart-ment which singled out Baghdad as one of the principle offenders against human rights.[16] This opinion was still being reiterated in November of the same year. In a further article the West's role in arming Iraq is repeated and utilizes evidence from Mr Sahib Alhkim, head of the London-based Organization of Human Rights in Iraq, to draw the conclusion that 'Western governments are now paying the price for betraying their much touted commitment to human rights'.[17]

The Guardian also sought to highlight Western naivety towards the wider issues surrounding the Gulf Crisis. In a front-page commentary piece, the newspaper blamed Western misunderstanding of the Palestine–Israeli situa-tion for undermining moderate Arabs opinion.[18] This, the article argued, increased the likelihood of Hussein being able to turn his current campaign into a wider general Arab cause. *The Guardian* and *The Times* both agreed on the brutal and monstrous act Saddam had committed by invading Kuwait. However, as *The Guardian* concluded the culpability of the West's complicity, some of the emphasis on Hussein was diminished and his image employed in a subtly different way.

Different attitudes to the responsibility of individuals or countries in the Iraqi invasion were not the only early divergence of opinion in the press. From the outset there developed varying views on how to remove Saddam from Kuwait that again incorporated his persona in different ways. Possibly in light of *The Guardian*'s views on partial Western culpability for the crisis, the newspaper quickly excluded any military option in facilitating Saddam's removal. Yet the extract below showed how intrinsically Hussein is identified with the crisis:

> The Gulf crisis which has matured over the past decade will only be resolved by the collapse of the present regime in Baghdad, and all legitimate means should be employed to work towards that end. This excludes military intervention on grounds of principle and practicality. But every trick of diplomacy should be used to seek an arms embargo – which to be effective must include lone operators (particularly China) as well as the established suppliers such as France and the Soviet Union – as well as a trade and credit boycott.[19]

The Guardian had previously stressed the role of other governments in aiding the invasion of Kuwait, notably by trading arms. Therefore, the above article suggested a course of action that is compatible with the newspaper's perception of the cause of the crisis by proposing an international embargo.[20] This opinion excluded any military action, which the article implied would be illegitimate. The report achieved this by stressing that all legitimate means should be used but excluded armed intervention. However, most important for the role of the leader figure is the continued identification of Saddam as the central cause of the crisis. The call for his regime's removal is presented as vitally important in settling a dispute that started not with the invasion of Kuwait but had developed over the 'past decade'. The conclusion being that Saddam's regime, a constant element over the past ten years, had been central to Middle Eastern problems.

The newspaper continued to propose sanctions as the only available option for settling the Gulf dispute. Iraq announced that the patriots of countries imposing economic sanctions would not have their safety guaranteed, effectively branding them potential hostages. In consequence, the newspaper warned that a military option was now out of the question, as the comment piece below argued:

> Frustration in the Gulf leads temptingly to the invocation of task forces and tactical bombing, but the military option is no option at all. The emergence yesterday of a potential hostage problem of vast dimensions only emphasised that this is far too complex a crisis for gunboat diplomacy.[21]

The editorial stance remained firmly against an armed response. Yet, there is an obvious contradiction between the newspaper's reasons for avoiding conflict and the endorsement of an embargo. The Iraqis were threatening Western civilians because of potential sanctions, yet *The Guardian* still promoted an embargo as the only way of dealing with the issue of safeguarding the potential hostages. In addition to this, the article reinforced a negative view of military intervention with the use of the phrase 'gunboat diplomacy'. The statement has negative nineteenth-century imperialist connotations and is used in the same way as proponents of military action often evoke 1930s appeasement as a historical precedent to reinforce an interventionist policy.

Editorial opinion in *The Guardian* continued consistently to support sanctions as opposed to armed intervention. The newspaper pressed for a full debate for and against war while giving sanctions 'many more months to work'.[22] In essence the suggestion was that a military build-up increased the likelihood of war and 'directly tugs against a policy – sanctions, in place and effective – which will in the end remove Saddam from Kuwait and give the obvious platform for wide-reaching diplomatic settlement'.[23] The policy remained consistent and the role of Saddam was reinforced by the comment that he personally be removed from Kuwait. The personalization implied that sanctions could drive Saddam out of the country; however, an embargo was more likely to have a direct effect on the Iraqi populace before President Hussein. Despite the constant editorial or comment stance, *The Guardian* did carry alternative views, such as Hugo Young's article, which criticized sanctions as skirting the realities of the real world.[24] Overall, however, the volume of opinion favoured the singular policy of sanctions, which meant that as Desert Storm began the newspaper faced an awkward dilemma. Either the newspaper stayed true to its ideal policy and risked being condemned as unpatriotic, or it changed tack and backed the war. In the end *The Guardian* compromised insisting that sanctions had not been given enough time while issuing the disclaimer that 'such feelings are inevitably stowed aside in battle'.[25] It is a policy change that sits comfortably with Noam Chomsky's general statement on the media closing ranks and backing government policy once the guns had begun firing.[26] While *The Guardian* had not consistently followed an interventionist policy, its decision to back the campaign effectively meant support for military action.

In contrast to *The Guardian*, *The Times*, while suggesting a considered and democratic approach to the crisis, was anxious that the British government should not rule out military options. In an editorial written early in September 1990, the newspaper responded to a letter that Paddy Ashdown, leader of the Liberal Party, had sent to Mrs Thatcher. In the letter, Mr Ashdown had urged the government to follow the policy of sanctions exclusively. *The Times* insisted Thatcher should not restrict the government's option to intervene and that the House of Commons should support her stance.[27] Bearing in mind the air war did not begin until January 1991, as early as late September 1990 the newspaper asserted that the passing of United Nations Resolution 670[28] marked the final non-military step.[29] *The Times* was actively supporting an interventionist agenda just over a month after the invasion of Kuwait. In relation to the approach of the above two newspapers *The Sun* exhibited some common elements of the personalization propaganda technique. *The Sun* initially shared the view of *The Guardian* and called for an economic blockade 'until Iraq quits Kuwait, gets rid of her tyrant ruler and returns to civilised behaviour'.[30] In this instance, the emphasis is on the Iraqi people to oust Saddam, the man once again personified as the causation of the crisis. As with *The Guardian* sanctions are seen as having the ability to compel ordinary Iraqis to solve the issue themselves, despite the relative shortsightedness of this position with sanctions ultimately weakening the general populace first. However, it was not long before the newspaper strengthened its position, insisting that if the 'Iraqis will not get rid of him, the West must do so'.[31] The *Daily Mirror* shared in the belief of the right of the government to intervene militarily in a war that it claimed would be justified.[32] An early *Daily Telegraph* editorial, by Defence Editor John Keegan, focused on the military options open to the West and as such sidelined debate on alternative options.[33] In essence, the overwhelming opinion in the British press, and most notably in the editorial policies of each of the newspapers, was in favour of armed intervention to remove Saddam from Kuwait. Consistently Saddam was personified as the reason for the crisis and it was action against him, in whatever form, that would bring an end to the hostilities. In the case of Kosovo, opinion was much more divided on the legitimacy and reason for intervention. However, a similar pattern of debate and conclusions is reached. Milosevic was consistently employed as the personification of the cause, indeed the personification of evil and the reason for the continuation of the conflict.

The Kosovo Conflict, in general, posed a more difficult situation for the justification of military action, especially a ground war. This is reflected in a greater number of articles, which were critical of government policy, appearing in the press. However, each of the five newspapers' editorial policies came around to backing the use of ground forces. For example, *The Guardian*, which had rigorously pushed for economic sanctions against Iraq, was quick to stress the need for ground troops if any military action against Milosevic were to succeed.[34] *The Times*' editorial position challenged the criticism that Kosovo was simply one of any number of conflicts in the world by reminding its readership 'this particular tragedy is being enacted on Europe's stage. NATO can and must act'.[35] *The Times* urged NATO to make urgent plans to send in ground troops to support the air offensive.[36] Under the clear heading 'Half Measures are not Enough' *The Daily Telegraph* warned after ten days of the air campaign that:

> To date, the conduct of the offensive has been marked by tough
> gestures, followed by panic at the prospect of deeper involvement.
> The lesson of the past 10 days has been that half measures are not
> enough. The allies should think back to the Bay of Pigs in 1961,
> when the failure of President Kennedy to support with air power
> an invasion force of Cuban exiles led to a fiasco.[37]

Once more utilizing a historical precedent to predict future failures, the
article insists on the necessity of ground troops for the successful completion
of military action against Yugoslavia. In this respect, the broadsheets
present a united front, unlike during the Gulf War. The difference here
does not reflect a more belligerent and hostile attitude adopted by the British
press, instead the certainty for the use of ground troops stems from two considerations. First is the historical and military assumption that air power
alone cannot win a conflict. Second, and more importantly, was the justification with which war was being waged. In the Gulf War Iraq's invasion of
Kuwait gave much clearer reasoning for intervention, in Kosovo the justification put forward was often that of humanitarian concern. Thus bombing,
it was seen, could not halt the Serbian actions on the ground, which were
generating the flow of Kosovan Albanian refugees.

During the Kosovo campaign, the tabloids struggled to sustain a consistent editorial policy on the use of ground troops. However, it is also in
the tabloids where the greatest evidence of weaving Milosevic into specific
war aims is most blatant. Initially, *The Sun* hypothesized that the allies
would probably have to send ground troops in to tackle Yugoslavia and
Milosevic.[38] However, as Tony Blair was insisting that ground troops
would not be sent into Kosovo in a militarily hostile environment, so
The Sun's editorial policy shifted and insisted if Blair did change his mind
they would not support him. In doing this *The Sun* claimed to be 'the only
national newspaper backing the British forces currently in, or close to,
combat' and suggested that those forces 'will remember who stood by them
in these most difficult times'.[39] The dramatic headline, 'Don't Send our
Troops off to Die' emphasized the newspaper's stance in a manner intended
to evoke an emotional reaction.[40] This is in stark contrast to the abandon-
ment of non-interventionist ideals when conflict commences and the press
purports to be supporting the troops. The newspaper retained this policy
consistently, after an initial delay in deciding upon what action to support,
and in doing so directly affected the opinion of the *Daily Mirror*. The
Mirror initially backed the use of ground troops if necessary and, in a thinly
veiled assault on *The Sun*, described 'one confused newspaper' which was
out of touch with its own readership for not backing the potential use of
ground troops.[41] However, the confusion was not confined to the editorial
staff of *The Sun*. The *Mirror* later insisted that Tony Blair should not jeopar-
dize public support for the campaign against Milosevic by sending in ground

troops, as any invasion of 'the mountainous province would cost British lives without saving Albanians, triggering a bloodbath the public could not tolerate'.[42] The *Mirror*, notably after revelations of Serbian 'rape camps', just two days later shifted policy again[43] and continued from that moment to call for the deployment of 'a substantial ground force'.[44]

In this respect, the *Mirror* was adopting a policy in line with previous conflicts and newspapers, and the media at large fought between themselves over policy and patronage. During the Falklands Conflict *The Sun* led the way with belligerent lambasting of perceived foreign and domestic opposition. Roy Greenslade, who was assistant editor at the newspaper during the conflict, has explained how editor Kelvin MacKenzie opted to open a 'second front' by attacking the anti-war *Daily Mirror*.[45] The ensuing battle for circulation figures saw *The Sun* brand the *Daily Mirror* 'traitors in our midst' while the *Daily Mirror* retaliated by naming *The Sun* 'The Harlot of Fleet Street'.[46] As far as the research for this discussion is concerned, such overt inter-newspaper rivalry was not as blatant or widespread. There was some barracking, as in the example above, concerning the use of ground forces, however the similarities of positions were greater than the differences. In the most recent Gulf War, the *Daily Mirror* reverted to a pacifist position in the escalation towards the crisis.[47] Numerous editorials sought to demonstrate the illegality of going to war and urged Blair to stand up against Bush. An honourable stance or a cynical ploy to exploit a commercial niche in the media market, the *Daily Mirror* stood at distinct odds with the main media policy that was far more oblique in any criticisms. However, as war approached the newspaper was again struck by the need to appear patriotic. Thus, the *Daily Mirror* promised to expose the truth behind the war, continue to condemn Blair, while at the same time standing alongside the British forces.[48]

Such a moral stance is severely undermined when the newspaper's subsequent opinion is analysed. After the cessation of hostilities, the newspaper praised Blair for having a remarkable century, which had earned the respect of his enemies and astonishingly claimed that he had come 'out well from the war in Iraq'.[49] Instead, the newspaper reverted to highlighting his domestic obligations and the battles on the home front that were to follow.[50] Such sentiments were very different from the vitriol aimed towards the Prime Minister before the 2003 conflict in Iraq. In the process of reporting the two conflicts analysed herein the press displayed similar traits. The overt vitriol of newspapers attacking each other was largely absent, especially if compared with the battles fought during the Falklands. Examples do exist in the Iraq War 1990–91 and Kosovo Conflict 1999 of diverse stances being taken by individual newspapers, however, much of the coverage supports the conclusion that a compatible, pro-interventionist agenda was most beneficial to the healthy circulation figures of all newspapers. Personalizing the conflicts with the enemy leader figures thus constituted a primary component of the war coverage.

During the Kosovo Conflict, the overwhelming emphasis of articles in the press called for the employment of ground troops as part of the war aims for driving Slobodan Milosevic out of Kosovo. However, it was *The Sun* that took the issue of personalizing the conflict to the extreme in the following article after NATO bombers had struck Milosevic's Belgrade mansion on the 22 April 1999:

NATO said it would hit Slobba where it hurts.
But he can never have expected they would blow up his bed.
It's hard to see how dropping a missile on Slobba's private house can be called hitting a military target.
But who on earth cares?
There's only one thing we should feel sorry about . . .
He wasn't in the bed at the time.[51]

In this article, the newspaper is effectively calling for the death of Milosevic. With the other forms of personalization discussed above, Slobodan Milosevic and Saddam Hussein had become the epitome of the conflicts and represented the best hope for the conclusion of hostilities. For *The Sun* the ultimate war aim in this case was the logical one if personalization of the leader figure is taken to its extreme, the elimination of Milosevic. As well as focusing public attention towards an identifiable enemy the personalization of events magnified the difference between the leaders and their people. Just as Nazism and Hitler were distinguished from the German people as a whole during the Second World War so too was this technique utilized during the 1990s. This level of hostility is made easier to present when the second part of the propaganda role of the leader figure is implemented, that is the demonization of the opponent.

Demonization

The demonization of the enemy leader figure is in keeping with the narrative formula of casting the combatants in the roles of 'good' and 'evil'. Once the enemy has been identified and linked with the conflict through personalization, the demonizing strengthens the negative connotations associated with him. For propaganda to be effective, it needs to address basic human elements, which stimulate emotions. Jacques Ellul summarizes this fundamental concept:

Propaganda must stay at the human level. It must not propose aims too lofty that they will seem inaccessible; this creates the risk of a boomerang effect. Propaganda must confine itself to simple, elementary messages (Have confidence in our leader, our party . . . Hate our enemies, etc.) without fear of being ridiculous. It must speak the most simple language, familiar, individualized – the language of the group that is being addressed, and the language with which a person is familiar.[52]

Central to the relevance of this issue is the concept of 'elementary messages' that Ellul notes can include hatred of the enemy. In conflict, the enemy is frequently portrayed as a brutal and violent person and by extension a potential threat to any peaceful, civilized society.

Once the leader figure had become the personification of the conflict, the press also began a process of demonization that exacerbated the negative connotations assigned to the enemy leader. *The Sun*, for example, dubbed both Saddam Hussein and Slobodan Milosevic with distinct titles emblazoned on its pages. The leaders were known as the 'Butcher of Baghdad'[53] and the 'Butcher of Belgrade'.[54]

The Sun also attacked Saddam Hussein for brainwashing and censoring his people and went on to complain that:

Even the way people speak has been censored. Western hostages are known as 'special guests' when dragged off to bombing targets. Words like invasion or occupation are completely forbidden. 'Fusion' is the word used to describe the invasion of Kuwait.[55]

Saddam Hussein is presented as a dictator whose oppressive regime even stifles an entire public's vocabulary. However, the newspaper fails to attack the governments of Great Britain and the United States for their obviously oppressive, under the above criteria, use of terms such as 'collateral damage' when obligingly reproducing statements from official military and government spokesmen.

The Sun was not alone in emphasizing the brutal nature of the opposing dictator, *The Guardian*, for example, claimed that in the ten years since Slobodan Milosevic had seized the Serbian leadership he had transformed 'into the most dangerous and ruthless man in Europe'.[56]

The demonization of the enemy leader can be split into two contradicting, yet mutually employed forms, with the person being described as both sane and calculating, as well as insane and irrational. Both have propaganda uses.

When portraying the leader figure as irrational or insane the accuser intimates that the enemy is not somebody who can be reasoned with. Dr Stephen Reicher, in an article for *The Guardian*, highlights the consequences of ascribing insanity.[57] He notes that if the current hostilities are a reflection of one man's madness there can be no logical reason for it, thus allowing observers to ignore the historical issues that could have facilitated the onset of conflict. With the conflict flowing from Saddam, 'we' are absolved from any responsibility. Furthermore, as Saddam is portrayed as aggressively insane there can be no reasoning with him and this in turn legitimizes military action against him. The ascription of insanity means that anyone associated with, or who supports him, must also be mad. Reicher's observations are validly transferred to the treatment of Slobodan Milosevic. The suggestion that the leader is insane or irrational is a propaganda theme witnessed in press coverage during both conflicts.

One of the prime examples of the employment of this form of demonization can be seen in relation to Saddam Hussein. *The Times* quoted at length reports that Saddam Hussein's handwriting confirmed his insanity:

> Iraqi brinkmanship relies heavily on President Saddam's reputation for unpredictable behaviour which, according to a report in an Israeli newspaper yesterday, bordered on the clinically insane.
>
> *Yediot Ahronot* said the Israeli secret service had commissioned an analysis of the Iraqi leader's handwriting which indicated he needed urgent psychiatric care. 'This man should be hospitalised immediately. He is a hasty decision-maker and has a tendency for radical mood swings, is ready to take extreme decisions and carry them out, has violent tendencies and is dangerous to his environment,' the paper said. The graphologist did not know his subject it added. The result will not comfort Kuwait.[58]

The Daily Telegraph also dedicated a paragraph to the same graphologist's assessment.[59] On the brink of conflict, the reproduction of this report confirms the insanity of Saddam and by extension the insanity of his likely invasion of Kuwait. What neither newspaper manages to demonstrate is any critical analysis of the source of these findings. The fact that the Israeli secret service had commissioned the report should cast some doubts on the credibility of the findings, even before one considers the reliability of studying handwriting to predict international diplomatic affairs. The source has been cited but without any critical analysis of its credibility and the statement reads as a clear assertion of Saddam's insanity. It is a conclusion with which *The Sun*, at a later stage, concurred. The newspaper attempted to back the credibility of the conclusion that 'Saddam Hussein is so crazy he is the most dangerous man in the world' by quoting a 'top psychologist'.[60] This method was repeated during the Kosovo Conflict when the newspaper stated that a 'top psychiatrist said yesterday he believed Milosevic suffers from "lust murder" and gets a sexual thrill from killing'.[61] *The Daily Telegraph*, in a subtler article but with the same conclusions, claimed Slobodan Milosevic had lost touch with reality and was emotionally numb and impervious to other people's pain.[62] The insistence upon the insanity of the enemy leader figure results in an acceptance of government policy towards the enemy and enhances the role of the leader in the war narrative. Furthermore, it bolsters the polarized view of conflict as a case of the sane and rational versus the irrational. As has been seen this can either be a conclusion drawn by the author of an article, an 'expert', or an official source. These are inserted to add credibility to the conclusions reached by the article. However, there are occasions when the opposite conclusions are reached.

By asserting the sane and rational behaviour of the enemy leader figure the domestic audience can be convinced that the person is responsible for their actions and, as a result of this, can be held accountable. This facilitates the association of the leader with the conflict through the demonstration of a coherent and planned policy. It allows the countries allied against the individual to associate the enemy leader with any atrocities that may be committed. Such assertions bolster the accusation that their actions were a result of a clear and conscious policy. Both the rational and irrational approaches are often employed simultaneously with little or no acknowledgement of the contradiction this creates. The overall impression generated is often that of a 'cunning madman', being both sly and unpredictable.

The rational behaviour of the opponent is also used to demonstrate a deep-rooted problem with the enemy leader's personality and prove that any one particular incident is in keeping with their character. By doing this the case for involvement is enhanced, as the likelihood is that without intervention such actions will occur again. Thus, *The Daily Telegraph* described Milosevic's assault on Kosovo as 'a stratagem by a man who throughout the last decade has been a step ahead of the West'.[63] In this sentence there could also be a veiled criticism of past 'Western' approaches to handling Milosevic, insinuating a need for a differing course of action or more intervention. However, the title of the article is 'Inhuman Logic behind Milosevic's Brutalities puts the Region at Risk'. The use of the term 'inhuman' invokes feelings of an irrational character whose actions would be hard to predict, this may help to explain why he had been able to stay 'a step ahead of the West' with the 'West' being seen as human and unable to understand his logic. Despite this, the article points to rational behaviour and a coherent 'stratagem' towards which Milosevic is working.

Other newspapers also ran articles countering the claims that either leader figure was insane. Just as *The Sun* made reference to 'top psychologists' to make credible their claims of Hussein and Milosevic's insanity, so *The Guardian* interviewed Dr Rajendra Persaud of London University who investigates the causes of mental illness, thereby adding credence to the article which drew the following conclusions:

> From previous analysis, Dr Persaud believes Saddam, like Hitler and Stalin, has absolute conviction in what he is doing, always trusts his own instincts ahead of anyone else, and believes there is

an invisible hand governing his destiny . . . But he shows none of the
signs of madness or mental illness, says Dr Persaud.[64]

In the article it is an inherent belief in the absolute right of what Saddam is
doing that drives his actions, not insanity. This conclusion also suggests that
with such determination a positive action must be taken against him, otherwise he is unlikely to stop. The association with Stalin and Hitler reinforces
the need for action and this type of association plays a central role in the
demonization of the leader figure.

When demonizing the enemy leader, aside from rational and irrational
explanations, another essential component is employed. The extension of
the leader figure's persona as the personification of evil, or simply as 'the
bad guy', is aided by the identification with established historical figures
that are clearly recognizable as undesirable. Just as history is used to provide
context to a crisis to assist the understanding that the media narrative is
presenting; so too are historical figures employed to instil instantly recognizable precursors. The most common example is reference to Adolf Hitler. The
'Hitlerization' of the leader makes the demonization easier and offers a
benchmark with which to compare personality characteristics. Reference
to historical characters, especially Nazis, is a theme that runs throughout
conflict coverage and is often intertwined with each of the other propaganda
themes, either overtly or indirectly.[65] Coverage of both the Gulf War and
Kosovo is littered with examples of the memory of Hitler being invoked to
aid in the demonization of either leader figure and this transcends the distinctions between broadsheets and tabloids. *The Daily Telegraph*'s Patrick
Bishop had no reservations in concluding that Saddam's invasion of Kuwait
was 'Proof of Hitlerian Determination'.[66] A different article carried the
pictures of front pages from four other Western newspapers, each of which
had reference to Hitler.[67] Not only was the demonization reinforced with
reference to Hitler, but also by showing other Western newspapers with
the same line of argument the article was defending its own use of the term
through demonstrating a wider acceptance of its validity. In addition to this
The Daily Telegraph, and indeed other newspapers, carried large sections
of speeches by figures such as Bush and Blair that contained references likening Hussein or Milosevic to Hitler, without critically analysing, or questioning the validity of using such phrases.[68]

The Sun was even more adamant about the linkage between Saddam
Hussein and Hitler. The newspaper claimed that Hussein hero-worshipped
Hitler, had a copper bust of him in his private study, collected Nazi relics
and even adopted some of Hitler's mannerisms.[69] By presenting this very
personal link between the two men, Hussein becomes associated with the
atrocities that Hitler committed and enhances the credibility of those calling to resist appeasement.[70] The *Daily Mirror* also stated that 'SADDAM
HUSSEIN IS the Adolf Hitler of the Arab world . . . His occupation of

Kuwait, like Hitler's early, easy and ignored conquests in Europe, is only the start of his territorial demands'.[71] Therefore, by comparing the enemy leader with Hitler, the conflict is not only personalized and the individual demonized, but it also introduces the concept of 1930s appeasement. In doing this the case for action, rather than inaction, in the face of an aggressive dictatorial protagonist, is strengthened. Intervention is demanded if the negative connotations of appeasement are not to be repeated.

To complete the Hitler analogy, which is widely utilized in both conflicts, the enemy leader will also be personally associated with atrocities and linked to a Second World War context. For example, an article in *The Daily Telegraph* bemoaned the inability of allied air power to have a swift impact on Slobodan Milosevic during the Kosovo Conflict, writing '[i]nstead he has calmly set about the most ruthless piece of social engineering in Europe since 1945, ordering the execution of hundreds of Kosovar civilians and the ethnic cleansing of hundreds of thousands more'.[72] In each or all of these elements the use of Hitler, Nazis or the Holocaust in comparison with a current enemy leader figure assists the demonization process. Not only is the violence deplorable, but also the Holocaust emphasis stresses the systematic and planned nature of the atrocities. As the personalization process has already defined the control asserted by the enemy leader figures over the events, they become directly linked to the war crimes.

The use of the Nazi analogy was in keeping with the rhetoric emanating from official government sources. This was especially the case during the Kosovo Conflict where the similarities were most striking and when humanitarian considerations formed the primary justification for intervention. In a press briefing George Robertson utilized the story of an Auschwitz survivor who claimed the scenes coming out of Kosovo reminded him only too well about the images of Nazi concentration camps.[73] Robin Cook reiterated such linkages and stressed the unity of NATO in light of the apparent resurgence of fascist ideology:

> The firm foundation for that [NATO] Alliance unity is our common belief that the revival of fascism which we have witnessed in Kosovo must have no place in modern Europe. NATO was born in the aftermath of the defeat of fascism and genocide in Europe. NATO will not now allow this century to end with a triumph for fascism and genocide.[74]

To what extent the press releases influenced the final content of the newspapers is debatable, especially without the explicit and honest comment of the authors. What is clear however is the attempt by official sources to provide the linkage and the subsequent repetition or compatibility of aims in newspaper articles.

Some newspaper articles did attempt to distance themselves from this formula of guilt-by-comparison with Hitler. Despite statements to the contrary carried on its own pages, a *Daily Telegraph* editorial insisted it was wrong to use any Hitler or Stalin analogy, as Saddam Hussein is a far smaller version.[75] However, a Max Hastings' editorial the following month defended the right to compare Saddam with Hitler as his record of brutality 'invites comparison with Germany's wartime leader'.[76] *The Times* ran an editorial that openly criticized the analogies to historical figures:

> The world may find it convenient to portray Saddam Hussein as a homicidal madman, to cartoon him as Hitler or Ghengis Khan, just as the world chose last week to portray Kuwait as a latter-day 'poor little' Belgium. Such parallels are dangerous . . . His conduct of the Iran–Iraq war was not that of a madman.[77]

The article dismisses comparison with historical predecessors but does so in a way that still asserts negative connotations. In this editorial the newspaper is following the rational argument against Saddam Hussein and dismisses his likeness to Hitler or Ghengis Khan because of his rationality rather than a failure to measure up against their standards of barbarity. Yet, despite some occasional reservations, possibly brought about by accusations elsewhere regarding the validity of using the Hitler analogy, the newspapers followed the official opinions of British and American military and political leaders in likening Saddam or Milosevic to Hitler.

Hitler was not the only historical figure to warrant such comparison and the demonizing effect was similar. In one article *The Times* ran, Conservative MP Michael Howard preferred to use the analogy of Mussolini's invasion of Abyssinia to describe Saddam Hussein's invasion of Kuwait.[78] While this lessened some of the negative connotations associated with genocide and the Nazis, the outcome was still similar; that appeasement was not acceptable. *The Times* even managed to incorporate five dictators in one article, which suggested Milosevic had the 'luck of the devil' and showed all the signs of being as difficult to oust as 'Mussolini, Gaddafi, Hitler, Saddam and Stalin'.[79] This demonstrated another aspect of the use of the historical figure to demonize. For the article on Milosevic *The Times* included Saddam. Thus, previous dictators become the blueprint for the next generation of alleged tyrants. *The Times* also stated of Milosevic that the 'Serb leader is a politician as cunning and deceitful as Saddam Hussein'.[80] *The Sun* asserted 'Slobba is no different to Saddam Hussein'[81] while the *Daily Mirror* informed its readers that Milosevic is being likened to Pol Pot and it 'sadly, is no exaggeration'.[82]

Association with historical parallels can ascribe negative thought processes in the reader and in doing so assist the policy aims of the domestic government. Comparison can also be made between British or American leaders to exacerbate the differences between the good and evil participants of the war narrative. The contrast occurs in one of two ways. First, the individual role of allied leaders can be played down, with the emphasis placed on the union of countries rallied against the enemy leader. This, as we have seen, has already been used when personalizing the conflict, whereby the right of intervention is justified through the process of democratic government and legitimated by collective action. During the Gulf War, for example, the *Daily Mirror* stressed with a rallying tone that never 'have so many nations, so quickly, and with such unity, rallied round . . . to face down an aggressor'.[83] The second method emphasizes the heroic nature of one's own leaders, which contrasts with the demonized enemy. Once again, this justifies the moral integrity of the chosen course of action.

The two forms are not necessarily mutually exclusive and within the same article while stressing the unity of the alliance the *Daily Mirror* praised the courage of George Bush and likened him to Franklin D. Roosevelt.[84] In this way, just as with the use of negative historical figures, the allies are compared with positive role models. *The Daily Telegraph* claimed that President Bush's military background meant, 'the code of the warrior and a belief that right must triumph over evil are integral to Mr Bush's ethics' and this was 'reflected in his determination that President Saddam Hussein's rape of Kuwait shall not prevail'.[85] This directly compares the two leader figures and draws out the inherent contrast that the personalization and demonization attempts to instil; that is the notion of good versus evil and right versus wrong. The demonization, though, is not limited simply to the enemy leader figure; it is often extended to a larger group.

Theme two: the portrayal of the enemy

The second propaganda theme prevalent in newspaper coverage of the Gulf War and Kosovo Conflict is the portrayal of the enemy. Just as the persona of the enemy leader figure is constructed, so too larger groups are defined as the enemy. This demonization of the masses can extend to an army, race or, less commonly, an entire country. The reason for demonizing a large section of a society is to create a viable enemy against whom it is justifiable to wage a war. This can justify intentional attacks against targets legitimated by their association with the leader figure or larger enemy. It can also dampen criticism of unintentional errors if culpability can in some way be apportioned to the enemy. The character of the enemy can be used to justify intervention where perhaps traditional means, such as an invasion of one sovereign nation by another, are absent. Furthermore, as with the contrast between the enemy leader figure and the 'heroic' alliance leader, the demonization of a larger group can provide a moral legitimacy for 'humanitarian' intervention.

The identification and demonization of a specific group is not a straight-forward process. Because of this there is not always a consistent policy towards sections of the enemy. During the Gulf War *The Sun* emphasized the alliance's efforts to minimize civilian casualties during bombing raids by claiming they 'regretted any casualties among civilians'.[86] In this instance Iraqi civilians are in no way demonized, while the actions of the allies in attempting to avoid injuring them is portrayed as admirable. The article also goes on to state that the civilians 'are the innocent victims of the cruel and demented tyrant who leads them'.[87] Once again the personalization of the conflict with Saddam is brought into the equation, removing culpability for any innocent lives lost from those actually carrying out the bombing. Civilians are not always portrayed as the innocent victims. In the following article the same theme concerning the removal of culpability is reiterated, but this time the full force of the accusations is not brought to bear solely on Saddam Hussein:

> Saddam might be a ruthless tyrant, but he didn't invade Kuwait on his own. And dictators don't stay in power unless substantial numbers of their own people are prepared, for whatever reason, to go along with them . . .
>
> Of course, we have no specific quarrel with Mr and Mrs Farouk Aziz, of 47 Saddam Terrace, Baghdad, and it would be unfortunate if a stray cruise missile were to destroy their home.
>
> But these things happen in wartime. And it should not be the responsibility of the British and American taxpayer to build them a new one.
>
> There would be some merit in leaving Iraq as a bomb site, to discourage other maniacs who fancy their chances against the might of the civilised world.[88]

In this example the Iraqi people are to some extent to blame for keeping Saddam in power and by extension for the invasion of Kuwait. Saddam, again personalized and demonized, is described as a 'ruthless tyrant' and a 'maniac', both of which could be used to excuse the Iraqi people, oppressed under a violent regime, from ousting Saddam. Yet, the author sidesteps this consideration by saying 'for whatever reason', thereby combining those who genuinely support Saddam and those too afraid to take positive action. In this way, by apportioning some culpability to civilians, the accidental bombing of residential areas can be dismissed as 'unfortunate'. Furthermore, the mentioning of a cruise missile, a 'smart' weapon, continues to underline the efforts the alliance is going to in order to avoid such incidents. The naming of the hypothetical residents Aziz is seemingly intentional, with the association with Tariq Aziz, the Iraqi Foreign Minister, being indirectly introduced. They live in 'Saddam Terrace' again associating them with

Hussein and in addition the article only mentions the home being destroyed, not lives being lost, sanitizing the hypothetical incident. Indeed they are still alive but their culpability means that the Americans and British have no responsibility for post-war reconstruction. The above passage ends with further reference to the unity of a civilized society against what must be deduced as an uncivilized one. This, therefore, fits within the narrative structure already developed in reference to the leader figure.

The demonization of an entire civilian population is rare. For numerous reasons it is not advantageous to portray a whole society in a negative light. International law and the need to maintain moral legitimacy for a conflict ensure that the killing of civilians is unacceptable with the Geneva Convention stressing that non-combatants must be treated 'humanely'.[89] This is especially true when attempting to hold together a fragile coalition where in the Gulf War, for example, the Arab members faced criticism by their own publics for helping the 'West' kill other Arabs. It is often hoped that a population may carry out the war aims for any alliance or coalition by removing the enemy leader figure themselves, as a result it would be unwise to damn an entire society and thereby possibly unite any domestic opposition behind the enemy leader. On other occasions military action may be justified as liberating an oppressed people who would not, obviously, be an acceptable target.

There is evidence of an effort to avoid the propaganda mistakes of previous campaigns. British propaganda during the First World War had demonized the German people and made a 're-educational process' a necessity in peacetime; to avoid this propaganda has to retain a degree of selection.[90] During the Second World War the British were anxious to highlight the difference between the German people and the Nazis. The Gulf War saw specific emphasis placed upon Saddam Hussein and *his* Republican Guard as the focus for hostilities. During the Kosovo Conflict the Ministry of Defence sought to re-emphasize the specific focus of NATO attacks. In the following example a MOD briefing by Doug Henderson combined the distinction of the Serbian people from their leader while simultaneously reiterating Milosevic's culpability. 'We have no quarrel with the people of Yugoslavia, as we have made clear. Indeed the British people and the Yugoslavian people have historically been good friends'.[91] In an extension of this theme the distance between the Serbian people and their leader was repeated to absolve the larger public from the atrocities committed by Serbian forces. George Robertson, insisted that the 'Serbian people know nothing of what is happening in Kosovo and so can be perhaps excused for seeing things differently, but the British and western publics must not lose sight of the real issues'.[92]

The reason for this approach can be twofold. First, the need for post-conflict reconciliation demanded a distinction and demonstrated a lesson learnt from the First World War. Second, the distinction does not absolve the publics of Western democracies from taking action and demands support for intervention. The same approach can also be used to explain the reluctance of Western democracies to declare war officially when intervening. Mr Henderson claimed the Kosovo Conflict had not been declared a war owing to the fact that it was 'not a war against Serbian people, it's not a war against the Serbian nation, it is a military action to persuade the Serbian government to see reason and to meet the very reasonable conditions which have been set by NATO'.[93] The use of these terms by official military briefers set the tone for the media war language that sought to separate groups in order to justify and legitimize intervention. Jacques Ellul summarized the necessity for this action and the role of the media succinctly: 'propaganda has to set off its group from all the other groups. Here we find again the fallacious character of the intellectual media (press, radio), which, far from uniting people and bringing them closer together, divide them'.[94] Understanding of conflict in relation to the specific war aims of the belligerent parties is facilitated by a clear definition of the enemy. However, the restrictions of international law with regard to non-combatants and the desire for reconciliation after conflict resolution requires a distinct, rather than a general enemy to be identified. Instead of tarnishing the character of a whole country it is far more common to isolate specific groups. In the Gulf War the Republican Guard were isolated for particular attention and their defeat seen as a vital war aim. Their portrayal as an elite force was significant and contrasted with the popular portrayal of the Iraqi conscript keen to surrender arms at the first sight of a coalition soldier. The Republican Guard were directly associated with Saddam Hussein, by doing this it was possible to justify the destruction of their units and thereby undermine a bastion of Hussein's power. In contrast the wholesale destruction of fleeing Iraqi conscripts on the Basra road proved less palatable for political and domestic audiences. However, when presented with certain scenarios, such as looting or murder, the average Iraqi soldier would once again be open to demonization on a general scale. This was essentially a result of perception as by committing such crimes they were the oppressors rather than the oppressed. There was a less divided attitude towards the enemy during the Kosovo Conflict. The Serbian police and army units were portrayed as brutal and willing murderers and as such deserved little sympathy from the press and general public.

As with the leader figure, the actions of the demonized section of the enemy's population can be portrayed as either rational or irrational. By rationalizing their behaviour and showing premeditated determination for certain actions, it is far easier to justify military action against them.[95] This is best seen during the Kosovo crisis. Debate surrounding the cause of the refugee exodus out of Kosovo centred on whether the coalition bombing or Serb brutality were the root cause. NATO's stance was clearly that the refugee influx into bordering countries had begun before any bombing.

In newspapers that backed the official version of events, articles were keen to stress the predetermined nature of Serbian actions to demonstrate a systematic abuse of the Kosovan's human rights. Hence, *The Sun*, in an open letter to 'our troops at war', insisted any suggestion that NATO were to blame 'for the plight of the refugees' was a 'great con' and that larger numbers of 'people were driven out of Kosovo **BEFORE** the NATO air strikes began than have left it in the week since'.[96] *The Daily Telegraph* also insisted that the 'systematic brutality of Serbian forces belies any suggestion that their attacks were a panicked reaction to Nato's air campaign' and that the Serbian offensive was 'planned well before the NATO action'.[97] The assertion each time is of the deliberate action of Serbian forces, which absolves NATO from any wrongdoing.

With regard to the irrational approach to the enemy's actions, the advantage is gained from asserting their maniacal behaviour. When presented with irrational behaviour it can be suggested that preventative action needs to be taken. It may be, as in the Gulf War and indeed Kosovo, that the armed forces may not stop at their current conquest and push on across further borders. Once again, as with the leader figure, irrational behaviour makes the enemy untrustworthy, fanatical or mad, all of which remove reasonable, civilized, diplomatic answers as a viable option, thereby, reiterating the need for military action.

The irrational approach can also be used to dehumanize the enemy. In the Gulf War *The Times* reproduced an interview with a returning US pilot, Lieutenant-Colonel Dick 'Snake' White, who likened Iraqis to cockroaches.[98] Dehumanizing enabled *The Sun* to comment on its front page that '[h]undreds of Iraqis fried in their tanks' without any emotion or degree of sympathy.[99] If the dehumanization is extended the enemy's character can become crystallized into a mechanical or robotic form. In the Kosovo Conflict *The Sun* referred to the 'Serbs' murder machine', creating an image of a robotic and mechanized approach to killing.[100] As well as drawing parallels with the Nazis' systematic annihilation of Jews during the Second World War, the presentation of the Serbs as a machine dehumanizes them. This allows the article to portray their destruction in terms of a 'smoking mass of twisted metal' with no reference to the loss of human lives, thus sanitizing their deaths.[101]

Whether utilizing a rational or irrational approach, the demonization of the character of the enemy enhances the good versus evil narrative. The most prevalent method of achieving this demonization of the enemy is through the use of atrocity stories. The use of articles referring to rape, torture, murder and theft evokes powerful personal feelings in the reader, with the outrage directed against the enemy. During the First World War the strength of the negative images of the enemy, 'the "Beastly Hun" with his sabre-belt barely encompassing his enormous girth, busily crucifying soldiers, violating women, mutilating babies' have become 'firmly implanted in the consciousness of the twentieth century'.[102] In many cases the reiteration of alleged atrocities, from dubious or unverifiable sources, is often produced in the press with little critical comment. It is an area of propaganda that is picked up and used by tabloids and broadsheet alike.

One of the most common forms is the utilization of women and children. One such example appeared in *The Daily Telegraph*, it cited Deborah Hadi, an American woman married to a Kuwaiti, who gave evidence to a US congressional committee. She described seeing 'Iraqi soldiers forcing a bayonet into the stomach of a woman in labour who had tried to enter a hospital'.[103] The newspaper made no attempt to discuss the validity of the story and, in another article by the same author that day, even admitted there were no figures, photos or names of witnesses to describe the atrocities taking place in Kuwait. Despite this the article insisted that a picture of systematic stripping was clear.[104] Without dismissing the fact that atrocities undoubtedly took place, the newspapers appeared to publish articles readily, without adequate confirmation of sources, which in peacetime would not be acceptable. One may argue that with a lack of information conflict does present a unique set of circumstances and this is a valid point. However, the fact remains that exaggerated atrocity stories were widely reproduced during both conflicts and even when they were exposed as fabricated the propaganda had already achieved its desired effect.

During the Gulf War, the clearest example of this method of atrocity story came with the alleged theft of incubators from Kuwaiti hospitals. *The Guardian* first mentioned the story via the evidence of Dr Ali Al Huwail, who had fled Kuwait. In his evidence he claimed to have buried fifty Kuwaiti children and witnessed Iraqis pulling the plugs from incubators.[105] The story was later repeated, this time with reference to a report compiled by Physicians for Human Rights, which mentioned 'three accounts of premature babies being removed from incubators and left to die'.[106] Indeed all five of the newspapers made reference to this particular story, which will be examined in more detail in the following chapter. The employment of this type of rhetoric was in keeping with atrocity propaganda widely utilized during the First World War.[107]

The nature of the justification for war in the Kosovo Conflict made the existence of atrocity stories even more necessary. With the main driving force behind military action being a humanitarian effort to save the lives of Kosovar Albanians, the atrocity story reinforced the necessity for fighting. In the Gulf War the brutal treatment of Kuwaitis and other nationals inside either Iraq or Kuwait simply reinforced the belief that Hussein was an evil tyrant and that his army must be driven from Kuwait. In Kosovo the British government faced a tougher challenge in generating and sustaining support for military intervention. In an article for *The Daily Telegraph* Alain de Botton highlights this distinction, '[i]n this new kind of warfare, sympathy replaces nationalism as the motivating factor. Mr Blair must persuade us to feel as touched by the fate of the Kosovar Albanians as by the fate of our own people in our own towns'.[108] In essence the employment of atrocity stories invokes emotional reactions from the reading public, thus stimulating a sense that 'something must be done'. As the press supported intervention in Kosovo the newspapers were filled with articles relating to atrocities and the fate of refugees. It must be noted that Kosovo was an air campaign. There was little in the way of visual material or newsworthy comment about the war. The most plentiful sources of information came from those fleeing the scene. This helps to explain the consistent repetition of various atrocities, and in doing so perpetuated the image that Kosovo was a campaign based on humanitarian issues.

Once more the emotive nature of atrocity stories, to bolster the demonized presentation of the enemy, meant that often broadsheets were as sensationalist in their coverage as the tabloids. The opening paragraph of a *Times* front-page article read, 'SERB forces have gone on a bloody rampage against Albanians in Kosovo, murdering scores of civilians, using entire communities as human shields and forcing thousands from their homes in an orgy of looting and burning'.[109] The paragraph left the reader in no doubt about the 'bloody' nature of the slaughter of civilians and it was not an isolated example. A later *Times* article claimed that not being satisfied with using 'human shields', 'shooting dead children' and burning homes, the 'Serbian border guards have taken to adding one more atrocity – rape'.[110] *The Daily Telegraph* mentioned 'that masked soldiers had slit the throats of young boys and then cut open the stomachs of pregnant women, skewering the foetuses on sharpened knives',[111] while also presenting human interest stories such as the epic plight of one 14-year-old whose mother had died in her lap.[112] A *Sun* headline exclaimed 'Kiddies Shot like Rabbits',[113] while the *Daily Mirror* described how one person 'saw soldiers pour petrol over a mother, father and two youngsters before torching them alive'.[114] The continuous repetition of these types of atrocity stories reinforced the image of the enemy as a barbaric and inhuman horde. Furthermore, by expanding the atrocity story theme further a new dimension to the image of the enemy could be created.

As with the leader figure, the continual portrayal of negative enemy characteristics leads to identification with the past. The Nazification of the mass was a clear evolution from the range of atrocity stories. This dimension of propaganda was most prevalent in Kosovo with the parallels between Slobodan Milosevic's ethnic cleansing and that of Hitler in the Second World War. However, this is not to say such associations were absent during the Gulf War. Allied leaders repeatedly raised the similarities not only between Hussein and Hitler, but also between their armed forces. As discussed earlier, newspaper reports often carried edited transcriptions of speeches which contained such rhetoric, including a *Guardian* article, quoting a Bush speech, which likened the atrocities in Kuwait with those conducted by the Nazi SS.[115]

In general though, the Kosovo Conflict produced some of the most explicit comparisons between the ethnic cleansing carried out by the Serbian forces and Nazi atrocities of the Second World War. The following article in *The Guardian* included Nazi references to reinforce a negative image of the Serbian forces, 'IN A CHILLING echo of the pogroms and camps of the Nazi era, sealed trains rolled into western Macedonia from Kosovo yesterday to disgorge a cargo of uprooted and dispossessed Albania civilians herded into the wagons at gunpoint by their strutting Serb conquerors'.[116] In this piece the Nazi connection is directly asserted and not merely implied. The mention of the 'strutting' Serbian forces conjures up images of an arrogant military force. It is the connection with Nazi Germany that gives the article its powerfully negative connotations, the effect of an article mentioning the arrival of sealed trains full of refugees would have had far less impact.

Despite this method of demonization by association and the above quotation, *The Guardian* made some attempt to remain open-minded about the possible atrocities being carried out. The editorial policy sounded a cautionary note insisting that not enough was known yet to use such terms as 'genocide' or 'ethnic cleansing', warning that as of that moment there was 'no hard evidence' of such crimes.[117] A later editorial reiterated this point of view, insisting that it was clear that the Serbs were guilty of driving out the Kosovans but that it was 'not established the crime is systematic killing'.[118] Therefore, despite printing an article directly associating Serb action with Nazi pogroms and camps, the editorial stance attempted to avoid some of the more sweeping generalizations being made. The newspaper insisted that the 'scale has already tipped, without adding atrocities which may or may not have taken place in any number'.[119] But while the direct assertions may have been cautionary, many articles throughout this and other newspapers carried indirect similarities, leading the reader to draw their own conclusions. For the tabloids, on the other hand, the similarities were obvious.

The Sun and *Daily Mirror* had no qualms in directly associating the Serbian forces in Kosovo with those of Nazi Germany. One *Sun* article mirrored *The Guardian* reference to sealed trains, saying survivors of 'Serb slaughter squads told yesterday how hundreds of them were herded on to trains in a chilling echo of the Nazi holocaust'.[120] In case any readers were left in doubt about the connection being highlighted, *The Sun* helpfully entitled the article 'NAZIS 1999'. In the same open letter to the British troops in Kosovo, which defended NATO air strikes against accusations of causing the refugee crisis, the newspaper reiterated the justification for war:

> Europe has not seen misery on such a scale since the Nazis extermi-
> nated six million Jews in the Holocaust.
>   In 1939, like you, our father and grandfathers went to war to halt
> the menace of Hitler and the Nazis . . .
>   Sixty years on, Europe is embroiled once again in war.
>   **And we will win again. Because right is on our side.**[121]

The connection was explicit, in doing so it justified the war and predicted a favourable outcome. The rallying call incorporated elements that can also be used for a single leader figure and still retain the same implicit message. The connection brings a historical event into a modern context to add gravity to the situation and to help explain the circumstances. However, just as important to this approach is the reference to a favourable outcome being achievable.

The *Daily Mirror* used another variation of this method when describing the deportation of Kosovans by train, explaining that '[t]he forced evacuation was reminiscent of SS troops sending Jews to the gas chambers, vividly portrayed in the movie Schindler's List'.[122] On this occasion the event was described with reference to a film, thereby visualizing the image, in a contemporary form. This reference is also significant because it was an analogy used on the same day by Major General John Drewienkiewicz of the Kosovo Verification Mission during a Ministry of Defence media brief-ing.[123] The article's title, '1939 or 1999?' also reinforced the Hitler connection.

Using historical association, notably with the Nazis, the press was able to demonize both the Serbian and Iraqi armed forces. The use of atrocity stories provided the framework from which to draw the association with Nazi Germany and also formed a part of those atrocity stories by placing them within the context of the Holocaust. This demonizing of the portrayal of the enemy particularly boosts the case for war justified on humanitarian grounds. Therefore, we see a consistent production of this genre of news item throughout the Kosovo Conflict and across the range of newspapers. In many instances, the emotive nature of the topic inspires a similar degree of sensationalism in the broadsheet and tabloid press alike.

During the Kosovo Conflict, however, there were a notable number of articles criticizing the government policy of a sustained air war. This high-lights a downside of the employment of humanitarian justifications for entering any conflict. Because Kosovo was portrayed as a concerted effort to help the plight of the oppressed Kosovan Albanians, air power alone was seen as insufficient. Thus, the humanitarian effort, which propelled the press to support intervention, actually fostered criticism of the adopted govern-ment policy. If the problem was on the ground with the atrocities and subse-quent refugees then, it was argued, ground troops were needed to resolve the crisis. This led, particularly in *The Telegraph* and *The Guardian*, to a call for ground forces. However, the significant factor remains that the employment of a humanitarian justification for war sustained support for intervention, even if debate remained about the best way to achieve the required goal.

The implementation of humanitarian justifications for war mirrors what Philip Hammond sees as the post-Cold War emergence of 'advocacy journalism' or the 'journalism of attachment'.[124] He argues that this form of journalism is a rejection of conventional journalistic neutrality and uses moral engagement to influence public opinion. Hammond notes that this style of reporting can appear selective and rather than adopting a fiercely independent stance, it often coincides with the policies of Western governments. It does indeed appear to be the case that the reporting from Kosovo bolstered the view that government action was correct in light of the humanitarian concerns. Although, as noted above, it did lead to some criticism of government handling of the conflict, if not actually questioning the right to be involved. But in the post-Cold War era the old justifications for conflict in a bipolar world have vanished. Now the distinction between 'us and them' must be made in different terms. The Gulf War provided a clear breach of international law, however, Kosovo appeared to be the more likely blueprint for future conflicts. It was a regionalized conflict with the line between legitimate and illegal intervention blurred by a number of factors. This is important, as Kosovo must not simply be seen in light of a war legitimated solely by humanitarian concerns.

The presentation of the enemy is, in many ways, an extension of the role of the leader figure. It has uses for the explanation, justification and continuation of conflict involving British armed forces. The enemy, as defined, is linked with the leader figure and many of the same characteristics and motivations are afforded to both. Reference to a defined enemy heightens the sense of difference between the general public of the opposing nation and the enemy as defined. This continues the efforts to defend against the accusation of waging a war against an entire nation. For propaganda to work effectively at legitimizing intervention the enemy must be clearly defined.

Theme three: military threat

The representation of the enemy's military capabilities serves key purposes in how conflict, or any potential conflict, is presented to the domestic audience. Evidence of the employment of this theme is clearly recognizable in British press coverage of the Gulf War and Kosovo. The discussion of the opponent's strengths and weaknesses, the presentation of the enemy, justifies intervention and explains the duration of the conflict. The portrayal of the enemy's fighting capabilities is split into two contradicting elements. Each factor reinforces certain messages for political and military advantage. During the coverage the military threat posed by the opposition's armed forces is either downplayed or enhanced. As with the rational and irrational depiction of the leader and the enemy, the twofold approach to portraying the enemy is not incompatible. Each approach justifies an action or event according to the particular circumstances.

Downplayed

The case for downplaying the enemy's military capabilities is relatively straightforward. For a government to foster public support for the conflict the war must appear winnable. Without such assurances support is likely to be severely limited and diminishing the capabilities of the opposition reassures public anxieties. A by-product of this is the encouragement of a low casualty rate. If the enemy is proven to be ill equipped and ill-trained, casualties can be minimized. A conflict that does not appear winnable or threatens vast casualty figures is highly unlikely to gain any significant public support regardless of the justifications for going to war.

There is also a certain degree of pride taken in one's own armed forces, stirring nationalistic feelings and reinforcing support for government and military alike. In this sense the war narrative, which requires a villain and hero, is reintroduced by contrasting the able and disciplined democratic forces against an ill-trained rabble. During the Kosovo crisis the perception of the Serb armed forces actually present in Kosovo differed greatly from the prevalent attitude shown towards the Iraqi army during the Gulf War. Serbian armed units were seen as cowardly, unprofessional and inhumane as their targets were often civilians. The fact that coalition ground troops were not required to fight their way into the area meant that a direct challenge to the perception of the Serbian forces was not required. The enhancement and degrading of the forces on the ground needed less consideration in the press while a ground conflict was seen as unlikely.

During the Gulf War, much had been made in the media of Saddam Hussein having the fourth largest army in the world and a million men in arms. To quell any possible fears of the capability of the Iraqi army, the *Daily Mirror* insisted they were 'in a much worse state than the West first believed' and that discipline was 'breaking down' and their equipment was 'becoming increasingly unserviceable in the harsh desert conditions'.[125] The article was produced under the headline 'Sad's Army is a Total Shambles' leaving the reader in no doubt about the efficiency of the Iraqi forces. *The Daily Telegraph* also produced a reassuring article in which the author suggested Saddam's army was far from an overwhelming military power.[126] He highlighted the fact that the bulk of the forces were conscripts, left over from the war with Iran. The article notes Saddam's failure to bring the Iran–Iraq war to a successful conclusion as evidence of his fallibility. The piece reassures those readers who may have been impressed with the figures regarding the size of Iraq's army being touted across the media.

The article also mentions that although his forces are weak they were still more than a match for Saudi Arabia. In doing so the message emanating from Western governments was reinforced; that Saudi Arabia needed bolstering to avoid it being invaded. As a ground war neared, these reassurances became increasingly important.

The Times utilized another method to reassure the public of the fallibility of the Iraqi forces. The newspaper ran an article by Air Chief Marshal Sir Michael Armitage, a former commandant of the Royal College of Defence Studies, London. In his assessment of the Iraqi forces he uses evidence from the Iran–Iraq Gulf War to conclude that they were 'ill-trained' and 'inept'.[127] As with reference to psychologists, doctors or academics during the demonization of the leader figure, the military threat of the enemy forces also invited comment from leading experts. Contemporary war has seen the widespread employment of military spokesmen and military experts by the media to offer legitimacy to the argument of articles. The most recent conflict in Iraq was no exception.

Enhanced

The view of the military threat of both the Iraqi army and Serbian forces was fluid and, at times, it was necessary to enhance the image of their capabilities. A principle reason for this was to prepare the general public for a prolonged diplomatic and military campaign. If the Western political and military leaders could convince the public they were facing a dangerous enemy, more time and preparation could be justified. During the initial stages of Western military action against Iraq, John Major stressed to the House of Commons that 'Iraq has a substantial number of men under arms. They have sophisticated weapons and, in many cases, they have considerable hardened military experience. There is a great deal yet to be done before the matter is resolved.'[128] The Prime Minister's statement encompasses the issues needed to calm overenthusiasm and prepare the public for a prolonged conflict. Such statements also act as a reassurance to the public that the commanders were acting to limit the number of potential allied casualties.

This enhanced explanation of the enemy forces also aided military and political planners in avoiding accusations of stagnation, especially during long periods of military build-up when coverage in the press could become repetitive. Thus, during the crisis in the Gulf *The Times* produced the following passage:

> This growing appreciation of Iraq's military infrastructure is one of the main reasons why allied commanders have sought to delay the land campaign. With such extensive stocks of ammunition, it seems likely that Saddam will have moved enough shells, bullets and missiles to the front to last months.[129]

The delay in activity is associated with a new appreciation of the enemy's infrastructure, which was now being enhanced. This reinforces *The Times'* view that there was a need for patience.

In the case of the Kosovo Conflict the Iraqi war once more became the benchmark against which to evaluate the current crisis. Thus, *The Sun* insisted Serbia would be no walkover and would be exceedingly more difficult than the Gulf. 'This time' the article warned 'the enemy's much more deadly. It's better armed, better trained and infinitely tougher'.[130] In Kosovo, much was made of the Serbian air defences that were seen as competent and covering a wide area, posing a substantial threat to allied air attacks.

It was important that the strength of the enemy was not overplayed, as the downplaying of it in other articles demonstrates. The creation of an enhanced enemy helped to justify the long build-up to conflict. During these periods newspapers would often talk about new phases that the war had entered which helped to break-up the monotony of press coverage. This was also done to demonstrate a continual onward movement and counter criticism of stagnation. Thus, in the face of a strong enemy and long war, progress was still being made, patience was the key and an enhanced military threat the justification for alleged inactivity.

The enhancement of the military threat also served two other related functions. By presenting the enemy as a strong force the policymakers could avoid accusation of bullying and slaughter. The press reiterated these enhanced perceptions of the opposing forces and in doing so limited some criticism of going to war against an enfeebled country. Furthermore, if the opposing force is presented as threatening then there is greater justification for its annihilation. If solely presented as an army of ill-trained conscripts their destruction becomes more distasteful.

Both enhanced and downplayed

Particular events can be used to both enhance and degrade the portrayal of the enemy's military threat. The Gulf War provides two interesting examples of this. In keeping with the association of the Gulf with the Second World War, the Iraqi system of fortifications designed to slow any advance was likened to the Maginot Line.[131] The Maginot Line had served British propaganda interests well during the initial stages of the Second World War and during the Gulf it again played a part in the assessment of Iraq's military capabilities.[132] *The Guardian* commented upon Iraq's defences through the use of implicit referral to the Maginot Line.[133] Michael Evans, writing for *The Times*, was more explicit in the comparison, using the heading 'Saddam's Maginot Line can be Broken'.[134] The article downplayed the importance of Saddam's system of fortifications suggesting that it was 'a very static sort of defence, with dense lines of infantry behind. It is not very sophisticated in Western eyes'.[135] The superiority of the West is reinforced and Saddam's defences were depicted as outdated. The very reference to the Maginot Line implies a flawed system of defence and an over-confidence in its practicality.

The Maginot Line metaphor was also utilized in reverse and at times by the same authors that sought to stress its weaknesses. As war loomed Evans backtracked on his previous optimistic appraisal of the line of fortifications, instead describing its breach by Western forces as 'one of their most dangerous challenges'.[136] The article refers to the bombardment of the defences by B52s, which had made the task easier, yet the emphasis from the same author had shifted to an enhanced respect for the defences.

Maps produced in the newspapers appeared to share a resemblance with earlier depictions of fortifications. Maps of the Maginot in the British press during the Second World War depicted a single consistent line. The Iraqi defences are also represented in a similar fashion. This gives the impression of a consistent system of fortifications, spread across the entire southern border of Kuwait. Overcoming such a barrier is not seen as an impossible task, instead the enhancement of the Iraqi defences allows for any potential delays or losses to be explained. In contrast, a swifter victory than the one expected enhances the credibility of one's own forces.

Another event that formed part of the military threat theme was the incursion of Iraqi troops into Khafji in Saudi Arabia.[137] This event allowed for a heroic image of the alliance soldiers to be reinforced even though the event demonstrated that the Iraqis were capable of mustering a counter-attack despite continuous bombing. The ability of the Iraqi troops was enhanced, thereby reducing the extent to which the invasion could be portrayed as an embarrassment. *The Times* did level some criticism at the coalition. Schwarzkopf was criticized for calling the large town a village and the entire event was depicted as a propaganda coup for the Iraqis.[138] However, the following day *The Times* was using the Khafji incident as a powerful portent to what lay ahead and claimed the incursion had 'sent a clear message that any battle to regain Kuwait City could last months rather than weeks'.[139] *The Daily Telegraph* reiterated the notion of the Khafji invasion as a propaganda coup for Saddam and added the incident demonstrated 'the cunning manner in which he is playing the weakest of hands'.[140] Yet, the same article also mentioned that '[n]o Western commander would allow himself to be party to a sacrificial thrust, which has cost his own troops' lives and some loss of equipment, to inflict negligible loss upon his enemies'.[141] In this respect the editorial is presenting both a rational and irrational view of Saddam. Rationally, by gaining a propaganda advantage, irrationally through reckless tactics. The distinction is once more drawn between his behaviour and that of more rational Western tactics.

As a result of these actions *The Daily Telegraph* called for more to be made of the allies' own activities as '[i]t is not politically helpful, especially in the Arab world, if Saddam's initiatives, however brutal or futile, dominate the front pages day after day'.[142] This point demonstrates once again the difficulty in providing positive and non-repetitive coverage of the allied war effort when there is a dearth of information generated by an air campaign alone. In general, however, despite a major breach of the Saudi border the criticism was limited.

The Guardian made some reference to the misunderstanding surrounding the invasion, describing the confusion as '[t]he one constant in the battle of Khafji'.[143] Yet, the newspaper was not immune from such misunderstandings, after initially referring to a 'small oil port'[144] the conurbation was upgraded to a 'city'[145] within two days. However, the most important issue derived from the Khafji incident, as shown with *The Times*' coverage, was that the battle pointed to tough fighting ahead. Khafji, rather than being seen as a quick and embarrassing skirmish, was thought to herald 'a new and grimmer phase . . . pointing to the tough ground fighting that lies ahead'.[146] In this respect the actual events in Khafji were sidelined. There was less discussion on what, if anything, had gone wrong. Instead the attention focused on how the results confirmed an overriding message emanating from the coalition forces; that this would not be a swift and painless war.

Western military planners enhanced the portrayal of the enemy threat during the Khafji incident for two reasons. First, it lessened the embarrassment of the invasion for the allies by stressing the 'cunning' and 'tenacity' of Saddam and his forces.[147] This made Khafji appear to be a more palatable distraction. If the effectiveness of his forces had been downplayed too greatly the invasion would have been far more difficult to explain. Second, the event reinforced the desired notion that the war would not be a short, easy victory, thereby preparing the public for casualties and combating impatience.

Overall, the presentation of the enemy's military threat plays a useful role in general propaganda messages during conflict. The process, being both enhanced and downplayed, is a careful balancing act and is employed according to the specific aims of the current situation. As the examples of Maginot Line-style reporting of Iraqi defences and the Khafji incident have shown, specific incidents can provide examples of both types of military emphasis, despite appearing to be incompatible. The direct military threat of the enemy forces also incorporates itself within wider implications of the enemy's strength.

Theme four: threat to international stability

A further component of the propaganda campaign to generate support for intervention in the Gulf War and Kosovo Conflict is the emphasis placed upon the threat posed to the international community. This is achieved by highlighting the destabilization a crisis can cause and by the potential terrorist campaigns that may develop from it. It is necessary to persuade the British public of the implications to them of Saddam Hussien's invasion of Kuwait or Slobodan Milosevic's actions in Kosovo. These implications must be seen to present a relevant danger in order to justify the risks associated with intervention. Furthermore, by reiterating the larger threat, the removal of the aggressor's military capabilities is legitimated.

When presenting international conflicts to a domestic audience policy-makers and the press are in essence emphasizing the general threat to their own region. To sustain a conflict public opinion needs to feel affected by the events taking place. One of the simplest ways of achieving this is to make the public 'feel that they are threatened by something outside the group which is both evil and dangerous'.[148] During the Second World War Hitler was able to achieve this by creating a number of threats to the security of Germany, most notably Jews and communist Russia.

In addition to fostering domestic complicity, the emphasis on regional implications is used to gain wider international support. During the First World War Britain avidly pursued propaganda to influence American opinion of the conflict. As Sanders and Taylor have demonstrated, British propaganda sought 'to foster a particular stereotype of the Central Powers as cruel, tyrannical regimes bent on world domination and, as such, were anathema to the democratic ideals cherished in Britain, France and America'.[149] By stressing the larger zone that can be affected by any given crisis, nations that may not have shared previous interests are bound together in the light of the current situation. In this sense it is always necessary in conflict to continue to reiterate the threat to the wider region to maintain and bind not only domestic but also international public and diplomatic opinion.

The construction and cohesion of alliances formed in the face of international crises are not always harmonious. In addition to binding a coalition through mutual concern, the British press displayed occasions when criticism of coalition members was used to shame those members into complicity. In advance of a proposed European Community meeting under the new chairman, Mr Jacques Poos, in Luxembourg, *The Times* and *The Daily Telegraph* both aired criticisms. The British press in general insisted upon a united front, in this case against Saddam Hussein but also against Slobodan Milosevic. The thinking behind this being that any perceived cracks in the international solidarity could damage the chances of the alliance's policies being effective. Any independent actions were seen as damaging to this approach. Thus, as the EC deliberated as to whether to send its own, as opposed to a United Nations, delegation to Iraq before the 15 January UN deadline, *The Times* launched an attack on their motives in the following editorial:

> The aim is supposed to be to impress the Iraqi dictator with the hopelessness of his isolation. For that, solidarity with the United

States is vital. If Mr Bush had publicly asked the EC to intervene, the mission would have a purpose. In the absence of any such request, Iraq may interpret an EC mission as the first crack in the western facade. Suez demonstrated the disastrous consequences of Europe and America failing to act in concert; and Saddam does not need reminding of that precedent . . .

If they lose their nerve, breaking ranks with Europe's rescuers in two world wars, Saddam will not be the only enemy of civilisation to profit.[150]

The United States is presented as the most important element for a unified approach to tackling Saddam. As any EC delegation would obviously not include America, this was deemed unacceptable and indeed damaging. Only with the blessing of Bush would the delegation 'have a purpose'. There exists a twofold attempt to utilize the historical image of US–European relations. Initially the veiled threat, with reference to Suez, reminds the reader that European action requires American backing to be successful. Second, the mention of the United States as Second World War saviours insists Europe owes a debt to America. Finally, the diplomatic effort is portrayed as 'breaking ranks' and therefore damaging, but more importantly any such action would constitute the EC losing 'their nerve'.

The Daily Telegraph reproduces this approach in its own response to a proposed EC delegation. The newspaper is explicit about why the United States should be allowed to take the lead in any negotiations, because it is they who are providing the bulk of military forces. The outcome of *The Daily Telegraph*'s editorial is conspicuously similar to that of *The Times*:

Above all, Europe should not seek a role in the crisis for the sake of its own misguided self-importance. It already has a role. This is to stand four-square behind its American ally – indeed leader – amid one of her greatest challenges for many years, just as the Americans stood by Europe for nearly five decades.[151]

The aims of the EC are deemed 'misguided' and the suggestion is that the institution should simply limit itself to backing the policy of the United States. Where *The Times* employed the historical references of the Second World War and Suez, *The Daily Telegraph* reminds its readers that Europe had enjoyed US backing during the Cold War. It is for these reasons that US attempts at diplomacy, such as sending James Baker to meet Tariq Aziz were welcomed. Although acting independently these moves were legitimated, if the above articles are to be believed, by the fact that the US had earned the right to intervene. Furthermore, what the above editorials highlight is the role that Britain identifies herself with. As part of the EC she should be regarded as partially culpable for its actions, however there is no reference to any British involvement in these European affairs. In addition the intervention of either the EC or America negates the role of the United Nations, when criticizing the EC the editorials insist they back the US and not the United Nations.

When attempting to stress the importance of a unified coalition efforts are not only made to bind countries together in the face of a common threat, but also some elements of shaming and reference to historical obligations are made to sustain unity. References to historical events, such as the Second World War, are in keeping with the employment of such techniques with regards to the leader figure and the image of the enemy. In essence the objective is to highlight what potential trouble may arise if the threat to the region is not faced and the crisis is allowed to destabilize a larger region. The underlying message remains that appeasement is no alternative.

The Iraqi invasion of Kuwait could not be portrayed to the public as an insignificant and distant conflict without any relevance to Britain if government policy was to follow an interventionist route. To avoid accusations that the Gulf War was simply a war for oil and to bind a larger coalition together, much was made of Hussein's ability to destabilize a larger region. If the issue of oil was addressed it was often to suggest that if Saddam managed to obtain even larger stocks of world oil he would use this to hold the world to ransom.

To emphasize the wider implications of Saddam's ability to destabilize a larger arena, the *Daily Mirror* insisted that any conflict against Saddam would be a '**just and justifiable war to preserve the peace, security and economy of the whole world**'.[152] In an article in *The Times* the author also incorporated the threat of chemical and nuclear weapons, which played a large part in much of the coverage of the Gulf War, into the theme of a more general threat. The invocation of chemical and nuclear weapons also reinforced his demonized image. The threat of these weapons is then extended beyond the relatively isolated region of the Middle East to cast a shadow directly over Europe:

> Saddam has acquired advanced chemical weapons, and his missiles will soon have the range to threaten Europe. His nuclear researchers, too, may be within two years of making atomic bombs. As he gets older, he will become even more impatient to accomplish his mission for Mesopotamia.
>
> If Saddam is allowed to survive this crisis, his enhanced prestige will propel him well towards becoming the leader of the whole Arab world. The price we would then have to pay to stop him would be greater still.[153]

In the article above the ability of Saddam Hussein to destabilize the region is tied in with his desire for wider political and expansionist aspirations. The conclusion is a call for his removal now or risk facing a greater threat in the future. The article makes reference to his age, suggesting he will become increasingly desperate to fulfil his ambitions as time advances. To enhance the domestic threat the piece predicts Saddam Hussein will soon have missiles capable of reaching Europe, thereby directly affecting the British public. The *Daily Mirror* reiterates a similar hypothesis, if in a somewhat more bombastic fashion, with its own comment piece about the Gulf War:

> It will be a war, unlike the Falklands, which could touch one way or the other every home in Britain. We will have to make sacrifices . . .
>
> In his ambition he would conquer and lead the whole Moslem world armed with nuclear weapons in holy war – a Jihad – against Israel and the infidel West . . .
>
> **From tomorrow** (the passing of the United Nations Resolution for Iraq to withdraw from Kuwait) **Britain has to unite as we did in 1939. For in a war it will be him . . . or us.**[154]

The *Daily Mirror* uses Second World War rhetoric to produce the same outcome as the *Times* editorial. Though utilizing different approaches the urgency of Saddam Hussein's invasion of Iraq is underlined and so too is the urgency to do something to counter his aggression. Both editorial and comment pieces draw attention to Saddam Hussein's wider goals. They refer to his pan-Arab intentions for a larger empire. The *Daily Mirror* emphasizes the religious connotations of this Arab unity by stressing that such opposition would amount to a holy war. This once more reiterates the narrative of a definable enemy against another block or grouping. It is interesting how the *Mirror* implies that the Falklands did not affect 'every home in Britain'. This would appear to be a further way of emphasizing the relevance of the current conflict, suggesting a much larger scale war and one which will become even more memorable, for good or bad reasons, than the Falklands campaign. However, what both articles do is to reinforce the notion that appeasement is not an option. *The Times* concludes that Saddam will only get more desperate with age and the *Daily Mirror* invokes 1939 and insists the struggle is one of national survival through the use of 'him . . . or us', thus implying that Britain must fight.

The Times also sought to portray action against Iraq as a final chance to demonstrate the viability of united international cooperation to uphold international security. The newspaper described the unified action against Saddam's army as an 'experiment' that 'must be made to work' on this occasion.[155] If not, the newspaper warned, each country would have to ally itself as best it could 'against the law of the jungle'.[156] The Gulf War was presented as a test for international solidarity. The failure of this would lead ultimately to a breakdown of unified action on any large scale. The reference to 'law of the jungle' suggests a chaotic, if not anarchic rule of law which would directly threaten Western, civilized, democracy. By fighting for the salvation of the international world order, British intervention in the Gulf War was justified and the likely outcome of non-intervention related directly to the domestic audience.

During the Gulf War, the international threat posed by Saddam Hussein was easier to establish than Milosevic's in Kosovo. Hussein had invaded another sovereign nation and the public was led to believe that he would invade Saudi Arabia as well. To introduce the fourth theme of propaganda into coverage of the Gulf War was therefore more justifiable owing to the evidence of Hussein's actions. The threat to international stability in Kosovo had a different set of considerations. The emphasis was placed on the moral and humanitarian justifications for entering the conflict. However, the nature of the regional or international threat was still employed to bolster justification for involvement.

In one significant respect, the Kosovo crisis held an advantage for the proponents of intervention by the very nature of its location in Europe. It was far easier for the press to draw relevance between people who shared the same European connections. However, the press still maintained an 'us versus them' distinction necessary for distancing the opposition in order to generate an identifiable enemy. There was a clear demarcation between the European Balkans and the Western democracies. However, the similarities with Gulf War coverage are remarkable, with the emphasis on how Kosovo would affect British lives explained frequently in the press.

Each of the newspapers, in their editorial policy at least, supported intervention of one kind or another in Kosovo, even if it were not military. The clearest examples of emphasizing the threat to international stability appear outside of *The Guardian* because the newspaper had pushed for a non-military policy until hostilities actually began. *The Times* carried an article written by Tony Blair for *Newsweek* magazine in which he insisted the conflict was being fought not for territory but 'for a new internationalism'.[157] This linked the crisis to a wider agenda. *The Daily Telegraph* was certain that Milosevic's 'authoritarian rule and racial policies present the greatest threat to stability in Europe' and that NATO was 'the only organisation capable of curbing his murderous ambitions'.[158] In this editorial, the newspaper directly asserts that Milosevic has the ability to destabilize the whole of Europe and in doing so the article was emphasizing the international threat necessary to stir public opinion in favour of intervention. By extension of this point the editorial concludes that the international threat requires an international solution and suggests the intervention of NATO. The approaches of *The Times* and *The Daily Telegraph* reiterated both the reason why intervention was necessary by stressing the proximity of the conflict and the potential political ramifications of the conflict spreading.

The tabloids followed the same method to establish the relevance of the Kosovo crisis to their readership. The *Daily Mirror*, while continuing to utilize the demonization of Saddam, suggested '[l]ike all dictators, his ambition recognises no borders. He will move into other European countries and won't stop until he is forced to'.[159] A further article in the newspaper entitled 'Evil Tyrant's Threat to all in Europe' claimed Slobodan Milosevic had developed a rational policy to destabilize other European countries through the flow of refugees.[160] These approaches justified intervention while underlining the association of Slobodan Milosevic with the calculated and rational policy of generating instability in European nations of close proximity. *The Sun* extended this theme of a wider international security threat to underline Britain's role by insisting the situation was 'not just Britain fighting for its own sake, but Britain bolstering and leading an uncertain alliance against a threat to world stability'.[161] The newspaper therefore saw Britain as being at the forefront of the alliance rallied to protect world stability. The additional installation of Blair as the central leading figure reinforces the implication that the conflict is one intimately connected to Britain's own welfare.

The ramifications of conflict in either the Middle East or the Balkans were not only portrayed as a threat to international stability. Another method was also employed which has greater implications for the conduct of future international policy. The international threat of terrorism, outside of the immediate conflict arena, threatens to challenge traditional approaches to portraying wars as winnable. It also provides a useful method of reiterating the importance of distant conflicts to domestic audiences. The threat of international terrorism against all coalition and indeed non-coalition members helps to gain international support and bind the nations together. Thus, all belligerent nations, whether actively supplying forces, sharing borders or providing other forms of aid, face the similar risk of international terrorism.

While bringing the war to the domestic front *The Times* was anxious that the role of international terrorism was not presented in such a way as to benefit the Iraqis in the Gulf War. The newspaper described terrorism as one of 'a myriad of weapons' utilized during a 'globally witnessed war', while headlining the article simply 'Scud Wars'.[162] However, in reference to media coverage of Scud missile attacks, the newspaper urged the public not to be panicked by media images and in doing so remove the fear and despair which is the terrorist's aim. Thus, the press brought the reality of war to a domestic audience with references to Iraqi or Serb retaliations via terrorist action. Yet, to emphasize the international threat and the justification for war, in this instance, the public was itself able to combat a form of enemy action, thus immersing them further into the war effort.

The international threat posed by conflict has shifted in the post-Cold War era. Previously two vast opposing blocs threatening nuclear conflict provided the explanation and justification for war and, via inter-continental ballistic missiles, brought the danger very much to the domestic sphere. In smaller, regionalized conflicts such as Kosovo the immediate dangers appear less apparent. The threat of terrorism is a mechanism utilized to facilitate a degree of public awareness regarding such crises, if not necessarily support for them. During the Gulf War, the much-vaunted 'smart' weapons were hailed as safeguarding Western lives and making the resolution of conflicts seem more obtainable. Kosovo managed to prove many doubters of the military ability to defeat an enemy by air alone to be wrong. However, 'smart' bombs have proved to be of little effect against eradicating the more frightening, unpredictable and fanatical forms that terrorism takes.

Theme five: technological warfare

The portrayal of weapons technology in the press is a component of the general war narrative. The form of portrayal employed to present technology during the war provides a further dimension to the other four propaganda themes. Ultimately, the discussion of allied weaponry reinforces the support for military action. However, there are distinctions between the Gulf War and Kosovo Conflict that raise wider issues regarding the propaganda value of this fifth and final theme. While undoubtedly having the potential to increase domestic support for conflict, there are also some inherent negative ramifications.

The Gulf War raised a particularly new interest in the role of weapons technology in conflict. By the time of the Kosovo Conflict the reputation of 'smart' technology had been partially tarnished. Despite this the unexpected conclusion of that confrontation could be used as a case for the reappraisal of the role of such weapons. However, despite a Gulf War dominated by technology and a Kosovan Conflict won by air power alone, the theme of technological warfare is not necessarily destined to become the most productive propaganda component for future conflict. As the most recent hostilities in Iraq have shown, technology alone does not ensure public support.

Modern Western weapons technology in whatever form is often used to support the arguments of pro-interventionists. In the instance of the British press the function of technology can be sensationalist, exciting and provide vital copy. In the run-up to conflict, discussion of weapons technology forms a consistent element of 'war' reportage. During the Gulf War and Kosovo Conflict there existed extended periods of inactivity or limited and secretive diplomatic wrangling. The approach of the press during the rise to war often heavily incorporates attention to the role of technology. As the majority of the newspapers provided little alternative to war, the extended periods of inactivity required some relevant copy to be written. Alternatively, often with tabloid coverage and especially during the run-up to Kosovo, the event would fall off the newsworthy agenda completely. When the issue was addressed a focus on military hardware provided relatively easy talking points and blended with the overall narrative structure that asserted the understanding that war was inevitable.

Modern weaponry also abetted those critics of a military, interventionist approach. By highlighting the effectiveness and precision of 'smart' weapons the arguments of peace campaigners could be countered and diminished. This traditional argument was summed up in the following *Sun* article:

> THE most astonishing pictures so far from the frontline have been those of Allied bombs and missiles hitting military installations in Iraq with surgical precision . . . Condemned by the 'peace' movement as weapons of mass destruction, they have in fact proved just the opposite . . . War is never pleasant. But modern technology has at least ensured that the spilling of innocent blood can generally be avoided.[163]

This piece and similar arguments stress the legitimacy of conflicts that utilize modern, 'lifesaving', weapons. Advanced weaponry such as described above further distances the two opposing sides, re-emphasizing the civilized versus uncivilized theme. The article mentions 'surgical' attacks, prompting images of a clean war; as such it is the Western powers with access to 'smart' weapons that can conduct 'surgical' warfare. The article, dated 19 January 1991, was written shortly after the instigation of the air campaign against Iraq in a period where it is certainly too early to make such assertions about the infallibility of 'smart' weapons. The only pictures available from the 'front-line', presumably the allied frontline and not in Iraq itself, in an air campaign would have been those from bombs or aircraft taking-off or landing. Furthermore, the author is confident that those buildings depicted from the camera of a bomb are military installations. In addition to discrediting the 'peace' movement, the article fails to question the validity of the pictures and leaves the reader with the impression that modern technology will save, rather than harm, lives. This pretence is soon downgraded when allied lives are potentially at risk. While precision bombing is the ideal it should not aid the enemy in any way, therefore if the range of allied targets needs to be expanded to further the coalition cause, civilian considerations are reduced.

The justification for escalating attacks on dubious military targets during the Kosovo Conflict is then related to the Gulf War precedent. In an article in *The Times* the escalation of the bombing campaign, after Milosevic had failed to concede when predicted, employed the Gulf War example to legitimize wider bombing of targets, which had the potential to endanger more civilian lives:

> However, just as the American-led coalition bombers of Operation
> Desert Storm had the authority to attack Iraqi government build-
> ings, power stations, strategic bridges, presidential palaces and any
> other facility that could be linked to President Saddam Hussein's
> war machine, so now NATO aircraft are being ordered to give
> Belgrade the 'Baghdad treatment'.[164]

The bombing campaign is not only justified via the humanitarian precedent, but, as with the leader figure, coverage of a conflict employs historical
precedents to legitimize the actions. There is no scope for discussing the
overall legitimacy of such actions, yet the implication is that because it was
deemed successful in the Gulf War this can be transferred to Kosovo.

Military technology, specifically 'smart' weapons, have obvious implications for justifying and legitimizing a humanitarian war. Yet, there are
inherent drawbacks to emphasizing the role such weapons play. By stressing
the 'surgical' nature of allied weaponry, errors resulting from the use of them
become far harder to accept in the eyes of public opinion. Both conflicts
provide examples where the propaganda theme of technologically dependent
warfare had the potential to cause more damage than create any significant advantage. Incidents such as the Amiriyah shelter bombing, the Iraqi
incursion into the Saudi Arabian town of Khafji and the Kosovan errors
that saw the Chinese Embassy in Belgrade bombed along with convoys of
refugees and the controversial targeting of the Radio Television Serbia
(hereafter RTS) building, were made harder to justify after the practical
infallibility of allied weaponry had been consistently reiterated in the press.
The Guardian attempted to suggest at the time of the Khafji invasion that
the Pentagon had left the public unprepared for the Iraqis to mount any
kind of offensive because of the focus upon hi-tech weaponry.[165] This led
the newspaper to the conclusion that Khafji proved hi-tech weaponry could
not replace the vital role played by the infantry in clearing cities of the
enemy street by street.[166] In this instance, the focus upon hi-tech weaponry
as the saviour of the allies in the Gulf was dampened by the Iraqi incursion,
which demonstrated that the alliance's tactics were less effective than had
been hoped or imagined. However, the blame was directed towards Pentagon briefings, briefings and sound bites that were regularly reiterated in the
British press.

In addition to the debate surrounding the effectiveness of modern
weaponry, limitations were also placed upon the extent to which civilian
lives were to be safeguarded. As mentioned above the moral justification
of avoiding civilian casualties is diminished when the lives of allied troops
are in danger. The distinction drawn out is that any allied-inflicted civilian
casualties are unintentional and thereby unfortunate. On an aspect of this
topic Max Hastings wrote for *The Daily Telegraph* that it was an 'irony of
a war against Iraq in 1991, as it was of the war against Hitler, that many

people in the outside world are far more concerned about the welfare of the enemy population than is their own leadership'.[167] Once again the Second World War analogy is woven into the fabric of an article espousing another propaganda theme. Reference to Hitler reasserts the demonization of Saddam. Because of a negligent attitude towards his own population the enemy leader figure assists a propaganda theme of those forces ranged against him. Unintentional accidents resulting in civilian deaths are depicted as unfortunate and still compare favourably with the enemy leader figure's portrayal.

The Times initially stressed the need for a moral, humanitarian approach to the bombing campaign against Iraq. This, the newspaper insisted, was vital to winning world and especially Arab diplomatic support and counter claims of waging war against civilians.[168] However, the culpability for any civilian deaths remained focused on the enemy leader. Although *The Times* had warned that precision bombing was the best form of diplomacy, such diplomatic considerations should, in the paper's eyes, never be allowed to dominate the agenda and that the 'allies must attack when, and only when, their generals conclude the time is ripe'.[169] In the build-up to a ground campaign the lives of coalition soldiers were far more significant than ensuring that civilians were not injured by increased bombing raids or more extensive use of 'dumb' bombs. The enduring sentiment was that at least the modern technology attempted to limit non-military damage and this in itself was an admirable quality.

One incident during the Gulf War that had the potential to challenge the alliance's bombing policy was the destruction of the Amiriya shelter.[170] The death of so many civilians had the potential to damage the coalition's credibility severely and undermine the public facade of a humanitarian conflict fought with smart weapons. However, this was not to be the case. Initially *The Times*, which had been calling for bombing for as long as the alliance leaders required for victory, was critical of government policy. The following editorial stressed the need to keep political and strategic aims in view as well as realizing the military significance of bombing:

> There is now a strong case for concentrating bombing on the Kuwaiti front and on obvious military encampments, and thus avoiding Saddam's obvious propaganda trap. Western publics will find it hard to believe that there are still targets in Iraq's towns and cities which it is militarily indispensable to destroy. Military spokesmen may continue to blame Saddam for 'causing' any civilian casualties, by his heartlessness and his intransigence. But that is only part of the story of war. It does nothing to diminish yesterday's tragedy, nor diminish the importance of trying to avoid it recurring.[171]

Whereas previously in *Times* editorials military rather than political objectives had taken priority, the Amiriya incident had shifted the balance slightly. The newspaper now called for a concentration of attacks in Kuwait, thereby limiting the opportunities for a recurrence of civilian losses in Iraqi cities. The editorial also mentions military spokesmen blaming Saddam although the paper itself refers to the incident as 'Saddam's obvious propaganda trap', this suggests what allied spokesmen were to argue that Saddam used the shelter for military purposes and the civilians as shields against attack. In regard to the use of smart weaponry and the success of the bombing campaign, the editorial mentions 'Western publics' finding it difficult to believe many more credible targets were left in Iraq. This impression would have been fostered by the over-optimistic battle damage assessments of the military spokesmen, which were consistently reproduced in the British press without critical analysis or cautionary note. In this regard, the overemphasis of the success of modern technological bombing meant that a long bombing campaign became harder to explain.

The cautionary tone of *The Times* was not echoed throughout the other newspapers. An incident that could effectively discredit the ability of modern warfare to conduct 'surgical' strikes was largely reported in line with official, Western, interpretations. Max Hastings from *The Daily Telegraph* reported it was the tragic truth that the war could not be swiftly concluded, with tolerable cost to human life, 'without accepting such episodes as that which took place in Baghdad yesterday as part of the price'.[172] The *Daily Mirror* had scant coverage of the incident and no editorial comment; *The Sun*, however, went to greater extremes. Not content with regarding the shelter bombing as a tragic mistake *The Sun* more than any other newspaper attempted to shift the focus of attention onto Saddam. Thus, the newspaper wrote '[i]f there were innocent victims, we grieve for them. But the real guilt belongs to Saddam Hussein. He could have had peace at any time. Instead he chose war'.[173] The editorial cast doubts over the loss of any innocent lives by using the word 'if' and in addition placed the blame squarely onto Saddam's shoulders.

The Sun's editorial was written in the context of some limited public criticism of the allies regarding the bombing from public figures such as Tony Benn. The newspaper reacted to this and other criticisms, attacking, for example the BBC and ITV's allegedly obedient screening of Saddam's propaganda images. On the previous day, when first reporting the incident, *The Sun* insisted the decision to bomb the shelter was correct.[174] The newspaper even went so far as to suggest that the 'smart' bombs used by the allies would not have caused the inferno seen and therefore Saddam's men must have started the fires after the initial blast.

The overall impression generated by newspaper coverage of the event was of a tragic mistake. Not only was it an accidental act committed by the coalition forces, but also it was an accident brought about by Saddam's

intransigence at prolonging the war. Despite the fallibility of modern technology, which still has to be targeted by humans, there remained no overt
criticism of a policy of reliance on such hi-tech weapons.

A number of incidents during the Kosovo crisis confirmed the precedent
set by the Amiriya bombing. While 'smart' weapons, especially during the
Gulf War, hailed a new 'clinical' era of modern warfare, mistakes were
not seen to discredit the reputation of such weapons. On the 14 April 1999
NATO warplanes struck a convoy of Kosovan refugees, mistaken for
Serbian armed forces. *The Daily Telegraph* reported the incident in the
following terms:

> THE death of a reported 75 Kosovo refugees yesterday is a tragic
> development that drives home the full horror of this war. We do
> not know whether the refugees were being used as human shields
> to protect Serb military facilities, or whether they were somehow
> mistaken by Nato pilots for enemy forces, or indeed whether Nato
> was responsible at all. But whatever happened, it is Slobodan
> Milosevic who is entirely responsible for creating the circumstances
> that led to their deaths. It is his regime that has driven more than a
> million people from their homes in a systematic campaign of ethnic
> cleansing, and then forced tens of thousands back from the border
> territories for his own despicable purpose.[175]

The editorial asserted that regardless of the circumstances the culpability
for the killings was solely Milosevic's. This approach mirrors official
channels of information when addressing such public relations mistakes.
NATO would initially deny reports, then attempt to deflect some criticism
onto Serb forces, either suggesting the refugees were human shields or that
they were actually killed by them. Finally, if there was an apology, it
would come at a considerable delay after the incident, thereby reducing the
impact of the event. In addition to this, as *The Guardian* reported on
Friday 16 April 1999, despite a belated alliance admission that the bombing
was their fault 'what happened on Wednesday does not alter the fundamental facts of this war. If the cause was right before, it is still right
now.'[176] The newspaper had argued the case for the use of ground troops
and employed the tragedy as a further justification for their deployment.[177]
The criticism was limited to labelling the conflict a 'flawed war'.[178] *The
Guardian* saw the only alternative to this imperfect confrontation to be a
diplomatic avenue, which would allow 'Milosevic to talk peace out of one
side of his mouth, even as he orders the ongoing emptying of Kosovo out
of the other'.[179] Despite its critical stance on the suitability of an aerial conflict, incidents where modern technology has demonstrated its infallibility
did not merit a high degree of criticism. Instead, once again, the introduction

of the enemy leader figure becomes the focus of an incident perpetrated by NATO.

In addition to the bombing of a refugee convoy, two other incidents had the potential to shatter the myth of the efficiency of hi-tech weaponry. These incidents were the bombing of the RTS media building and the destruction of the Chinese Embassy in Belgrade. The RTS bombing was controversial because of its dubious nature as a legitimate target. The Chinese Embassy attack, an alleged oversight by military target planners, threatened an international propaganda disaster. Yet, as with the Amiriya shelter and the refugee convoy, the incidents were not highly criticized in the press. On the day following the RTS bombing *The Times'* front-page article was a human-interest, refugee story.[180] The newspaper only carried one article relating to the bombing with no editorial or comment piece. The newspaper's official line was, therefore, in accord with Western policy-makers.[181]

The Sun, which backed an air war, said the RTS bombing was tragic but that the innocent people who died had done so because the bombing campaign had to be stepped up, concluding 'the bigger evil is the ethnic cleansing carried out by Slobba'.[182] Meanwhile, the *Daily Mirror* claimed it 'was a vital blow against Slobodan Milosevic's evil propaganda machine'.[183] In each case the RTS story quickly fell out of the news agenda. The *Daily Mirror* was clearly reiterating the allied justification for the bombing of the RTS building. Such a controversial incident as destroying a television and radio station producing domestic news warranted scant debate in the British press, despite the obvious implication for journalists across the world. Were the bombings to have been in London or Washington the outrage and debate regarding legitimate wartime targets would no doubt have been far more intense.

The situation with the Chinese Embassy bombing on 7 May 1999 could have potentially produced major international ramifications. *The Daily Telegraph* noted that '[s]uch is the belief here in the infallibility of Nato technology and intelligence that most Serbs do not believe the attack could have been accidental'.[184] Here at least there was some recognition of the incompatibility between the alliance's emphasis on a clean, humanitarian conflict, and the realities of war. It would be unrealistic to believe there could be no mistakes during a conflict and these do, to a degree, have to be accepted. But the lack of critical analysis of any of these events highlights a bias towards the official line of argument that does not appear so easy to justify. *The Sun* had no editorial comment on the Chinese Embassy bombing at all. The *Daily Mirror*, while asking that similar errors are not repeated insisted '[m]istakes happen in war and The Mirror remains 100 per cent behind Mr Blair in his mission to repel and defeat Milosevic, even if innocent civilians have to die in the process'.[185] The ready acceptance of such events conveniently avoids the re-evaluation of the 'surgical', 'humanitarian' and 'clinical' perception of modern hi-tech warfare that the press utilize both for their own publishing requirements and via the readily reproduced official Western channels of information.

The acceptance that mistakes happen or that such issues were outweighed by the overriding moral legitimacy for intervention mirrored the official spin surrounding the Chinese Embassy bombing. While regretting the incident NATO Secretary General Javier Solana stressed in a press conference that 'NATO never has, and never will, intentionally target civilians. As you know, extraordinary care is taken to avoid damage to other than legitimate military and military-related targets. The bombing of the Chinese Embassy was a deeply regrettable mistake'.[186] The MOD briefing of the same day adopted a similar tone to the above NATO excerpt in stressing the regret of the British government. Robin Cook went on to emphasize that a military campaign, such as the one being conducted, could not 'guarantee there would be no civilian casualties'.[187] During his statement, Mr Cook repeated the moral justification that 'it was the brutality of President Milosevic that compelled us to take military action'.[188] NATO spokesman Jamie Shea then attempted to shift the focus away from events in the briefing the following day, claiming he had 'nothing to add' to the previous day's statement.[189] In essence this approach mirrored the newspapers' response to the story, which was to drop the issue swiftly. When the MOD briefing of the 9 May 1999 raised the subject, it did so to re-justify the interventionist policy. The statement by the Minister for the Armed Forces Mr Doug Henderson alluded to the impact upon public opinion:

> NATO has made mistakes, these mistakes have sometimes distracted the public presentation of our case, that is unfortunately inevitable but the world knows that action began because Mr Milosevic would not be persuaded to stop the ethnic cleansing and the killing.[190]

Without the discussion of such tragedies and the implications for lost, civilian, human lives, conflict is ultimately sanitized. The press appears to accept the official responses to tragedies and re-emphasize the enemy's actions in instigating and sustaining conflict. The reports echo the sentiments of government and the military, either through a process of drip-feeding information to the press or through a compatibility of interests. Newspapers' pages were filled with stories regarding the efficiency of Western weapons technology and the morality of their cause. Mistakes such as the bombings of the Chinese Embassy, RTS building and Amiriya shelter sat uneasily with this overriding legitimization of conflict.

Modern technological warfare allegedly targets the leader figure and his forces alone. It is an acceptance of this degree of precision bombing which led the *Daily Mirror* to conclude that '[w]ith an 80 per cent success rate, there could hardly have been a better start. It should save much bloodshed' when describing the initial phases of the Gulf air war.[191] The comment piece uses official military figures, with no analysis of what the success rate actually meant, either simply landing on target or actually putting forces and units out of action. Furthermore, this accurate bombing is said to save much bloodshed, yet the acceptance of this sanitized war by the public did not always serve military requirements.

General Norman Schwarzkopf tried to emphasize that war 'is not a Nintendo game. It is a tough battlefield, where people are risking their lives all the time'.[192] The balance between the objectives and the representative portrayal of events during conflict has slipped in favour of a sanitized version of events. Michael Ignatieff sums up the impression generated by news coverage of modern war in reference to the Kosovo Conflict when describing the crisis as a 'virtual war'.[193] The watching public in the West were asked to view the spectacle rather than participate and have their emotions stirred but only in a manner comparable with those of a sports fan.[194]

The consistent portrayal of video images by coalition spokesmen facilitated the impression of a sanitized war, which ultimately leads to a computer-style acceptance of the violence and increases the entertainment value of conflict. Even the continual use of the term 'in theatre' to describe the battlefield conjures up images of a show or leisure activity. *The Daily Telegraph* reproduced quotes from returning airmen flying missions in the Gulf that described Operation Desert Storm as 'just like it is in the movies' and claimed that the build-up to a sortie was akin to 'preparing for a big ball game'.[195] The *Daily Mirror* went further and described pilots' missions as '[j]ust like Luke Skywalker manoeuvring his fighter into the heart of Darth Vader's space complex' and emphasized the action on the video images from the fighter-bomber's cameras with comic book reference to 'POW!', 'ZAP!' and 'WHAM!'.[196] All of this prose contributed to the establishment of a virtual war conceptualization of the conflict.

During the Kosovo Conflict *The Sun* also used cartoon references when comparing the race between coalition and Russian forces into Kosovo to the fictional Wacky Racers.[197] Added to these themes, the entertainment value and inherent sanitization of war is enhanced by the depiction of 'firsts', such as the first Internet war in relation to Kosovo, or the continual references to the escalation in bombing so that one day was always the biggest so far.

Not all of the excitement and entertainment value surrounding modern technological war was welcomed. *The Guardian* carried an article with criticisms by Antoinette Fouque, founder of France's Women's Liberation movement, who claimed '[t]he Gulf war theatre has become the ultimate in pornography with missile launchers, cannon and rockets blasting off in a show of phallic eroticism'.[198] Despite the pornographic nature of war coverage, according to Fouque, the image of modern technology can lead to a sanitization of war, which then lends itself to entertainment. This is in no way discouraged by the press who stand to gain in a competitive market from a readership eager to buy their newspaper.

The discussion of modern weapons technology inherently requires a contrast with the weapons brandished by the enemy. While modern technology is presented as personally attacking the enemy leader in a clean and clear fashion, the opponent's weaponry is utilized to enhance the demonization of the leader and the enemy overall. This meshes with the war narrative that has been consistently employed during both conflicts. The enemy's weapons are described as outdated and inferior when attempting to reassure public opinion, yet devastating weapons of mass destruction in order to bolster the justification for intervention. As the most recent war in Iraq has demonstrated, the realization that such powerful weapons may not have existed can generate adverse repercussions.

The weaponry of the enemy is also demonized and by connection so too are the users of such weapons. During the Gulf War, for example, *The Daily Telegraph* likened the Iraqi Scud missile to the German V-2 rocket, continuing the trend of associating the enemy with Nazi Germany.[199] However, to avoid any concern about the potential potency of this weapon the same author, John Keegan, reassured readers that just as Hitler's V-1's, V-2's and Me 262 jet aircraft had no effect on the outcome of the war, neither would Saddam's Scuds.[200] But while these weapons may have little or no effect on the outcome of war, the negative connotations help to sustain public support against the enemy. The opponent's chemical, biological or nuclear weapons or even barbaric employment of conventional weapons contrast distinctly with the clean surgical image of the allies. Furthermore, the removal of the enemy's 'dirty' weapons becomes 'essential in order to justify the West's massive military and political commitment'.[201]

The modern technology employed during war has another, further contrast. As Philip Taylor notes in his book *War and the Media*, the Iraqis depicted the war with the West in terms of faith versus technology.[202] Their technological inferiority was of less significance to their inspiration to fight than their faith, or so Saddam Hussein sought to portray; however, the thousands of Iraqi conscripts who surrendered without a fight is evidence to the contrary. For the coalition and the public, military advantage was engrained in the coverage for the benefit of propaganda aims. During the Gulf War, the allied mentality was perhaps faith *in* technology, a belief in overwhelming firepower to win the battle. By the time of the Kosovo Conflict there were concerns that 'smart' weapons alone could not win the day and that technology alone could not ensure victory. However, the successful conclusion of the Kosovo crisis through air power appeared to have reinstated the faith in technology and the implications this would have for a future world order:

What that means is that there are now no places on Earth that cannot be subjected to the same relentless harrowing as the Serbs have suffered in the past six weeks. What that implies, it may be judged, is that no rational ruler will choose to commit the crimes that have attracted such punishment. The World Order looks better protected today than it did the day before bombing began.[203]

Conclusion

Each of the five themes discussed above can be found in the British press reportage of the discussed conflicts and have reappeared during the most recent war in Iraq. These themes are not confined to the two conflicts analysed here, or indeed the five selected newspapers studied. The five common elements demonstrate continuity in propaganda coverage that transcends time and nature of conflict. The themes evolve in a fluid system to match the type of war being conducted and the reasoning behind it.

The first and second themes, that of the enemy leader figure and the portrayal of the enemy, are the foremost elements of the five. The need to identify the enemy is essential before any campaign can be conducted and it provides the domestic and international legitimacy for intervention. However, the establishment of a viable military threat is the next valuable component. During the Gulf War, Saddam Hussein's large army was emphasized and as such so was his immediate threat to the region. With the emphasis on military might the fifth theme of technological warfare becomes more important as the allies stress their military superiority. The widespread television coverage and newspaper pictures depicting an array of weaponry also aided this.

During the Kosovo Conflict, there was some criticism of a reliance on an air war as opposed to sending in ground troops. With a sceptical belief in the ability of modern warfare to protect the Kosovar refugees the fifth theme plays a less significant role, while the perception of the enemy, in light of humanitarian concerns, is enhanced. With regard to the most recent conflict between Iraq and a US-led coalition, the establishment of an international threat through the insistence upon the existence of weapons of mass destruction was uppermost in the justifications for intervention.

With each theme interchanging, it is difficult to predict definitely the way in which propaganda will influence future press coverage. However, there does appear to be a decline in the reliance on the technological warfare theme to provide comfort and moral legitimacy. As the recent Gulf War has shown, the world has not seen the end of large land battles between opposing armies. However, the end of the Cold War diminishes the significance of vast opposing alliances facing each other. The biggest threat is now harder to define and as September 11 and subsequent crises have shown, the fear of international terrorism has replaced the large-scale threat of Soviet invasion. What makes the terrorist imagery particularly potent for the propagandist is its irrationality and unorthodox nature. September 11 proved that military might and modern weaponry was no match for unorthodox tactics; 'smart' bombs cannot win the fight against terrorism. As such Kosovo appears to be an anomaly, where air power did succeed and intervention on humanitarian grounds provided a legitimate foundation for conflict.

In essence, the role of the leader figure and image of the enemy both hold consistent roles in propaganda, but increasingly the international threat to justify intervention in any conflict will be sought through the emphasis of an international terrorist threat.

6

PRESENTING ALTERNATIVE OPINIONS

Introduction

Propaganda to justify intervention is not only evident in the forms discussed previously. An important component comes in the existence of, and reaction to, alternative opinions. It is necessary to do more than regurgitate incidents of opposition to the current policy across the various newspapers. While these incidences are important, the attitudes towards them and omission of other details speak volumes about the British press and their attitudes towards the conflict. For example, while many newspapers produced at least a limited number of articles criticizing the policy pursued, often the consistent editorial policy had a pro-war bias.

The examination and analysis of the five central propaganda themes evident in the British press has highlighted a consensus between official government and military policy and the printed media. Evidence exists to suggest the formulation of a consistent and coherent 'structure' to provide the context and narrative for going to and sustaining involvement in conflict. This 'structure' transcends the nature of the individual conflict and reinforces the dominant official policy of intervention. The existence of such a pattern in the portrayal of conflict could suggest an overt censorship regime, dictating the presentation of any crisis to the willing or unwilling press. This would be in contrast to the positive attributes often associated with a free, liberal press, which supposedly reflects the enlightened society within which it operates. If the notion of any element of freedom of speech is to be believed, then another reason for the consistent repetition of such messages is necessary to explain the convergence of ideology between the state and the media.

One explanation for this supposed consensus between the press and government policy is the media's willingness to censor itself voluntarily.[1] This allows overt censorship to be avoided in all but the most severe of cases and maintains the balance between a free media and free state, which is in the interests of both parties. This explanation, in the eyes of Mort Rosenblum, has its roots in a coherent and traditional system:

> Britain, despite its long tradition of a free press, has a custom of voluntary cooperation with the government. Under the D-notice system, if officials suspect that an editor is about to release sensitive information, they can invoke national security. A D-notice is not legally binding, but in Britain's peer-driven society, it is almost always enough.[2]

This view can be utilized to support the accusations of both sides of the argument regarding British press censorship during time of international crisis. On the one hand, the DA-Notice censorship system is not overt and overpowering, enhancing the image of a democratic and liberalized free press.[3] The acceptance of this view of the press is beneficial to both parties in legitimating the coverage and conduct of any given war. A seemingly free and unrestricted press superficially reflects an open, honest and just conduct of war. When the opposition is demonized and personalized in the form of an autocratic dictatorship, the comparison between Western democracies and totalitarian regimes is mirrored in their respective media. In an international arena where liberal democracy is championed as the superior mode of government, notably by those nations that employ it, so too self-satisfying gratification can be taken from the superiority of one's own news system.

Conversely, Rosenblum's description also lends credence to the argument that government holds too great a deal of authority over the British press. The DA-Notices stand as an obstacle to totally free reportage but the reluctance of the press to test these boundaries would suggest a deeper concern about the potential repercussions of speaking outside of the officially sanctioned news agenda. If Rosenblum's peer-driven explanation is to hold true then the last section of society that can hope to benefit or influence the media or government can be the public. With the press seeking to retain contact and healthy relations with MOD and political sources, they strive to enhance their standing within the political elite. While the public ultimately holds the government accountable the widespread electoral apathy and infrequent elections, allied to the first-past-the-post electoral system, reduces much of the immediate influence of the public on their elected representatives. Combined with an increasingly dominant executive the British system of government in the second half of the twentieth century is accused of being 'neither a parliamentary regime, nor a particularly democratic one'.[4] This leads to the question of public participation in the decision-making processes of going to war and of attitudes to not only government policy, but media interpretation of events.

Opinion polls attempt to shed some light onto the question of public attitude, however these results can be manipulated to fit within a desired context, or omitted where they do not. Mass Observation directives also give a limited, but illuminating, angle on current events that cannot be found by analysing press reports, with the exception of letters pages to some extent, or the memoirs of prominent figures in the establishment.[5] While no single source may provide an airtight synthesis of public opinion in Britain, it is a necessary consideration when examining the influences of and influences upon the British press.

The difficulty of assessing the influences surrounding the press is one that has stimulated previous academic discussion. Edward Herman and Noam Chomsky argued that newspapers propagandize in favour of the status quo and the pair produced a five-filter propaganda model to assess newspaper coverage during conflict.[6] Subsequently Richard Keeble has attempted to validate Herman and Chomsky's model in his PhD thesis by applying it to the Gulf War.[7]

Another of the other fundamental debates surrounding media exposure and conflict is the relationship between 'live' television coverage and government policy. Nik Gowing of the BBC addressed the issue of the so-called 'CNN effect' and concluded by challenging the assumption that real-time television directs foreign policy.[8] Interestingly, with regards to the influence of various media outlets, Gowing states instead that the power of television images is indirect and as a result of newspaper editorial policies.[9] Arguing from the alternative perspective Piers Robinson also used the theory of a policy–media interaction model to assess the 'CNN effect', with the use of the 1995 Bosnian and 1999 Kosovo Conflicts.[10] As previously mentioned the basic model predicted that where government policy was uncertain, news and media coverage would be extensive and critical. Conversely, where the government line was certain, news coverage would be indexed to the 'official' agenda. The conclusions claimed that generally, 'there were no indications of policy uncertainty' in the US government strategy of non-intervention concerning committing ground troops.[11] Robinson concluded that critical media coverage was unable to alter US policy. However, this rather simplifies a diverse situation where opinion was not split between two diametrically opposed schools of thought. Although both commentators have predominantly sought to demonstrate the influence or otherwise of a free or censored press, any polarized definitions are difficult to justify. Instead, only general conclusions can be drawn. An element of judgement must be employed to ascertain a predominant rather than an overwhelmingly dominant mode of thinking.

The diffuse characters opposed to intervention represent the diversity of circumstance between both conflicts. Those who objected to military action did so from radically alternative ideological positions. Alex Bellamy, in an article referring to Kosovo, highlights how the anti-war lobby made up a curious collection of individuals.[12] Bellamy notes how John Pilger and Noam Chomsky found themselves alongside American strategic realists Michael Mandlebaum and Henry Kissinger, and with right-wing British Conservatives such as Boris Johnson. During the Gulf War such variation in opposi-

tion to conflict was also evident, from traditional peace campaigners, isola-
tionists and, to take one example, Enoch Powell's opinion that intervention
was based on an ill-conceived notion of collective security.[13] With a plethora
of reasons for opposing war, it is difficult to deconstruct the arguments
for and against intervention into any bipolar model. The diversity between
the conflicts raised differing objections based on the variance in the justification and nature of the two conflicts. However, through an examination
of a number of sources, a general overview can be obtained which allows a
qualitative, if not quantitative, assessment of views opposing armed intervention.

The official policy of Western governments during both crises included an
element of military intervention. When forwarding this opinion it was
important in military and political views to win over public support. With
the range of modern technology allowing domestic news to be reached by
a global market, this battle for public opinion was not simply a case for
acquiring and sustaining domestic support, but also 'selling' the idea of war
to the world and cementing international alliances.[14] An essential requirement of the government's media policy was to promote the justness of
their cause, with the free and honest flow of information being a vital
component of this respectability. A seemingly impartial and free-speaking
media carries more credence than a state-controlled institution.

Such impartiality brings with it a degree of pressure, as any evidence of
official intervention can be strongly objectionable. In attempting to portray
a sophisticated and independent media, an unreal representation of the
media's impartiality was constructed. As Philip Hammond notes in reference
to the Kosovo Conflict:

> It would have been remarkable if Western news coverage of Kosovo
> had not been characterised by propaganda. Yet Nato frequently
> contrasted Yugoslavia's state controlled media with the freedoms
> enjoyed in the West. As Blair put it in a 10 May speech: 'We take
> freedom of speech and freedom of the press, for granted . . . The
> Serb media is state-controlled. It is part and parcel of Milosevic's
> military machine'. Such claims were themselves part of Nato news
> management, entirely hypocritical.[15]

For propaganda purposes distinctions were extracted between the types of
government practised by the aggressor and the Western powers. Effectively
this was a comparison between totalitarian dictatorships with inherent
negative connotations and the freedoms of democracy. In the same vein
differences were highlighted between the media systems operating on both
sides, however the evidence of the British press' output challenges the validity of this comparison. The true test for a free and representative Western
press comprises a number of variables. The simple number of articles voicing

concern at odds with the interventionist approach does little to shed light upon the general impressions created by the newspapers. Furthermore, the reaction to and treatment of 'alternative' views must also be considered. Public perception cannot be adequately measured through opinion polls alone and neither can the diverse nature of opinion, ranged through a mix of sources, against the intervention of the British government in either the Gulf War or the Kosovo Conflict. This chapter will attempt to highlight the range of objections presented in the British press and form a qualitative analysis of their implications.

Preventing war

At the beginning of any international incident the first public source of information regarding the crisis will often be the media. Readers or viewers can construct a reaction to an event in response to the way the incident is conveyed to them. Stephen Badsey sums up this position of power thus:

> [T]he mass of the public lack prior understanding of any crisis in which their governments might deploy military forces, and is therefore heavily dependent upon the media for perspectives and attitudes towards the military actions taken, a process usually known to the media themselves as 'framing' or contextualisation.[16]

If this perspective is adopted, the British media has an initial period where the nature of their reportage boasts an ability to shape public perception of a crisis. This, in turn, raises the question of obligation and duty, with one having to consider whether the British press is obliged to pursue peaceful, democratic means as a desirable objective over armed intervention. Initially, in the case of the Gulf War, there was indeed a reluctance to advocate a massive military response, or at least an attempt at a practical and limited approach to the invasion of Kuwait. However, the extent to which this was a genuine desire to promote a peaceful end to the crisis, or a reflection of official government and military reaction, is open to debate.

Initial reaction to the Iraqi invasion of Kuwait was cautious. *The Guardian* reserved some room for criticism of the West's role in the events. A front-page comment piece by Martin Woollacott argued that:

> The West has only itself to blame for much of this. The position of moderate Arab states was gravely undermined when the US broke off its dialogue with the Palestinian Liberation Organisation. More generally, the failure of the US and Europe to put real pressure on Israel at a time when wrongs were being righted around the world has [been] discredited both in the eyes of many Arabs.

> Saddam's chances of turning his brutal adventure into a general upheaval in the Arab world may not be high, but the West must signal a new even-handedness. It must make clear that after dealing with the occupation in Kuwait it will turn its attention to the occupation of the West Bank. Justice is not divisible.[17]

Elements of the personalization and demonization of Saddam with the phrase 'his brutal adventure' still exist, but there was a notable degree of opposition towards the previous attitudes and policies of Western governments. This does not sit squarely within the traditional conflict narratives of an isolated aggressor facing a determined and legitimate opposition. The article seeks to complicate the issue by discussing the Middle East in general, a policy which Saddam Hussein was actively pursuing to bolster Arab support and which the West sought to subjugate to a peripheral, if non-existent, component of the events. Any wider association of foreign policy elements had the potential to damage the coherence of international condemnation. The West were aware that the question of Israel provided Saddam with two desirable outcomes: to split Arab opinion and at the same time elevate himself to the figure of leader of the Arab people.

Possibly because of the initial uncertainty over the culpability of the West, *The Guardian* editorials sought to promote economic sanctions as the most likely and desirable form of reaction to Saddam's invasion of Kuwait. The newspaper insisted that it was only possible to follow one track at a time and that a blockade of Iraq and a purely defensive force in Saudi Arabia, stretching into months and maybe years, was the desirable solution.[18] Initially *The Times* was similarly reticent in predicting an aggressive policy to oust Saddam Hussein's forces from Kuwait. The newspaper dismissed the notion that a US-dominated counter-invasion force, requested by the Emir of Kuwait, was a valid option. Instead the editorial suggested the 'waiting game has its potency, enough to make it worth resolute prosecution'.[19] However, the broadsheets in question herein did not universally share this view.

The Daily Telegraph initially forwarded a more robust response. An article by Peter Almond suggested the most likely action was a blockade, but that an air strike against a prominent Iraqi target was also an option.[20] However, he rules out any land assault. The following day an editorial by Defence Editor John Keegan summarizes the military options available to the West.[21] The editor concluded that Saddam's invasion of Kuwait did indeed bear comparison with an early Hitler coup. The insinuation was that Saddam would use the invasion of Kuwait as the first step to further expansion, just as Hitler had continually tested the resolve of Europe with a number of aggressive moves. Furthermore, he suggested an embargo would force Hussein's hand into further aggression against Saudi Arabia's oil reserves. Thus, the conclusion was that an international military force, in addition to the embargoes, should supplement the Saudi Arabian air force.

The Daily Telegraph reaffirmed its stance against the invasion nearly two weeks after the event, insisting that 'world opinion remains convinced that Saddam's annexation of Kuwait is intolerable'.[22] Not only is the invasion 'intolerable' but also the newspaper supports this with a reference to a universal world opinion against the action.

Generally, the initial broadsheet response was cautious and limited and clearly reflected the government policy. It is a stance summed up by the following *Times* editorial:

> Both the American and British task forces know what they are about. At this stage they are not about a military recapture of Kuwait, nor a land invasion of Iraq in the hope of toppling Saddam. Both would be awesomely expensive, would be hard to sustain over time and would strengthen Saddam's position internally and among Arabs already nervous of appearing to support 'American imperialism'.[23]

The cautious response envisaged limited Western military intervention and dismissed any wider objections, such as a regime change in Baghdad, as untenable. The newspaper highlighted the importance of maintaining international support and denying Hussein extra advantage. The editorial went on to assert that the 'prospect of Western troops isolated in the desert for months on end is not attractive. So far, Mr Bush has been exemplary in foreseeing the risk of this; his diplomacy to avoid it has been commendably successful'.[24] Thus, the desire for a political settlement was portrayed as a commendable objective that fulfilled the requirements of international law and supplemented the underlying assumption that the West negotiates while the barbarian invades. The ultimate conclusion and desired policy for *The Times* is, as a result of this appreciation for the role of diplomacy, suitably refrained:

> There is all the more reason, therefore, for the US and Britain to keep their military objectives in the Middle East limited and clear, including the authority under which they are being pursued. The United Nations security council is the basis for the multinational offensive against Iraq. Moderate Arab support is the basis for defending Saudi Arabia. That is why British forces are being asked to risk their lives in this distant conflict. That is why their cause is just.[25]

Multinational cooperation was the foundation from which the legitimacy of intervention was constructed. By issuing clear and limited objectives the

West hoped to assuage likely Arab objections to their intervention. The defence of Saudi Arabia was a vital component in generating international support. Without a clear and present danger to the surrounding Middle Eastern countries, their likely reaction would be more cautious, yet the assertion that Saudi Arabia was under threat hastened the need for a quick and emphatic response. This approach fits within the international threat propaganda theme constructed in the previous chapter. Furthermore, the insistence of a clearly involved Arab basis for support and the backing of the UN Security Council lessened the critical perspective that the United States or other Western powers were simply exploiting the situation for their own gain. In view of such a noble and ultimately 'just' explanation of the length to which intervention should stretch, any change of policy would, assumingly, have met with a limited degree of opposition in the press or at the very least sparked a debate over shifting principles. This, however, did not seem to be the case.

The broadsheets were not blind to the developments of Western political and military thinking over the invasion of Kuwait. Some articles even appeared that suggested an escalation in the objectives and means to secure those objectives, which exceeded the official response to Iraqi aggression. *The Guardian*'s Martin Woollacott, in a comment piece, highlighted the growing divergence between the United States' declared policy and the actual assembling of a force capable of a larger role. He asserted that although the declared objective of US policy was Iraqi withdrawal from Kuwait, 'the real aim is to bring about an internal crisis in Iraq which will end with Saddam's removal from power, and perhaps his assassination'.[26]

While this reaction did not ultimately lead to a call for US-led ground troops to oust Saddam, the objectives had certainly shifted to include the encouragement of internal opposition to evict Saddam, not only from Kuwait but also from political authority in Iraq altogether. This appreciation of a shift in policy was emphasized even more clearly in *The Times*. The newspaper followed suit and spelt out what Martin Fletcher described in terms of a widening gulf between the stated and potential objectives of the West:

> As week two of the Middle East confrontation ended, it was apparent that there were two 'gulfs' involved, one with salt water and a capital 'G', and the other without. The lower-case, rapidly broadening gulf was between the administration's publicly stated plan for defeating Iraq through rigidly enforcing sanctions and its real strategy.
>
> The latter, it became increasingly clear, involves a massive military build-up in Saudi Arabia and the surrounding seas, which far exceeds the purely defensive requirements of the desert kingdom and which this week assumed a conspicuous potential for offence.[27]

This realization was at odds with the predominant broadsheet view that US and Western policy would be restricted to the objectives set out by the UN Security Council. It exceeded the mandate by which the current policy was implemented and in doing so made a mockery of the 'just war' theory upon which the coalition were basing their objection to the Iraqi invasion.[28] If the press were supporting the previous policy, the recognition of this development should have caused a degree of debate as it conflicted with the purely limited aims that had thus far been promoted. However, instead of criticism *The Daily Telegraph* editorial line followed this escalation and by 29 August 1990 it was promoting 'the removal of Saddam's aggressive capabilities . . . Any outcome which does not achieve this will amount to failure – tragic failure'.[29] In light of its earlier aggressive stance, in comparison with the other broadsheets, the newspaper then backtracks partially warning that 'it will be a sorry reflection upon the Western public and the media which influence it, if its will and patience cannot now endure a pause'.[30] The editorial policy of these three newspapers recognized the likely escalation of US involvement, which was more belligerent than current international law legitimized; however, there was little opposition to this shift. Instead, the editorial policy developed in line with political and military options. In this respect, the broadsheet's initial calls for a limited reaction could be seen to mirror Western policy and take its opinion from that presupposition, rather than two independent opinion formers arriving at mutually compatible conclusions.

The recognition of a shift in the military capabilities of the US-led forces did inspire some limited form of debate. Once again, however, the decisions could be used to benefit either side. On the day that the Fletcher article on the widening gulf appeared in *The Times*, the same newspaper published an editorial entitled 'Democracy Expects'.[31] In this article, the newspaper warns that a recall of Parliament would do little to increase public understanding of the crisis and raise the political temperature. Despite this, the editorial insisted that armed conflict was no ordinary government measure and Parliament should be recalled to discuss the matter. Tony Benn, on the other hand, writing in *The Guardian* on 6 September 1990, warned that 'Parliament should not give Thatcher a free hand'.[32] In his view and from the standpoint of someone opposed to armed intervention, any recall of Parliament was seen as a way of the Conservative-dominated legislature legitimizing the escalation to war through the approval of Parliament. Benn believed public opinion was moving against the war and that sanctions, if given sufficient time, were bound to work. The two newspapers were thus divided. The issue of a recall of Parliament was portrayed as either a limited objection to potential policy change, or, not dissimilar, a move to provide a legitimate mandate for war. Not surprisingly, the traditionally conservative *Times* emphasized the democratic role of Parliament in the decision-making process, while the left-wing Benn saw the likely vote of approval as another step towards eliminating opposition to greater armed intervention. Whether they were a limited objection or a mandate for war, the views echoed the voices of the ruling elite without severely challenging government policy in the process.

The political stance of *The Times* was further highlighted at the beginning of September 1990 as the newspaper began to crystallize its views on the need for more stringent opposition to Saddam Hussein. Paddy Ashdown, leader of the Liberal Democrats, had written to Mrs Thatcher insisting that Britain should limit herself to sanctions alone. In a view which supports the *Times'* request to recall Parliament the newspaper believed the Prime Minister ought to keep her options open claiming the 'tactical equation of any conflict over Kuwait could well require military action against Iraq . . . The prime minister understands this and deserves ungrudging support on Thursday from all sides of the house'.[33] The initial call for flexibility or, as distracters may argue, complicity, was reinforced towards the end of September. *The Times*, under the title 'The Mood Hardens', hailed UN Resolution 670, which banned sanction-busting flights to and from Iraq or Kuwait, as the final non-aggressive action against Saddam Hussein. 'If this fails', the editorial asserted, 'the next step must be military'.[34] From this point the gulf between the stated aims of the Western powers and the physical reality of the military build-up was tackled not by a questioning of policy, but through the process of mimicking the hardening resolve. Where *The Times* had sought to expose the widening gulf it did not go on to challenge the implications and legitimacy of this shift, instead the goalposts moved to accommodate the change. By 1 December 1990 the editorial policy was openly promoting the destruction of Saddam Hussein as a 'vital interest' and warned American credibility was at stake if the policy was not pursued.[35] Once more, this objective exceeded the UN security resolution 687 that authorized the setting of the 15 January deadline for Iraqi forces to withdraw from Kuwait. The momentum towards a greater war had already begun before the commencement of the air campaign and more optimistic pieces even started to hypothesize about the structure of the Middle East after the defeat of Saddam Hussein's Iraq.[36] Meanwhile, in an article that demonstrated that tabloids are often not alone in sensationalist calls for drastic decisions, Michael Evans of *The Times* believed Washington and London would live to regret the decision to remove the nuclear deterrent from the war-rhetoric.[37] In conjunction with the build-up of military forces and options, *The Times* increasingly espoused a more belligerent line of argument. In this sense, the newspaper followed Robinson's model of a certain policy line leading to a lack of criticism. However, in contrast to Robinson's theory, criticism was not evident when the official policy was unclear or changing.

The above selective view of the evolution of broadsheet attitude towards the growing Gulf crisis demonstrates little in the way of consistent opposition to the evolution of government policy. Even when the policy was recognized as shifting and exceeded the international mandate available at the given time, the press felt no obligation to criticize the change of stance.

The Kosovo Conflict witnessed a significant difference in *The Times'* editorial approach towards government policy:

> Tony Blair needs urgently to explain why it is right for Britain, a middling power, to be so heavily engaged in the cause of peace. This question will be asked even if he persuades the country that Kosovo cannot safely be left to burn. He must convince anxious citizens that British troops will be there to serve the cause of European peace, not to fly the flag in support of his ambitions to demonstrate Britain's 'leadership in Europe'. He must guard against future accusations that the British people, whose support for this country's high military profile is a national strength, were in this case not given the full reasons for putting troops in harm's way. The people of this country understand well that a trading nation with global interests must be prepared to deploy its forces where international stability is threatened. But informed public assent is the indispensable basis of public support.[38]

In the above editorial the newspaper argued for the public's right to know why troops should be sent to war. In this instance, *The Times* to some extent is labouring behind government policy, and notably a Labour Government policy, of action in the name of international stability or humanitarian obligation. Blair's stance is seen as having a dual purpose, which included portraying himself as a leader of Europe. The newspaper appealed to the necessity of public knowledge in order to facilitate an informed opinion. The demand resembles the debate on the recall of parliament during the Gulf War, but the circumstances over intervention in Kosovo differed.

The Times editorial neglects to suggest any alternative conduit of information aside from parliamentary discussion. The media themselves are rendered an ancillary consideration in the formation of attitudes regarding government policy. Where uncertainty over the cause and likely effects of an international crisis is found, the British press has looked to the government to explain their policies and inform public opinion. This raises questions about the role of the media during such crises. The media is surely obliged to explain matters as best they can. Hiding behind issues of government censorship and national security are unacceptable when British foreign policy is not yet crystallized into a firm military commitment. However, as the analysis of broadsheet coverage during the build-up of the Gulf War above shows, the press is often seen to take their lead from official sources rather than adopt and adhere to genuinely independent principles. As the events escalated and the US-led coalition began to take on an offensive capability, this definitive and positive policy line attracted little media criticism. In the case of the Kosovo Conflict, such considerations existed, but the issue was blurred by additional considerations unique to that particular type of conflict.

Kosovo did not 'enjoy' the invasion by a clearly definable hostile nation, impeding upon its sovereign territory. Furthermore, as critics would often stress, Kosovo lacked the wealth of natural resources and potential threat to the international economy that Iraq's capture of Kuwaiti oil posed. The 'enemy' was far harder to define and traditional prejudices regarding the barbarity of eastern European peoples perpetually willing to fight among themselves flourished, be it in the guise of the ever war-ready Serbs or the suspicious, terrorist activities of the KLA allegedly funded by drug-smuggling activities. The aims of the Western powers were therefore harder to explain and justify, because of this, the policy of the British and United States' governments was often perceived to be muddled and confused. If Robinson's model were to be validated, such ambiguity would increase the influence of the media and result in more critical coverage of the crisis. In this respect, the Kosovo Conflict provided a different set of obstacles in the battle for positive public opinion. *The Times*, during the Gulf conflict, criticized the government for not informing the public of the issues during the build-up to the crisis. However, when policy shifted from the declared aims the press was slow to highlight the rising disparity between rhetoric and reality. Where policy was not yet fully crystallized the Robinson model predicts critical media coverage. However, the press merely seems to mirror the official policy until a formal policy can be identified. In the build-up to conflict, the press should be awash with alternative views to crisis management and a plethora of opinion while military action has yet to be proclaimed the only option. However, this does not appear to be the case and the press appear as willing as official government channels to push ahead swiftly for an aggressive resolution.

Peace initiatives

One way to measure the theory that newspapers mirrored the government line, even when this was uncertain, is to examine British press coverage of peace initiatives during both conflicts. By doing this, it is possible to establish whether the official policy line was followed almost exclusively, or whether views opposed to this traditional opinion were given equal credence and therefore created a balanced overview of the crisis, its belligerents and the variety of options open to policymakers. This is not the forum for a comprehensive debate of every peace policy initiative instigated during

both crises, but the examination, however superficially, of such issues consti-
tuting a vital element of views other than the recognized political or military
mainstream.

Despite the fragmented understanding of Balkan issues amongst the
British public and media, much of which was recorded in the pages of newspapers, letters pages and through Mass Observation responses, the Rambouillet Conference offered a surprisingly central focus for peace talks over
the crisis concerning the Former Republic of Yugoslavia (hereafter FRY)
and Kosovo. The talks have subsequently been the subject of considerable
political and academic debate and heralded as either another opportunity
to impose imperial will upon a weaker European neighbour, or the last
significant chance for Slobodan Milosevic to drop his 'barbaric' policies
and fall in line with international, Western, civilized norms of diplomacy
and human rights.

For the supporters of Rambouillet the talks constituted an achievable
opportunity to secure peace. In the view of Alex Bellamy 'Rambouillet
offered the best possible chance for long-term peace in the region' and he
is critical of what he views as an anti-war lobby which utilized only selective
reading of the Rambouillet agreement to support their cause.[39] As a former
lecturer in Defence Studies for King's College London, Bellamy has argued
against what he perceived to be the academic and public acceptance of the
anti-war agenda. He goes on to argue 'that the FRY showed no intention
of engaging in serious negotiation'.[40] William Walker, the American head
of the Organization for Security and Cooperation in Europe (hereafter
OSCE), supported this view.[41] Bellamy described Slobodan Milosevic as a
control freak and insisted Rambouillet proved that Milosevic never intended
to find a settlement. From the opposite perspective, Noam Chomsky has
argued that the Rambouillet terms were presented in a manner of 'accept
them or face the military consequences' and as such had no validity under
international law.[42] Meanwhile, Philip Hammond believes Rambouillet was
designed to fail and simply provided a pretext for the NATO bombing.[43]

The question then raised is whether the media, or indeed politicians and
the military, espoused any alternatives, other than war. If diplomatic man-
oeuvres such as the Rambouillet conference were simply attempts to lay
diplomatic efforts finally to rest and achieve legitimacy through the process
of peace initiatives, rather than the achievement of an actual policy, then
the media had neglected its role in presenting the facts to the public. Furthermore, the media perpetuated the view of the status quo and in doing so failed
to provide credible alternatives to the official policy.

Much of the above criticism appears justified in the case of the Gulf War.
The press often seemed to follow the official line. In doing so the pro-
interventionist argument dominated the debate or, as critics would suggest,
the lack of any debate. The editorial policies of the press presented the

strongest hint at the direction the printed media were willing to take over the Gulf crisis. The dominant editorial opinion supported the government policy, if sometimes under the guise of supporting the troops once they had already become embroiled in the conflict. However, the lack of sustained opposition in the early stages of the crisis, before intervention, points to a more general desire to 'wait-and-see' rather than develop, if not strong opinions, then at least viable alternatives.

While occasional articles appeared criticizing policy, or questioning the legitimacy of intervention, the overriding perspective was pro-war. It is this failure to provide information that John Pilger objected to most. Pilger insisted that if war commenced 'the British media – which unlike Iraq's, is said to be "free" – will bear much of the responsibility for a "patriotic" and culpable silence that has ensured that people don't know and can't know'.[44] In the same article, he notes how President Bush's speeches were quoted uncritically almost everywhere and attacked John Simpson and Robert Fisk for their pro-war/only war stance. *The Guardian*, in which his opinions were printed, did not support this view editorially and his voice was one of only a few willing to adopt such a stance and find a platform upon which to air it.

In both conflicts, the intervention of British troops secured the way for a more coherent backing of government policy. The attitude of the *Daily Mirror* summed up the closure of alternative opinion as a topic worthy of debate over Kosovo: '[o]f course we do not like this bombardment. Neither does Tony Blair or President Clinton or any of the world leaders involved . . . But we like the alternative even less. It is no alternative at all, in fact'.[45] Through asserting the unacceptable nature of alternative opinions, the case against intervention is dismissed conclusively. This approach also diminished the likelihood of inter-newspaper arguments as the editorials adopt similar positions. As has been discussed in Chapter 5, during assessment of the enemy leader figure theme, the Gulf War and Kosovo Conflict have produced only sporadic examples of overt rivalry. This is in contrast to the rivalry of *The Sun* and *Mirror* during the Falklands. It is also at odds with the 2003 war in Iraq whereby the *Mirror* initially attempted to establish a clear, anti-interventionist agenda, yet its criticism of Tony Blair was dropped after the war and the British forces were supported during the hostilities.

While the West insisted on portraying itself as the pursuer of peace in both conflicts, the reality often appeared to be at odds with this claim. Bush insisted the US were committed to 'go the extra mile for peace' yet critics would argue the avenues open to provide alternatives other than war were severely limited. There was an underlying or consistent thread running through the US and British attitudes to peace initiatives, not only during the Gulf crisis but also prevalent over Kosovo. During both conflicts, there existed an intransigent nature towards peace initiatives other than those sponsored by these two powers or the US specifically. A succession of peace initiatives failed to propel the US or Britain into serious consideration despite protestations that all diplomatic efforts were being stringently explored.

At Rambouillet, the conditions stipulated by the West were non-negotiable. Equally, Gulf peace initiatives fell short of Western demands. Washington and Riyadh rejected King Hassan of Morocco's September 1990 five-point peace plan. Then on 8 October 1990, the Temple Mount killings in Jerusalem threatened to establish linkage between the Palestinian problem and the Iraq crisis.[46] Dilip Hiro, who has outlined many of the peace initiatives put forward during the Gulf crisis,[47] believes this incident meant the US became less responsive to any new attempts for a negotiated settlement while escalating the objective to overthrow Saddam Hussein.[48] This view was backed by Bush's 15 February 1991 call for Saddam Hussein to be overthrown. None of the initiatives, it was argued, met the uncompromising standards held by the US and Britain. The initiatives were criticized for falling short of the requirements stipulated by the UN or NATO. However, in contrast the US was willing to promote alternatives that exceeded these benchmarks.

A variety of peace initiatives was necessary to promote the perception of striving for diplomatic resolutions to both crises. In reality, peace initiatives were limited to those officially endorsed by the US. In this respect the range of alternatives was limited and discredits the US view of 'going the extra mile for peace'. *The Guardian* had some concern about Bush's motives in pursuing the diplomatic solution. When Bush offered to meet Iraqi Foreign Minister Tariq Aziz in Washington and send James Baker to Baghdad, the journalist Simon Tisdall believed President Bush's remarks were designed 'to convince an increasingly critical public and Congress that he was doing everything possible to avoid a conflagration'.[49] In light of *The Guardian*'s preference for sanctions to be allowed more time to work against Saddam, a degree of scepticism is understandable. In contrast, other newspapers were all too willing to follow along with the perception of the Western peacemaker versus the belligerent dictator. Shortly before the 15 January deadline set for Saddam to pull out of Kuwait, *The Daily Telegraph* editorial opinion was confident that the US was indeed making every effort to avoid military intervention:

> Between now and next Tuesday, the world will continue to cherish a slender hope that Saddam will act, even at the eleventh hour, to save his own people from the catastrophe that otherwise threatens them . . . Mr James Baker's visit to Geneva ensures that no reasonable person can doubt the lengths to which America has gone to achieve a solution by peaceful means. Responsibility for war, if it comes, is now seen to rest squarely with Saddam.[50]

The paragraph above also reinforced the personalization of the conflict with the figure of Saddam, while reducing the role of the West in the culpability of war. These actions fall within the propaganda processes of personalization discussed in Chapter 5. In addition, this view of good versus evil or black and white appreciation of events is further emphasized within the text above. The assertion that 'no reasonable person can doubt the lengths' gone to to find a peaceful solution allied the doubters with the irrational policy of Saddam Hussein. The vacuum between the two opposite alternatives is filled by insisting on the irrationality of seeing the US-sponsored peace efforts as anything other than comprehensive. This belief in the overriding comprehensiveness and legitimacy of US-backed peace initiatives meant that alternative views could be isolated and ignored.

Aside from direct criticism of an interventionist policy, alternative peace proposals were often derided and portrayed in a negative way. Just as the West insisted on a solid 'us against them' coalition with a unified front, so too were alternative peace proposals, not officially sanctioned by the US, often criticized as a betrayal of that unanimity. One example of this is *The Times*' treatment of the European Community (hereafter EC), who planned to send a delegation to Iraq before the UN deadline. The editorial insisted the trip would have been worthwhile if it had been backed by Bush, but as it had not the EC efforts would be interpreted by Saddam Hussein as the first cracks in international condemnation of his actions.[51] In tandem with this policy, Colin Rallings, Michael Thrasher and Nick Moon argued that the setting of the 15 January 1991 deadline was vital in preparing public opinion for the fact that this date represented the last hope for a peaceful outcome.[52] Through these processes the public were groomed to accept the fact that US demands for a negotiated settlement were the only legitimate peaceful alternatives to hostilities and these had to be adhered to within the timescale of a US-backed deadline. These suppositions, duplicated in the press and applicable to both the Gulf War and Kosovo Conflict, limited the acceptable range of policy alternatives and reinforced the dominant government agenda.

This reading of the attitudes towards peace initiatives still demands that the fundamental question, of whether the media are obliged to provide alternative opinion, be answered. As Matthew d'Ancona has commented, the debate surrounding media censorship is not simply a question regarding disclosure of potentially valuable information to an enemy:

> The debate has become more nuanced when other grounds for censorship or self-censorship were subjected to editorial scrutiny. Was the 'national interest' best served by an obsequious press which toed the line, or one which sought to inform the public at the possible cost of embarrassing the executive or impairing 'morale'? How far was it the responsibility of the media to shore up the resolve

of the general public and to protect its sensibilities from the consequences of the decision to go to war?[53]

The debate is divided and this division exists within the media as well as
amongst academics. It does appear that despite denials from the military,
politicians and the media, the road to war on terms dictated by the West
and most significantly the US is the dominant doctrine presented to the
public. The traditional complaints regarding national security do not provide a substantial enough explanation of this support during both conflicts.
While it is true that an overemphasis of views opposed to conflict could distort the influence of the anti-war lobby, the press falls far short of reflecting
even the most limited opposition to official policy.

Unintentional support

In addition to omitting vocal opposition to military intervention, the newspapers reinforced the dominance of the pro-war agenda through unintentional or subliminal sources of reference. Much of the battle for public
opinion draws parallels with historical understanding of rudimentary propaganda techniques. Robinson's model of clearly defined aims leading to a less
critical media is echoed by Richard Connaughton who stressed the need to
set out exactly what aims are desirable:

> Precise, unambiguous aims, and therefore the concept of what con-
> stitutes success, contribute towards the validation of the principle
> that a state should pencil in an outline withdrawal plan or plans
> concurrently with the formulation of the plans for the force inser-
> tion. That is a statement difficult to contradict for it has long been
> an historical maxim that it is folly to start a war without having
> some idea of how it will end.[54]

Connaughton highlighted the relationship between clear policy aims and
a structure for the understanding of what constituted success. Furthermore,
he insists that foresight is needed to develop alternative plans in order to
ensure that a desirable conclusion can be reached under a variety of circumstances. More specifically, he argued that the consensus of public opinion
'has to be linked to a precise aim'.[55] The difference between a clearly stated
aim and the repetitive use of significant phrases or policies is a small step
between the ideals of enhancing public understanding of government policy
and embedding a propaganda message. Similarly, General Sir Peter de la
Billiere had developed his appreciation of the influence of the media since
the Falklands crisis:

I had found, first, that if I could win reporters on to my side they would do a lot for the forces, and second, that if I put over a consistent message, that message would start to filter into the hearts and minds of people in the United Kingdom. Further, that message would permeate through to every level of British society, because if one influenced the people of Britain, one began to influence politicians as well – and support across the whole political spectrum was essential for the kind of major overseas operation which we were mounting.[56]

The theory of a consistent message filtering through to the public would not appear out of place on the pages of a book discussing propaganda techniques. de la Billiere clearly saw the media as a conduit for information, which could be utilized to influence both the government and the governed. He envisaged 'the media as a weapon, to put over a positive message, so that what we were doing would attract the support of both politicians and members of the public throughout the free world'.[57] The media, in his opinion, were not therefore simply a peer-driven institution self-censoring to appease their political masters. Instead, they were a tool with the ability to influence public opinion and in doing so affect political decisions. In this respect, he was hinting at the need to establish a military agenda separate from political aims and to win public domestic and international support for this. His methods utilized public opinion and hoped to bypass traditional forms of parliamentary democracy to influence the political agenda. The media thus enjoyed a significant role in the interaction between the state and society. Some of the more obvious occasions in which the press supported the government line have been discussed. However, as de la Billiere's comments allude to, the constant repetition of a theme is a desirable objective. This can also be achieved through more subtle processes.

The press attempt to add credibility to their stories through less blatant assertions than simply agreeing with the status quo. 'Experts' are used routinely to substantiate the argument being developed and augment the reporter's own views. Such 'experts' can take a variety of forms, such as doctors, academics or ex-military figures. Many newspapers employed retired generals to predict and evaluate military strategy, subconsciously performing a number of psychological roles. In the first instance the employment of 'informed' sources and the variety of opinion sought reinforces the traditional appearance of a democratic and free press able to express wide-ranging views. In addition the use of an 'expert' asserts authority and adds credibility to a view, which often complements the official propaganda. This also strengthens the reliance of the public on such information. The use of an 'expert' demonstrates the need for greater understanding of a subject than a simple layman can hope to grasp, this has the negative effect of reinforcing the feeling that some people have of hopeless disinterest and depression about events which they cannot fathom and have no opportunity to influence.[58] From a political and military view, such a response has the positive repercussion of quelling some opposition. Finally, retired generals are also reluctant to criticize the military.

The use of expert opinion was not universally welcomed in the political and military arena. As well as fears regarding national security some critics were annoyed, probably because of an understanding of the influence of the media, that the main issues of war were being overlooked and the press were simply distracting from the military job in hand. A Major in the 32 Heavy Regiment Royal Artillery was one such critic who was relieved to see a reduction of such 'informed' speculation of the war:

> However, at least there has been a marked reduction in the amount of bollocks from experts and indeed the incidence of spotty weaklings bumping their gums in TV studios has been dramatically reduced. This is probably as well, even the normally demure Mrs S has taken to shouting 'Bollocks' as a reflex action as soon as 'an expert' rears his spotty head. We are of course now inundated with pollution experts on 'oil slicks'. Bad form Saddam, will Green Party declare war on Iraq?[59]

Clearly not enamoured by the use of such experts this single opinion would seem to reflect a wider apprehension towards not only the media, but also any commentators outside of the official military structure. However, the reinforcement of particular messages through the utilization of individuals and organizations to bring credibility was widely employed in the British press in both the Gulf War and Kosovo Conflict. One such group was humanitarian organizations; the utilization of these by government characterizes the limited and selective role afforded to opposition groups.

Humanitarian reports issued before and during international crises can often be a source of criticism of government policy, yet in the incidences of the Gulf War and Kosovo Conflict organizations such as Amnesty and Human Rights Watch were quoted in support of the official propaganda campaign. Such selective use of these reports reinforced the government credibility by seemingly demonstrating independent opinion in favour of their actions. For example, *The Daily Telegraph* referred to an Amnesty International report when discussing Iraqi atrocities in occupied Kuwait.[60] The same author, Charles Laurence, utilized this method again in late February and revealed that the 'Foreign Office endorsed Amnesty's damning indictment of Iraq before it was forced to abandon its Kuwait City embassy, and accepts the estimate of 7,000 Kuwaitis killed and 17,000 missing'.[61] The latter article mentioned that Amnesty International had not added to the material it presented in December 1990, as they were unable to corroborate the witnesses' evidence. Despite this, however, as late as the 22 February 1991 this source was being reproduced.[62] Reference to these organizations supported the official propaganda, in this case concerning the perception of the enemy. However, the exclusion of other details presented by such reports reveals a telling insight into the omission of opinion opposed to conflict.

The most infamous incident of Gulf War propaganda was not unique to this conflict alone and demonstrated a well-used formula of generating a negative propaganda perception of the enemy. Atrocity stories occur regularly during conflict and facilitate the demonization of the enemy as well as often emphasizing the personalization effect and potentially enhancing the opponent's military threat. During the First World War, for example, false atrocity stories were generated that included the bayoneting of children and the rape of women.[63] Such atrocity stories have been perpetuated in subsequent conflicts and the Gulf War was no exception.

One of the most often cited incidences during the Gulf War was that of Iraqi soldiers stealing incubators from hospitals and leaving babies to die. The initial reaction to these claims from *The Times* utilized an 'expert' to play down the story. An article by Christopher Walker quoted a former Icelandic hostage, Doctor Gisli Sigurdsson. The evidence of the doctor corroborated the assertion that shooting was the most common punishment for any crime, but it did not support the incubator story. Instead, the rumour was dismissed as propaganda.[64] However, eight days later the newspaper ran the following article: 'MORE than 300 premature babies in Kuwait were left to die when their incubators were looted by the Iraqi military forces, Amnesty International says in its first comprehensive report on human rights violations since the Iraqi invasion'.[65] The article suggested Amnesty International had confirmed the story through interviews with doctors and nurses, apparently not the same doctor quoted previously. Without assessing the validity of the sources and despite the fact that the newspaper had already printed a report rubbishing these claims from a respected source, there is no scepticism about the validity of these allegations. The lack of any alternative opinion is dismissed through the wholehearted reliance on the reputation of Amnesty International.

The Times was not alone in this respect. The *Daily Mirror* ran a story under the heading 'Iraqis Gouged out Victim's Eyes'.[66] The article cited Amnesty's figure of 300 premature baby deaths after the removal of incubators.[67] Despite the title, the article devoted less than half the story to human rights abuses and more to the Bush/Baker Iraqi peace initiative. This dual approach once again re-emphasized the contrast between Bush the peacemaker and Hussein the aggressor.

The Guardian's Simon Tisdall, who had cast some aspersions over the motives behind Bush's efforts to 'go the extra mile for peace', was more willing to accept the Physicians for Human Rights report that noted three incidences where premature babies were removed from incubators.[68] This estimation falls well below the Amnesty International figures quoted two months earlier. The story was reiterated to reinforce the moral justification for military intervention. After the Amiriyah bunker bombing by the US, American Lieutenant General Thomas Kelly was quick to point out that Saddam Hussein had fired scuds at civilians, gassed Kurds and 'pulled the plugs out of incubators in Kuwait'.[69]

The issue of moral legitimacy for intervention attained even greater importance during the Kosovo Conflict where human rights abuses were depicted as the major justification for military action. The human-interest aspect of the crisis held a greater resonance than suggestions of a threat to international security. The official policy espoused placed greater emphasis on the moral imperative to intervene. In a speech given in Chicago, Tony Blair denied Kosovo was an internal matter, claiming that intervention was necessary.[70] Dan Keohane views this emphasis on moral legitimacy as part of a wider Labour government policy to be more assertive about human rights, which made intervention unavoidable in light of this declared stance.[71] There was certainly enough evidence available to support the claim of intervention on the grounds of humanitarian support. The organization, Human Rights Watch, produced a report in 1998 to explain some of the violations in Kosovo and it placed much of the blame upon Slobodan Milosevic's shoulders.[72] In another Human Rights Watch report, based on research carried out between September and December 1998, the predominant blame for the atrocities is levelled at Milosevic and his summer-long offensive.[73] The report criticized Milosevic's propaganda and disinformation campaign that 'has served to whip up xenophobic nationalism and fears of an international anti-Serb conspiracy, a central pillar of President Milosevic's rule'.[74] Furthermore, a press release issued on 29 January 1999 concluded that the attacking and killing of civilians in Racak was deliberate.[75] Such reports offer valuable points of reference for those trying to justify intervention in the name of humanitarian necessity. By making reference to these independent and apparently impartial reports, Western governments can bolster support for their policies by appealing to the public's emotional responses.

These important sound bites are often extracted out of context and the overall impression of humanitarian organizations supporting intervention can be misleading. In essence, the omission of vital sections of the reports amounts to a form of censorship of views opposed to conflict. As the press have access to these reports, they do not have to refer to the statements selected by politicians and military leaders and are, therefore, carrying out a form of censorship. While the press reproduced some aspects of the results of research by humanitarian organizations, other findings were less palatable. A Human Rights Watch report produced after the Kosovo Conflict concluded that while they found no evidence of war crimes there was

evidence that NATO violated international humanitarian law.[76] Of particular note was the organization's finding that the bombing of the Serb Radio
and Television building and seven bridges did not constitute attacks upon
legitimate military targets.[77] The report goes on to criticize the disparity
between confirmed deaths and their own findings, which were three to four
times higher. Reports appearing before or during the crisis often contained
references criticizing the enfeebled position of Western democracies and
their prior reluctance to act on allegations raised by humanitarian organizations, as well as criticizing Milosevic. Yet, this dual apportioning of blame
was not transmitted into the public arena with the evidence selected to
support the West's stance.

After the Kosovo Conflict the criticism continued. Another Human
Rights Watch report published in March 2000 was unable to corroborate
stories circulated during the crisis concerning rape camps. During an MOD
press briefing by Robin Cook, it was claimed that young women were being
taken from refugee columns and 'forced to endure systematic rape in an
army camp'.[78] Mr Cook declared that this completed 'the pattern of brutality of Milosevic's forces'.[79] The humanitarian organization's report alleged
that NATO had publicized the existence of the camps to justify their policies:

> As a party to the conflict, NATO used premature and unsubstan-
> tiated claims of humanitarian law violations to justify the continua-
> tion of the bombing campaign and may thereby have undermined
> more careful reporting on abuses. NATO's use of insufficiently sub-
> stantial allegations provided Serbian officials with an opportunity to
> denounce all rape reports as mere propaganda.[80]

In using selective and unsubstantiated findings, Human Rights Watch
believed NATO actually aided Serbian propaganda by undermining their
own credibility. As Western governments referred to the existence of such
camps, comments that were reproduced in the press, the apparent backing
of humanitarian organizations added credibility to these statements.

Amnesty International also criticized the NATO campaign and a number
of bombings 'which may have breached international law'.[81] Amnesty produced a report in 1998 detailing the abuses in Kosovo and asserted that
only the high level of media scrutiny had prevented a further escalation of
the atrocities.[82] Governments did not utilize such evidence until it coincided
with the objective of military intervention. This was true also for the Gulf
War, in the same Amnesty report that was cited in reference to the incubator
story the organization made it clear that it took 'no position on the conflict
in the Gulf, and does not condone killings and acts of violence perpetrated
by the parties to the conflict'.[83] It goes on to criticize the international community for failing to act on information made available to the world regarding human rights violations. This failure to act was repeated by Andrew

Whitely of Middle East Watch, a division of Human Rights Watch. In his testimony before the House Foreign Affairs Committee, a week before the UN deadline for Saddam to withdraw, he noted that:

> Information provided by human rights groups today about Iraqi human rights violations in Kuwait are receiving a great deal of attention from the Bush Administration, and indeed the President himself. We regret that similar attention was not paid to Iraq's well-known record of gross abuses of human rights when the United States was in a position to influence the situation.[84]

However, such criticism was not widely reported whereas the more spectacular and gruesome contents of the report provided essential propaganda material. This selected use of humanitarian organizations slanted the coverage in favour of a pro-war bias and constituted censorship of opposition views. Despite Middle East Watch concluding that the allies conduct of a *safe* war had fallen short of a *legal* war and that 'these shortcomings appear to have involved deliberate decisions by allied commanders to take less than the maximum feasible precautions necessary to avoid civilian harm' the overriding impression generated by the media focused attention on the atrocities of the enemy.[85] This is intended in no way to belittle the atrocities carried out in both Kuwait and Kosovo, which, as Philip Taylor has noted, it appears in the case of Kuwait had not been exaggerated.[86] However, the manipulation of the stories and omission of other aspects of such reports, including criticisms of the interventionist policy, failed to provide a balanced view of events and the position of humanitarian organizations concerning military intervention.

Opposition during the conflicts

As well as a misinterpretation of opposing views, both conflicts generated vocal opposition to armed intervention. The treatment of opponents of war, more than the amount of coverage afforded to them, is a revealing indicator of media attitudes to the conflicts. As has been noted, the reasoning behind the opposition varied but the resulting criticism received was equally apparent.

During the Gulf War Saddam Hussein's use of Western hostages as a bargaining chip with those governments allied against him aroused a great deal of human interest in the media. However, while the majority of the press and politicians refused to be held to ransom, in a typically British reaction to alleged acts of terrorism, some prominent figures were willing to seek a more pro-active role. Edward Heath was one such person who sought talks with Saddam to secure the release of British citizens. *The Guardian* backed the move at a time when it supported the use of sanctions.[87] It is, therefore, perhaps unsurprising that this broadsheet advocated a reasoned response to the hostage situation yet *The Guardian* was an isolated voice on the issue.

The reaction of *The Sun* was more typical. The tabloid viewed any outspoken opposition or discussion of compromise as tantamount to treason. This attitude accounted for *The Sun*'s editorial of 17 September 1990 entitled 'Traitor Ted!', which reported that Edward Heath believed Saddam should have access to Kuwaiti islands and a share of the disputed oilfields.[88] As such, this approach was in keeping with the unanimity policy associated with the peace initiatives. Meanwhile, in adopting a consistent approach to opponents of war, Tony Benn was vilified as *The Sun* claimed Benn needed 'a hospital full of shrinks' because of his condemnation of war.[89] On this occasion the demonization technique, which was successfully employed against Saddam Hussein, is directed towards those deemed to support his actions. Hussein was often depicted as a madman and anyone supporting his objectives was tarnished with the same brush. Here Benn's support for a compromise earned him negative coverage. This association was mirroring the techniques employed by politicians to rally support for the Gulf effort.

As well as condemning alternative views explicitly, newspapers devoted space over to the interventionist argument that also sought to denigrate opinions opposed to intervention. *The Daily Telegraph* ran an article that quoted John Major's speech to the House of Commons as the government was supported in a vote by 534 to 57. In this speech, Major stressed that:

> What we are seeing in Kuwait is an attempt to eliminate the state by a dictator who has shown himself to be a through force for evil . . . Those who caution delay because they hate war – as we all do – must ask themselves this question: how much longer should the world stand by and risk these atrocities continuing.[90]

While attempting to divert criticism of war-mongering the insinuation is that those appealing for peace are condoning the atrocities committed by Hussein's forces. In this respect the treatment of views opposed to conflict are closely intertwined with the dominant pro-intervention propaganda. This approach was identified by at least one columnist writing for the *Daily Mirror*:

> **BRITAIN is no longer divided into those who think war is the only tactical solution, and those who think sanctions could have done the job.**
> Instead, the split has been manoeuvred by the warmongers into a phoney one between the brave and the cowardly.[91]

Such comments were rare and the overriding emphasis stressed the negative connotations of anti-war sentiment.

During the Kosovo Conflict, there is evidence of a moral vocal section willing to espouse policy options that could critically be termed in the language of appeasement. Writing for *The Times* Simon Jenkins regularly contributed opinion against favouring military involvement based primarily upon Kosovo's geography and the potential for wider European ramifications if NATO failed to act, which contradicted the overall editorial policy. Jenkins insisted the only option available was to not bomb, especially as nothing in the UN Charter, according to him, gave the US and Great Britain the right to intervene. He warned that each 'bombastic intervention makes things worse. But to make them worse only to make us feel better is the height of immorality'.[92] In Jenkins' view, any intervention on humanitarian grounds would simply be the result of a misplaced moral conscience. The main reason for this appears to be the absence of a clear right or wrong side. This echoes the views of critics who have highlighted the West's failure to intervene in other similar disputes:

> A minority of Kosovan militants have been encouraged to believe that Nato troops will help them to win their freedom from the Serbs. They have committed atrocities, and provoked counter-atrocities from the Serbs. They have provoked a powerful and ruthless Government to repress areas of the country which it had previously ruled undemocratically but not murderously.[93]

With this line of reasoning the Kosovans lose their status as the victims, which makes supporting them undesirable. Furthermore, blame is apportioned to them for the atrocities, stripping a vital component of the pro-war initiative away from supporters. Jenkins' opinion is thus:

> The fact is we should have left Kosovo's separatists to fight their own battles, as we normally leave separatists round the world. We should have afforded such help as charity can supply. But charity no longer wins headlines. Only bombs do that. When the blood flows, we yearn to meddle. When the meddling is mixed with macho-ism, it gets out of hand. It has now brought Nato possibly and Kosovo certainly to a catastrophe. Of course the fault lies with monstrous Milosevic, but not all the fault.[94]

Jenkins therefore found himself part of the diverse anti-war lobby, but his views were isolationist rather than pacifist. The passage also contained the realization that the pro-war agenda enjoyed the benefits of providing entertainment to the reading public as opposed to the intricacies of diplomatic wrangling. However, unless more articles like his appear there remain few willing to criticize the policy of intervention. Newspapers may sell on the back of exciting news but in doing so they leave themselves open to criticism that they only supply one side of the agenda.

Writers such as Jenkins were placed in the unenviable position of seemingly promoting a policy of non-committal, a policy that he defended as 'not a policy of cowardice or appeasement'.[95] Mick Hume, also writing in *The Times*, was even more critical of the Labour Government's reason for intervention. He argued that the moral purpose of the war had done little to aid the people of the region and had actually precipitated a humanitarian crisis in an effort to project an image of an ethical Britain.[96] Instead, Hume believed, the real purpose of intervention was to give 'Mr Blair's Government an aura of moral authority and a sense of mission. It is about projecting a self-image of the ethical new Britain bestriding the world'.[97]

Media commentators were not alone in criticizing the government policy over Kosovo. From the outset around a dozen Labour MPs from the left-wing Campaign Group objected to NATO interference. Their numbers included Tony Benn, Tam Dayell, George Galloway and Alice Mahon. Their views and others from the Left of politics were criticized for failing to address real-world issues and made them 'bystanders to evil'.[98] However, as Dan Keohane has pointed out, the objectors were not restricted to the Left of the political spectrum, he noted the number of Conservatives espousing isolationist sentiment. Douglas Hogg, for example, believed Britain's strategic interests were not sufficiently at risk to justify intervention.[99]

This diversity of criticism could not break the monopoly held by pro-interventionists and left the opponents open to criticism from across the political and public arena. Blair and others openly condemned Alex Salmond, leader of the Scottish National Party, for daring to compare the bombing of Serbia with the Blitz of Britain during the Second World War. The reason for this is clear; to work, the demonization of the enemy had to be absolute. The Western leaders had sought to ally Milosevic's ethnic cleansing with the Holocaust, just as Saddam's invasion of Kuwait was hailed as the first step towards greater conquests. Western propaganda could not allow its policies to be tarnished by association with negative historical connotations. The media was, in John Pilger's opinion, guilty of 'egging on the moralising aggressiveness of the Prime Minister'.[100] Such comparisons also make the public think about the enemy as human beings, something to be avoided when promoting a sanitized conflict against a demonized enemy.

The media continued to facilitate a negative opinion of those calling for peace. During the Gulf War John Keegan undermined the foundation of non-interventionists. He believed the 'political resolve of the alliance, despite media focus on anti-war sentiment in the United States and hesitations in the Arab world, appears to strengthen'.[101] He clearly drew a distinction between coverage in the US and Arab nations, with the resolve demonstrated in the United Kingdom. Thus, while acknowledging the presence of opposition the existence of such opinion in Britain is not deemed worthy of mention. His views are probably based upon his optimistic opinion that victory would be relatively easy for the allies and the more antagonistic stance of *The Daily Telegraph*. Other *Telegraph* writers insisted that Americans simply needed strong leadership[102] and belittled opponents by referring to them as 'Peace Groupies'.[103] Meanwhile, a protest in which red powder was thrown at MPs in Parliament was accused of diminishing the gravity of the discussion.[104]

Accusations of diminishing the gravity of a situation were a key way of belittling the opposition. Anti-war protesters were systematically categorized through association with marginalized, radical or undesirable elements of society. In addition to 'loony left' or 'hippy' analogies, opposition was categorized along with the Second World War policy of appeasement and its inherent negative implications. For example, a comment piece in the *Daily Mirror* urged those advocating peace at any cost to 'remember what happened to Neville Chamberlain'.[105] However, *The Sun*'s columnist Richard Littlejohn, when commentating on the peace protests being held at Trafalgar Square, encapsulated the most comprehensive criticism:

> As the UN deadline passed out crawled the usual collection of 'students', Godbotherers, Guardian readers, gays, Communists, Trots, men with beards and duffle coats, men with ponytails, wimmin in men's shoes and old hippies with worn-out Country Joe And The Fish LPs.[106]

Clearly avoiding the constraints of modern political correctness the above comment piece encapsulates the plethora of insults and stigmas associated with peaceful protest against intervention. The bias in favour of the pro-war agenda is multiplied by the lack of reasoned opposition opinion reproduced in the press and by the willing reproduction of official interventionist statements. This is often done without serious critical analysis. This type of coverage hampers serious, intellectual debate and reflects poorly upon the notion of a civilized, independent and questioning media. Serious evaluation of a cross-section of society, without resulting to name-calling, would reflect a far greater degree of moral legitimacy. This could be achieved without compromising support for the government, if that were the editorial aim of a newspaper. Instead, by affiliating non-interventionist ideals with minorities in society and negative stereotypes, the press often reflects little more than a bigoted and biased conduit for pro-war propaganda.

There are some figures in the media that openly state that they do not believe in the necessity to produce a balanced and objective representation of events. Max Hastings found it ironic that many people were more concerned with the welfare of the enemy than their own leadership.[107] For Hastings the moral legitimacy of the allies' cause was unquestionable when evaluated against the actions and character of Saddam Hussein. Because of this, he 'remained unconvinced of the case for displaying "objectivity" as between the allies and Saddam, when even the most generous moral assessment of his deeds already in the war suggests that he is an exceptionally evil man'.[108] The good versus evil narrative is used here to dismiss the notion of retaining an objective press. However, this contradicts one of the moral legitimacies that help to make up the West's justification for war, namely its free, democratic and objective state and media.

Hastings was not isolated in his opinion, Richard Littlejohn attacked the BBC for its even-handed reporting of the Gulf Crisis and was 'sure Saddam Hussein appreciates their support but, frankly, who gives a toss?'.[109] The observation was obviously worthy enough to comment upon but characterized the flippant dismissal of any coverage deemed unpatriotic or pessimistic. Indeed, the ideals were reiterated by a cartoon in *The Sun* depicting the BBC as a puppet to Saddam.[110] These attitudes reflect a recurrent debate about the role of the BBC during conflict, which finds itself a target for those who deem its output to be unpatriotic. Phillip Knightley notes that during the Falklands War 'the BBC, criticised in the past as a bastion of British conservatism, an arm of government, part of the Foreign Office and so on, found itself this time accused of "damaging the war effort"'.[111] In the House of Commons during the Gulf War, one Member of Parliament accused the BBC of being unable to distinguish between good and evil, highlighting in the process the deemed necessity of presenting conflict in terms of black and white depictions.[112]

Establishment individuals were also not immune from such criticisms. *The Sun* branded Sir Patrick Cordingley 'Brigadier Bigmouth' after his assertion that the public should expect heavy losses; the newspaper believed Saddam Hussein 'will be encouraged by foolish, alarmist statements from a commander who should know better'.[113] Criticism of Cordingley was evident despite the fact that he was an authoritative figure and one involved in the military effort, exactly the type of character who would normally be utilized to provide authority and expert credibility to pro-interventionist articles.

In spite of such attempts to dismiss the relevance of objectivity out-of-hand there remained, throughout both the Gulf War and Kosovo Conflict, a number of issues that raised questions regarding the benefit of government action. These incidents created the opportunities for dissent to be voiced with a degree of confidence.

Two examples can be extracted and analysed in order to compare press attitudes to key events during both conflicts; namely the right of intervention and civilian deaths. Both these issues had the potential to divide opinion and both were relevant to each of the conflicts under discussion. At the start of the Gulf War, the right of intervention debate was assisted by the clarity of the events. The Iraqi invasion of Kuwait was a clear breach of international law and provided an identifiable victim and aggressor, although this is not to assert that everyone agreed with this evaluation of the circumstances. Some aspects that opponents of intervention sought to utilize clouded the issue. The question of Kuwait's oil reserves led to accusations that the West was merely contemplating intervention in order to secure the economies of the developed world. Indeed, when briefing his men General de la Billiere insisted that the principle reason for their being there was to safeguard Saudi Arabian oil.[114] He did not attempt to hide this as an objective of the British military presence.

In addition to the territorial justification, the question of morality was raised. While the Pope condemned the war on 3 February 1991, John Major actively sought to gain the blessing of Archbishop Robert Runcie and Cardinal Basil Hume, who gave their personal and private reassurance that it would be a just war.[115] Armed with such support, criticism from the church was isolated and those continuing to voice their opposition were discredited in much the same way as peace protestors were. When thirty church leaders produced a document which stated the Gulf War would be unjust, Damian Thompson, writing in *The Daily Telegraph*, felt obliged to point out that the Dominican order had become known for its left-wing stance.[116] By doing this, any moral objection to war could become politicized and associated with other left-wing organizations opposing war that, as we have already seen, have been discredited.

The right of Britain to intervene in Kosovo did not facilitate support with such ease. The debate over whether Kosovo constituted an internal, domestic matter or warranted international intervention, dominated the thinking of those on either side of the intervention agenda. Without a clear victim and aggressor, the main justification for intervention rested on the moral legitimacy for action. Those supporting intervention to halt Milosevic's aggression against ethnic Albanians believed in the absolute justification of military involvement on humanitarian grounds. Nicholas Wheeler, writing after the conflict, has argued that the slaughter of civilians should not be subordinated to the requirement that intervention needs always to be authorized by the United Nations Security Council.[117] Yet, the press did not universally accept this argument and initially some commentators were sceptical of the reasoning behind intervention. One such critic was John Laughland of *The Times* who argued that this relatively new justification for intervention was flawed because 'the bogus notion of human rights can never provide a basis for either the rule of law or morality'.[118] This concept meant some writers believed that non-intervention was the only option available. Humanitarian and moral obligations had played a role during the Gulf War in aiding the demonization of Saddam Hussein and his forces, yet it was only part of a wider framework of justifications. In Kosovo, it was the utmost consideration. This led Patrick Bishop to conclude that short 'of deploying Nato troops to protect the civilian population – which would effectively mean declaring war on Serbia and backing an independent Kosovo – there is nothing new for the outside world to do'.[119] Also in *The Daily Telegraph* Alice Thomson suggested no action should be taken and warned that strategists at home 'should remember the lessons of Vietnam and Northern Ireland. Armies cannot end wars fought by civilians'.[120] In this example, historical precedent is once again employed to justify a current policy line. Much as references to the Second World War bolstered the pro-war agenda so too do perceived less successful conflicts, such as Northern Ireland and Vietnam, benefit the protestors. Despite the obvious differences between the two examples both are prolonged conflicts that caused a drain on human lives and a subsequent strain on public opinion.

Those people against intervention included *Daily Mirror* writer Paul Routledge, who consistently challenged the right and reasoning to intervene. The newspaper's Chief Political Correspondent saw the killings in Kosovo as simply another episode in the bloody history of the Balkan people and even felt the necessity to remind readers that a single shot in Sarajevo had instigated the First World War.[121] His criticisms led him to attack Blair's decision to intervene and claimed he was lying about having UN authority to bomb.[122] Aware of his isolation Routledge felt the need to state under the title of one of his articles that his was a 'controversial view'[123] and to deny that he supported Milosevic's ethnic cleansing.[124] His isolation was not eased by the *Daily Mirror*'s interventionist editorial stance on the issue.

The incidence of Routledge's criticism offers a very good indication of the scale of anti-war opinion printed in the press. While a number of examples of opposition can be extracted, the overall opinion generated by the newspapers is often different, for example the *Daily Mirror*'s editorial policy being at odds with Routledge's beliefs. In contrast to Routledge the *Mirror* used the threat of the wider implications of events in Kosovo to demand action not only 'to stop this carnage on Europe's doorstep but to prevent it spreading closer to our own shores', while reiterating Milosevic's status as a butcher in the title.[125] It was, the newspaper insisted, time to stand up to Milosevic the 'bloody tyrant' and Milosevic the butcher.[126] With the editorial policy dominating the newspaper's views on the conflict, Routledge's opinions, while significant for their existence, constitute a token voice of dissent in the clamour for intervention.

Where criticism of government policy became more prevalent was not in reaction against intervention, but in accusations of a lack of involvement. The non-committal of ground troops by Britain and her allies was seen to be a grievous oversight, especially in relation to the stated objectives of NATO. In contrast to the Gulf War the Kosovo crisis demonstrated the fallibility of the humanitarian argument for proceeding with intervention when the means employed do not tackle the root of the troubles. The *Daily Mirror* had been critical in the early stages during the Gulf War of government inaction regarding the hostages, yet the later escalation of forces quelled any opposition based on insufficient commitment.[127] During the Kosovo campaign, NATO insisted intervention was necessary to safeguard the Kosovan Albanians from Milosevic's attempts to subject the region to ethnic cleansing, however they were only willing to commit to an air campaign. This led to accusations that NATO policy was not only failing to alter the situation positively on the ground but also actually causing an escalation of the violence. Richard Gott of *The Guardian* believed that 'the sudden Kosovo population displacements were triggered by Nato bombing and by the decision of Western governments to impose impossible conditions on the Serbian sovereign state'.[128] In addition to questioning the competence of the NATO strategy, this argument intimates a disapproval of the wider legitimacy of intervention into the affairs of a sovereign nation. It undermined the reasoning behind the intervention and claimed that as the war escalated the humanitarian crisis was 'relegated to playing a purely propaganda role' in the eyes of one *Guardian* journalist.[129] In this atmosphere, the press pushed for greater military commitment on the part of the allies to enforce the objectives with which they claimed they gained the right of intervention.

Writing after the war Susan Carruthers has stated that the '"war for human rights" may have been worth killing for, but it wasn't worth dying for'.[130] This phrase demonstrates the negative perception of humanitarian intervention that fails to alleviate the circumstances that justify the war. NATO's failure to deploy ground troops and proceed only with an air war could be interpreted in line with Carruthers' statement. Her observation certainly echoed the dissent found in the printed media. Reinforced by the widely accepted historical belief that air power alone could not bring a decisive victory, the press pushed for stronger action. As Peter Goff has questioned, if 'Milosevic was a world-endangering demon, why were Nato not prepared to discuss the possibility of sending in ground troops or even flying their planes a little lower?'.[131] The incompatibility of aims and strategy caused greater dissent than the overall debate of whether or not intervention was justified. Matthew Parris of *The Times* was critical of the discussion at Westminster that he viewed as 'an alternative to action',[132] while Patrick Bishop thought it was difficult to see how the West's aims would be secured by the air campaign alone.[133] Bishop's views were expanded by the *Telegraph*'s editorial policy, which consistently called for an escalation of NATO's role in Kosovo.[134] The newspaper was critical of Labour's handling of the crisis, more so than the legitimacy of intervention, and believed that Tony Blair was failing to win the support of, what it called, the 'informed readership' of the broadsheet customers.[135] The aim of the allies to return the Albanians to their homes was, in the *Telegraph*'s view, becoming an ever more distant prospect as the Blair government continued its inept conduct of the campaign.[136]

Other newspapers followed this line of limited criticism of the strategy but not the legitimacy of NATO intervention. Jonathan Eyal of *The Guardian* claimed the biggest humanitarian disaster would commence once the air assault had begun,[137] while Hodgson and Kaldor both produced articles promoting the use of ground forces.[138] For *The Sun*, support of Blair led to a slightly confused editorial policy over ground troops, initially resigned to the need for them, but later agreeing with Blair's decision not to use such forces.[139] The *Daily Mirror* for its part vented its frustration at Britain's 'spineless allies' who threatened to undermine Blair's determined position.[140] The effect of such criticism of government policy was made more difficult to evaluate owing to the conclusion of hostilities. The victory of air power over Milosevic's regime meant that the voices calling for greater intervention were silenced and even compelled John Keegan to admit in print that he had been wrong to presume air power would not be sufficient.[141] Yet, what the opposition does show is the strength of the pro-war agenda. Critical objection to the government policy over any form of intervention in Kosovo was severely limited; however, when the criticism was aimed at promoting greater government intervention the editorial policies were more than willing enough to voice their opinion.

This brings us onto the second potentially contentious situation. The issue of allied forces causing civilian deaths had the ability to rouse opposition and vocal condemnation of military action. Just as human interest stories about civilian victims could be utilized to positive propaganda ends, so too could it be potentially divisive. Targets that were of a militarily dubious nature had the potential to attract condemnation from organizations and governments who may otherwise be sympathetic to the West's aims. During the Kosovo Conflict in mid- and late May, the United Nations High Commissioner for Human Rights, Mary Robinson, was critical of Serbian killings but also clearly censured NATO, calling for a halt to the use of cluster bombs.[142] However, it was not only the direct threat posed to civilians that affected allied policymakers, poor handling of the issue could easily damage the public relations war. Geoffrey Best, writing in *The Daily Telegraph* during the Gulf War, was sympathetic to the difficulties faced by the coalition forces and believed that the removal of civilians from danger areas was as much the responsibility of the defender as it was for the attacker to avoid them. He was more concerned with the language in which the coalition justified them and insisted that it was no longer enough to hide conveniently behind political jargon and describe civilian casualties as 'collateral damage'.[143] The potentially divisive issue could have challenged the stalwart support afforded by the British press, however, the pro-war agenda was in large able to subjugate the issue and keep the public focus on the larger military and political aims.

Perhaps the most notorious event involving civilians during the Gulf War was the bombing of the Amiriyah shelter in Baghdad. On the 13 February

1991 the building was struck causing the deaths of hundreds of civilians. The coalition claimed the bunker was deliberately hit and that it served a military purpose. In defending their decision, they tried to insist Saddam Hussein was to blame for having placed civilians in a military installation in an attempt to deter an allied attack. The television footage showing the despair of relatives and the destruction wrought had the potential to question public support of the strategy of the allies. Yet, the shelter bombing in fact caused surprisingly little concern in the British press. *The Times* was swift in attacking the television coverage of the bombing describing it as 'a hopeless medium of analysis'.[144]

The incident appeared to cause more inter-media argument than criticism of government or debate between the newspapers. *The Sun* asserted that high-explosive smart bombs would not have caused the inferno witnessed and thus believed the fire had been started by Saddam's men.[145] Instead, the newspaper sought to criticize the visual coverage of the event. *The Sun* argued that television coverage was 'biased', basing its opinion on a selective opinion pool. The newspaper referred to a phone-in it conducted, which revealed 2,600 people believed ITV and BBC had shown favour to the Iraqis while 139 thought they supported the allies.[146] As already stated, this belief was reinforced by a cartoon published by the newspaper that depicted Saddam Hussein as puppet-master to the BBC. Instead of utilizing the incident as a basis for reassessing coalition strategy, the shelter bombing did little to deter the support of the conflict. Instead, television channels willing to show the footage were attacked for providing Saddam Hussein with a propaganda victory, when in effect it was the allies who had handed the initiative to Iraq. The incident demonstrates the ready acceptance to publish opinion poll data based on a very selective audience. The poll fitted within the editorial comment of the newspaper and was reproduced accordingly; it provided little insight as to the diverse reactions of a general public.

This response was symptomatic of a wider dissatisfaction with the role of the media in the Gulf War. News channels and the media inside Iraq and Baghdad were seen to be at the mercy of Saddam Hussein's propaganda machine. In keeping with the supposed distinction between the free, Western press and the state-dominated Iraqi media, the location of such news providers as CNN in Baghdad was heralded as alien to the concept of independent Western journalism. CNN was attacked by Robert Fox as a 'conduit of the propaganda of Saddam's men' and believed its rise to prominence marked 'a change in television journalism, where spectacle and the personality of the purveyor now precedes the dull but necessary sorting of rational fact'.[147] Increasingly this argument is forwarded in opposition to the alleged benefits of 24-hour, live news coverage. The demand to meet regular deadlines, the reliance on personality and resort to emotional reportage appear to diminish some of the positive attributes of global, live news. Newspapers

are therefore in a position to provide the opinion and debate often unacceptable or unobtainable in visual media, however it appears this is not a challenge they have been able, or desire, to meet.

From the military's perspective, General de la Billiere also had his mis-
givings about the media's influence in Iraq:

> The principle of a free Press, as I understand it, is that the media
> report everything which happens. Reporters in the heart of enemy
> territory were completely muzzled and could send out only what
> Saddam Hussein allowed them to. They were, in effect, mouthpieces
> for the enemy, whose aim was to destroy and kill our servicemen. I
> therefore thought their reports should not have been broadcast or
> published, for they served no purpose as far as the Coalition was
> concerned and in my view offered no real extension of the informa-
> tion available to the public.[148]

His words are revealing. The issue of a free press as opposed to the inti-
mated state-controlled media of Iraq is raised. The association is drawn
between the enemy and the death of servicemen, insinuating that by revealing the Iraqi side of the war the media were contributing to the death of
servicemen. However, the supposedly free press in the West still has to be
censored for reasons of national security. He insists that reports were of
no use to the coalition, yet this is not the purpose of a 'free press' designed
to report 'everything that happens'. As allied forces, with the exception of
a limited number of unilaterals, controlled the only other sources of information, his statement was actually stressing that the public need nothing
other than the coalition depiction of events. However, de la Billiere does
admit in the same book that he used CNN in his war room in Riyadh to
update him on the attacks in Baghdad and this left him in no doubt they
were hitting home.[149] Obviously, this provided, if his earlier statement is
to be believed, the public with no extension of their understanding of the
conflict. As for the Amiriyah bombing, de la Billiere believed that it served
a dual purpose and that Saddam deliberately and willingly placed civilians
there to protect the site.[150] For elements of the press, such as the *Daily
Mirror*, the easiest way of tackling this difficult issue was to afford it as little
coverage as possible and deliver no editorial criticism. Amiriyah failed to
ignite a wider debate on the legitimacy and justification for war with Iraq.

Kosovo had its own potentially divisive issues, the most prominent among
them being the accidental bombing of the Chinese Embassy and, the event
that will be examined here, the controversial bombing of the Radio Television Serbia (RTS) building. Human Rights Watch criticized the incident
for endangering civilian lives to a degree disproportionate to the military
gain.[151] Once again, the event failed to provide the catalyst for widespread
disapproval. For the large part, the press avoided making any controversial

statements; *The Times* waited until the following week before declaring that the building did not constitute a military target.[152] *The Sun* reminded readers that despite it being a sad event the greater evil was Milosevic's campaign of ethnic cleansing. Meanwhile, the *Daily Mirror* declared the attack a 'vital blow against Slobodan Milosevic's evil propaganda machine'.[153] In total, the slaughter of civilians in a militarily dubious target raised little public debate or editorial criticism. Furthermore, it failed to muster any substantial support for suspending hostilities or re-evaluating targets.

Civilian casualties and the news coverage they received were a concern for the military and political planners; however, it appears this concern was overestimated. The press failed to utilize the events to attack the present policy, preferring instead to back government policy. It was a missed opportunity to display objectivity. The public was offered little in the way of critical commentary of events and was partially shielded from the reality. While this appears unacceptable, it is difficult to appreciate what public opinion is actually willing to accept and what it actually wants to be shown. Public opinion is a difficult medium to measure and is easily utilized by both the anti-war protestors and the pro-intervention lobbies to support their case. Opinion polls are traditionally offered to substantiate particular claims regarding opinion on the domestic front; however, their relevance can be criticized. Richard Connaughton has argued that there is a danger in drawing conclusions from opinion polls, which attempt to devise simple questions for an unsophisticated public when in fact they are actually complicated scenarios.[154] Despite this type of criticism, opinion polls are regularly commissioned or reproduced in the British press during conflicts. When politicians and military leaders attempted to justify the interventionist policy, reference was often made to the political consensus encapsulated in UN security resolutions but, as Clyde Wilcox concludes, this did little to demonstrate any possible world public consensus.[155]

Those opinion polls that did appear predominantly reinforced the support for government policy. During the Gulf War *The Daily Telegraph* printed the results of a Gallup poll that proved that 'Britons remain firm on the use of force',[156] while an ICM poll in *The Guardian* suggested 54 per cent of those questioned believed the government should do all it could to drive Iraq out of Kuwait.[157] A report cited during the Kosovo campaign in *The Daily Telegraph* by Gallup demonstrated how public support had risen from 58 per cent in late March 1999 to 72 per cent in April.[158] However, to what degree these figures actually represented any coherent public opinion is questionable. Individuals were often divided and sceptical of policies and the intricacies of these opinions were not given justice by simplistic opinion poll results.

Another selective source of public opinion, Mass Observation directives, gives a slender insight into some of the criticisms and concerns held by the public. Many of the comments reveal the uncertainty of people to form coherent and educated opinions on the conflict, yet there is a notable appreciation of the content of the media coverage. One female observer during the Gulf crisis succinctly encapsulated one of the hypocrisies exhibited by *The Guardian* when she mentioned that although its letters pages were filled with pacifist sentiment 'overall the media seem happy about the situation. I suppose it sells newspapers'.[159] A newspaper with strong liberal backing was at odds with its readership.

Other replies were more critical of the press, not for apathetically supporting the war to increase sales, but by actively involving themselves in blatant propaganda. The same respondent went on to complain that the 'propaganda, as opposed to news, on the radio (and) T.V., has become blatant'.[160] Yet despite this appreciation of the propaganda content of the news the respondent goes on to display reactions suggesting at least one message was seeping through by commenting on the likelihood of severe casualties in hand to hand fighting because of the Iraqis' practice in Iran. This mimicked the enhanced 'battle-hardened' interpretation of Saddam's forces, where it was believed the Iraqi army was a realistic challenge to the coalition forces, for reasons discussed in the previous chapter. Thus, while demonstrating an awareness of aspects of propaganda these enhanced views of the capabilities of the Iraqi army were still prevalent. Other reports contained references to Saddam and Milosevic as insane or compared them with Hitler; one example declared Hussein 'is a megalomaniac, as Hitler was', again mirroring some of the more obvious propaganda messages encapsulated in press coverage and official briefings.[161] While the examples mentioned provide an extremely limited dissection of public opinion, they demonstrate some of the intricacies and shifting opinions of a public who may be sceptical of some aspects of the news they digest, but willing to reproduce other facets.

This mixed approach to news coverage was also evident over the justification and right of intervention in both conflicts. Some believed Britain was right to intervene and that the government had sought a peaceful solution[162] in order to avoid a future disaster.[163] Other opinions ranged from believing intervention was a mistake and actually exacerbated the situation[164] to criticism of the policy pursued and the clarity of the West's objectives.[165] The criticism that the military or government had not clearly stated their objectives was often repeated, yet the predominant reaction does not appear to be a clamour for greater knowledge, instead respondents often resigned themselves to having little or no opinion on a subject that they knew little about. Some found the coverage depressing and shielded themselves from the repetition of such scenes in the media.[166] The feeling of being overwhelmed by coverage, but without developing a clear enough understanding of events, also prevailed.[167] In this respect, the coverage of the Kosovo Conflict demonstrates a public sympathy for the Kosovar Albanians, yet the basis of a war on humanitarian grounds was not sufficient explanation for many people. They remained confused with regards to the objectives, especially when the means employed did little to stem the refugee flow. As saturation coverage brought extensive scenes of suffering, many people found the events too depressing. This shielding of oneself from the horrors of war, coupled with the sanitation of descriptions of conflict by official sources and the media, led to an increasing sense of detachment from events as people became removed from the realities of war.[168] The overwhelming interpretation gained from the Mass Observation reports is the degree to which the media dominate the public's understanding of a crisis. Whether they agree or disagree with the opinions raised the media provide the most substantial benchmark with which to explain one's own interpretation of the events.

Opposition since the conflicts

Much of the criticisms regarding the reporting of both conflicts have understandably occurred since the cessation of hostilities. There has been considerable academic debate afforded to issues surrounding the media. Patrick Bishop has criticized the Joint Information Bureau (JIB) during the Gulf War, accusing it of presenting only good news and exercising control wherever possible, but all the while professing the right of journalists to disseminate information freely.[169] His major concern was the lack of urgency displayed by the media pools in transmitting reports, a criticism that had been widespread during the Falklands Conflict almost a decade earlier. However, in Bishop's reports for *The Daily Telegraph* there is a lack of criticism at the time, instead his articles echo the official propaganda themes of Hitlerization and a cautionary, yet unconvincing, effort to enhance the credibility of the enemy.[170]

Criticism was also levelled at the degree of inconsistency between the information supplied to the US and British media. Anton Antonowicz, writing for the *Daily Mirror* during the Gulf War, drew a distinction between the level of openness displayed by the US and British governments and complained of a 'disease of secrecy' evident at the MOD.[171] There were criticisms that the US correspondents were given information that was then contradicted or denied by British sources. However, journalists writing of the US experience also used the same argument when comparing their own information with that afforded by the British military. For example, John Fialka of the *Wall Street Journal* claimed that British media consumers learned about the actions of their forces faster than the US audience did; this was partially due, in his opinion, to the British military facilitating the use of satellite technology.[172]

The military were keen to claim that they did not attempt to mislead the media during both crises and insisted they provided the best material available to them.[173] Whether or not this was the case, the briefings became a vital source of information as the access was restricted in both conflicts and, as has been noted, sources deemed to be influenced by the enemy were criticized for their overt objectivity. The briefings came to dominate the agenda for the day and in a move that appears deliberate, as the allies attempted to focus the news in line with their own requirements.

The pool system received less open criticism actually during the crisis and there were those willing to believe the official argument that the best information was available. Christopher Bellamy, Defence Correspondent of *The Independent*, wrote after the Gulf War that he believed 'the military high command did everything it could to help'.[174] His view may have been more positive regarding the military because of his own background of serving in the Royal Artillery, therefore maintaining a more sympathetic approach to the military desire for secrecy. Richard Kay of the *Daily Mail* has also subsequently stated that the media ground rules appeared reasonable,[175] yet he went on to highlight the degree of control the military still retained when recalling the outset of the ground campaign where correspondents were pre-briefed and in effect subject to a form of embargo.[176] This loss of freedom, according to Julia Burkart, meant that the press continued to mouth the information fed by the military briefers.[177] The pool system also fragmented the media and dented hopes of providing any sense of a united front against the military on the part of reporters.

Aside from the practicalities of reporting the news, the actual necessity for going to war has been debated. A major part of the military and political propaganda was designed to win public support for the conflicts through the justification of the cause. This battle appears to have faltered on occasions, most notably during the Kosovo crisis when the legitimacy for intervention was more clouded. However, the Gulf War was not universally accepted as a worthy cause, one US officer concluding that he became increasingly convinced that Saudi Arabia and Kuwait 'aren't worth fighting for'.[178] Such reactions are perhaps understandable, as Patrick Bishop points out; the Gulf War was fought in the name of human rights, as was Kosovo, yet the tyranny remained after the war.[179] Others have criticized the aims of the Gulf War in terms of a desire to protect world trade partners rather than out of any sense of moral duty.[180] Even when the moral argument is accepted as valid, Noam Chomsky criticizes the selectivity of the West when deciding on which occasions it should act, while ignoring other equally deserving cases worldwide.[181] Michael Ignatieff argues that the Kosovo Conflict was a virtual war because without casualties to the NATO forces the hostilities ceased to be fully real.[182]

Such attitudes reveal the often radically conflicting assumptions about the reasoning behind, and the clamour for, war. What much of the criticism has focused upon has ranged from one polarized view to another with a profound difficulty apparent in producing an argument that adopts aspects of both sides. Thus, Max Hastings has criticized the admiration given to such writers as Robert Fisk, who received more plaudits by attacking the US and UK policy than John Keegan's articles, which correctly predicted a swift and comprehensive allied victory in the Gulf.[183] Martin Shaw has criticized Hammond and Herman's book *Degraded Capability*, which sought to attack Western policy but realized there was little merit in the Serbs' case and instead merely downplayed the extent of the slaughter.[184] However, there is merit in attempting to understand both arguments and highlighting the more obvious consistencies between the two conflicts that reveal continuity in the way wars are presented. In identifying the propaganda themes applicable to both conflicts and highlighting the lack of opposition given by the press to the pro-war agenda, it is clear that the British press have tuned into the national psyche and appealed to traditional sections of our culture and national identity in an attempt to bolster public support for the war effort. The press demonstrates an awareness of the government's attempts to shape public perception of war, yet does little to challenge this openly. Instead, it is often left to journalists, historians and public figures to write their 'untold stories' after the event and in doing so highlight the discrepancies between the supposedly free, democratic press and the reality of war reportage.

Conclusion

Opposition in the British press during the Gulf War and Kosovo Conflict was muted. The media demonstrated an ability to self-censor that meant that overt censorship remained limited while the desired effect was just as pertinent. The editorial policies of the newspapers provided a relatively consistent thread supporting the pro-war agenda and dominated the discussion of conflict, edging debate critical to intervention to the periphery of the argument. Both conflicts displayed a similar level of opposition, but Kosovo differs over the type of criticism. Here the argument moves away from the theory of a censored or self-censored media mimicking the daily propaganda messages presented for public consumption by political and military figures. Kosovo demonstrated willingness on behalf of the media to challenge the government policy and demand more intervention, in doing so, it demonstrated that the press is able to criticize official policy if necessary. The issue then becomes one of whether or not the media do follow official propaganda or if they simply share a desire, for commercial purposes, to promote war.

The essential factor in ascertaining the degree of support afforded to the interventionist agenda comes from the newspapers' editorial policies. The press systematically supported moves towards armed intervention, even before government policy was fully dedicated to such a venture. In this respect, the press, despite a number of important examples opposed to conflict, can be said to support the government policy by way of mutual compatibility rather than overt censorship. This in turn fits conveniently within the government and press' desire to present a facade of a free press working within a democratic society.

Such assertions, however, should not be taken as fixed rules. Commentators such as Robinson have sought to produce polarized theories establishing the nature of the relationship between the media and the State.[185] Alternatively, the 'CNN effect' has been heralded as a new component of this relationship, while Gowing argues against its influence.[186] What appears is that a degree of grey area must be factored into the equation.

Generally, the press appears to have a duty to present alternative policy options in the sense that they certainly have a duty to highlight policy changes that go against their own previous assertions about the correct course of action. Instead, as has been discussed, the newspapers mirrored the government policy and adapted to the changes with little comment or discussion. This effect runs contrary to Robinson's inverse model. As the examples of peace initiatives demonstrated, the press echoed the official policy line. Peace initiatives that were not sponsored by the US or the allied nations were derided. Conversely, policies that exceeded the mandate established for legitimate intervention were not challenged.

As General de la Billiere's words demonstrate, the military positively pursue the dispersal of a message through the media. It should not be surprising then that various subtle techniques are utilized to enhance the perception of the Western actions. It should also be unsurprising that groups such as humanitarian organizations are exploited to support the interventionist argument, while critical opinion by the same organizations is omitted from the public forum.

On the occasions when alternative opinions are aired in public, the press and politicians deride the individuals or groups. They are explicitly labelled traitorous or associated with groups that carry negative connotations. Alternatively, the anti-interventionist arguments are belittled and subsequently their arguments can be branded as diminishing the gravity of the situation. Even when potentially hazardous situations, such as military mistakes and civilian casualties occur, there is little deviance from the well-established interventionist agenda. On the contrary, during the Kosovo Conflict the biggest anti-government coverage was actually for more, rather than less, intervention.

Instead of critical and illuminating press coverage of British foreign policy, the two examples shown have demonstrated complicity with government policy. Much of the debate has occurred after the conflict and often by those who were unwilling to criticize at the time. The untold stories appear after the conflict by those who were capable of telling it during the event, an occurrence that destroys the myth of an objective and effective media system capable of exposing the propaganda campaigns that promote intervention.

CONCLUSION

This book has sought to prove a general propaganda theory, demonstrating a consistent model of propaganda used to justify intervention during a conflict. The existing discussion has often focused upon a theoretical analysis of propaganda techniques, illustrated by relevant examples. Alternatively, broad discussions of conflicts through a given period have been created. The object of this research has been an attempt to strike a balance between a broad overview of propaganda and the press against specific examples. Any analysis cannot offer a definitive answer, just as no definition of propaganda is universally accepted.

The nature of any analysis is also defined by the theoretical framework, or definition, which is utilized by the commentator. The variations of conceptualizing propaganda are diverse, echoing the educational and societal groundings of the various writers. Nevertheless, despite the differences there appear to be two major disputes that shape the understanding of what constitutes propaganda. First, one can point to the debate concerning whether or not such a concept as modern propaganda exists. As discussed in Chapter 1, some commentators such as Jacques Ellul have argued that propaganda as it exists today is a result of the development of mass society.[1] Only through this concentration of people, with more efficient and wider dissemination of information, can modern propaganda exist. Thus, he draws a chronological distinction between the forms of propaganda. Other commentators, such as Philip Taylor, trace propaganda from far earlier precedents to the present day.[2] The analysis carried out herein has essentially concerned itself with propaganda from the turn of the twentieth century up to the modern period. This is not to suggest any adherence to the school of thought promoting the necessity of a mass society with its associated elements of information dissemination. Mass society has indeed brought significant developments in the field of media and the sociological structure of society has altered. These progressions may have been alien to earlier generations, however many of the propaganda techniques would probably not have been. Further research will prove whether modern propaganda techniques can be applied retrospectively.

The second major quandary or debate between propaganda theorists is just how permissive any definition should be. In this instance, one is inclined to agree with Ellul's approach in the sense that propaganda classifications should be liberal. Thus, to those students of propaganda that seek or espouse a more rigid structure, the findings presented herein may be too inclusive. In defence of this line of argument, one must consider whether or not propaganda can be a subconscious act or whether it must be deliberate and premeditated. Because many propaganda techniques rely on socially engrained prejudices or fears any definition should, in my opinion, incorporate an appreciation of subconscious regurgitation of propaganda messages. These pre-installed elements make much propaganda acceptable and dilute the impact of more radical policies. However, by accepting this, one is aligned to the more permissive definition of propaganda. Whatever line is adopted, and the definitions are by no means incompatible polarized interpretations, there must be recognition that no classification can achieve absolute and universal acceptance. Furthermore, although a unique model is offered here, it by no means precludes the validity of other models. Just as propaganda should not be viewed in absolute terms, so too can the definitions overlap and share components.

If one accepts that no single definition can be incontrovertible, the only way to explain the processes and techniques is either to re-evaluate the evolution of propaganda theory or utilize case studies to analyse the implementation of propaganda and derive the reasons for the implementation. The two are by no means mutually exclusive. This study has attempted to incorporate both but the conceptualization of the theory has dominated the discussion. The research and findings are also geared towards understanding the reasons behind the propaganda techniques used, in other words it seeks to establish what benefit the propaganda served. There is a clear distinction to be drawn here with the analysis of how effective propaganda is; this will have to await further research. In essence, it is simply enough to suggest that the lack of vocal opposition to the conflicts and the use of propaganda is worthy of study. As the country and the media largely acquiesced to conflict, arguably the propaganda could be said to have been effective.

This brings us on to the interrelationship between the propagandists and the conflicts, in this case the first US-led Gulf War and the Kosovo Conflict. The methodology adopted meant a number of comparisons were attempted simultaneously, namely between the conflicts, between the newspapers and subsequently between the propaganda techniques. The two crises occurred in the post-Cold War era; as such, one is analysing the British press in a mass society. Entwined with this concept of a globalized information network is the continuing influence of the individual, in other words the journalists and their effect on the messages.

183

The two conflicts are not an arbitrary selection although it is hoped that the findings of the five propaganda themes can be applied to other conflicts. As already mentioned, both conflicts occurred in the post-Cold War period and both in a modern mass society. However, the differences between them are numerous. The Gulf War and Kosovo Conflict provide between them a number of 'firsts', such as the title of the first live war and the first war fought in the Internet age. They also represent extremely different types of conflict in style, geography, international significance and scale. These differences aid the development of a propaganda model by showing continuity where diversity exists. They also help the historian and student of propaganda to look beyond the First and Second World Wars while at the same time offering a theory that could be applied there also.

The diversity between the two case studies offered here meant that the justifications for intervention in each example differed. For the propagandists their approach had to be adapted to the circumstances presented and the argument for involvement suitably constructed. It is for this reason that the five themes of propaganda must be viewed in terms reminiscent of an undulating wave. Various themes rise to prominence and are at times superseded by others. Without regurgitating the argument already presented, an example can be forwarded. The Gulf War had a clear trigger to the events; the invasion of Kuwait meant that the war could be pitched in terms of an international threat that needed to be acted upon. In contrast, the evolution of the Kosovo Conflict was less defined and the international nature of the situation was clouded by the discussion as to whether the crisis constituted an internal matter. Subsequently, the justification for intervention was based on appeals to humanitarian principles. Thus, the demonization of the enemy was of paramount importance. In each case, these justifications shifted over the course of the conflict with the other themes never disappearing completely.

In this approach to propaganda, it becomes the reason for the justification, just as much as the method employed to transmit the argument, which needs consideration. However, it is not as simple as to suggest a strict linear movement of propagandist to propagandee via the media. Propaganda is more than a stimulus–response formula where the propagandists dictate their message irrespective of any public reaction. Public opinion is not a blank sheet upon which can be dictated, erased and dictated again, the message of the day. Propaganda must act upon the immediate stimulus and the traditional concepts inherent in public opinion. The nation-state offers the grounding of public attitudes towards specific ideas. It is this propaganda, enlisted to activate subconscious attitudes, which can also help to perpetuate propaganda without the need for specific, predetermined, thought. An example of this in Britain would be attitudes to democracy. Advanced in this country as the most respectable of the forms of government and shaped by our history of ideological struggles, the average citizen has a positive perception of democracy. In this respect the propagandist can utilize this when supporting justification. Distinctions are drawn between the liberal principles of our free democratic state, against the intolerant, irrational and belligerent principles of the enemy dictator.

In light of this element of resort to subconscious concepts to make the propaganda message acceptable, one must ask how far overt restrictions on the flow of information can influence the perception of an event portrayed in the press. The potential for strict censorship during war certainly exists with the *Green Book* standing as testimony to this. The analysis of this document in Chapter 3 proves the scope of censorship can potentially be wide. Most significant about the shift in MOD media policy since the Falklands Conflict has been the removal of the burden of responsibility for transmitting news that does not contravene security from the shoulders of the military and onto the media. In effect, the media are being asked to censor themselves. This reality runs contrary to the perception the MOD attempt to put across. In this respect the often-mentioned statement that the restrictions were rarely utilized, points towards an unwillingness to test these boundaries, rather than a liberal policy being in place. Combined with the assimilation of journalists into the war effort and an economic incentive to provide exciting news, the aims of the media and government during war appear to be far from the incompatible objectives of security versus the public right to know. Instead, during conflict they share compatible aims. This could help to explain the transmission of propaganda themes in the press, through simply either overlooking them or appreciating that they also benefit the commercial press.

Theoretically, therefore, the *Green Book* has the potential to censor news and assists the transmission of propaganda messages designed by political and military representatives. However, this does not explain the existence of all propaganda during conflicts. In the push for war, before British troops were involved, the press failed to present a case against intervention. Absent were the forms of demonization and personalization so readily utilized once the wars had begun. In the period where government policy was uncertain, the press presented a pro-interventionist agenda, ignored the issue or remained indecisive. On the rare occasions when opposition was promoted, the policy shifted once combat commenced. Free from the constraints of MOD restrictions there remained little in the way of sustained opposition to intervention. But, more worryingly, there is evidence of a pro-interventionist agenda that often went further than the government was willing to contemplate. Thus, the *Green Book* should not be forwarded as the reason for supporting intervention, because the majority of editorial opinion supported action even before such restrictions came into force.

The similarities between the five newspapers analysed herein have been greater than their distinctions. The propaganda themes transcend tabloid and broadsheet formats as well as traditional political affiliation. The research

185

has revealed a willingness to adopt an interventionist approach with only limited examples of overt rivalry between the newspapers. Commercially, each is vying for market share with each other, the wider press and other forms of media. However, the ability for conflict to sell newspapers appeared to dilute grounds for rivalry between them. This is not always the case, as has been noted. *The Sun* and *Mirror* fought an overt battle during the Falklands Conflict. In the recent Iraq war, the *Mirror* attempted to form a bastion of pacifism to increase market share and increase its distinction from other newspapers. However, the need to be seen to support British forces tempers overt criticism, a fact that Western governments appear to rely upon.

The study has also demonstrated the narrowing of ideals and style between tabloids and broadsheets during war. Many radical ideas and calls for further intervention are espoused regardless of broadsheet or tabloid formats. The broadsheets resort to similar propagandistic traits to those of the tabloids, further blurring distinctions between the types of newspaper. As some broadsheet titles adopt smaller formats, such similarities are further enhanced. We discover that despite an increasingly diverse media, incorporating visual and instant formats in addition to the press, the range of opinions does not increase comparably. In essence, the editorial policies of the five newspapers considered increasingly begin to represent a very similar body of opinion, which strengthens the propagandistic messages contained in their pages.

As the interventionist agenda develops into a discernable ideal the five themes of conflict propaganda become evident. Once again, the propaganda themes begin before the commitment of British forces into hostile action and, as such, fall outside the remit of the *Green Book*. The five themes identified support the interventionist agenda during the Gulf War and Kosovo Conflict. Since writing, the world has seen further conflict in Iraq and, once more, the same methods of propaganda appear to have been utilized to support war. During the war against Iraq in 2003, the leader figure was evoked once more as was the demonization of the enemy. The use of atrocity stories continues to add credence to interventionist arguments despite the discrediting and disillusionment with them post-1918.

During both US-led Iraq conflicts, the story of mobs stealing incubators from hospitals was utilized to invoke a sense of outrage or disgust. During the 1990–91 conflict Iraqi soldiers were accused of removing babies and leaving them to die, this enhanced the demonized image of the enemy. Looting formed part of the atrocities that often included theft from houses and shops and the rape of women in the same sentence. In 2003, the looting in Baghdad appeared initially to be welcomed. The perception portrayed by the military and subsequently the press explained away the incidences as part of the 'joy' at the apparent dissolution of government control.[3] As a symptom of the overthrow of Saddam's regime, and essentially a symptom

186

of Western efforts, the looting was initially excusable. However, as the peace appeared uncontrollable the Iraqi people were once again portrayed as the obstacle to reconciliation. The looting appeared to begin to echo the coverage of the first US-led Gulf War with references to an 'orgy of looting' and a 'plunge into lawlessness'.[4] The question then arose that if 'you can't stop the hospitals losing their incubators . . . then how on earth are you going to help create a nation which is demonstrably better than its pre-decessor?'[5] In both incidences, the incubator story contains an element of humanitarian appeal and a challenge to traditional British concepts of civility. However, humanitarian appeals alone do not sustain the campaign and other parts of the five-theme model are required. At present, it is the threat of terrorism, or the threat to the international community, which dominates the agenda. The military threat and the international threat have shifted from weapons of mass destruction to terrorism, changing as the requirements for justifying policy alter.

The role of technology is also important in contemporary discussions about British and US foreign policy. The Gulf War of 1990–91 appeared to tarnish the image of smart weapons and their capabilities in light of post-conflict revision of events. Kosovo, however, was a war won through air power alone, sustaining the importance of technology during conflict. However, this is only part of the argument concerning the use of technology in propaganda. The significance is to be found in its ability to make conflict appear more acceptable. Technology offers the opportunity to minimize Western casualties, a concern of public opinion. Furthermore, conflict continues to be sanitized through both censorship and the video game image of war perpetuated in the media. In these respects, technology continues to aid the justification and public acceptance of war.

Contemporary conflict has also demonstrated the role of opposition in the British press during times of crises. War sells newspapers, as does novelty, thus the *Mirror*'s effort to oppose war could cynically be viewed as exploiting a market niche. Most telling, however, has been the shift towards criticism of government policy, post-invasion. The press has proved they are capable of critical analysis after the event. Some questions need to be asked of the role of the journalist in these issues. Post-conflict reveal-all stories of their exploits raise their profile and introduce issues that should have occurred at the time. There is some evidence that a reappraisal of their role could be forthcoming. Recently Nick Robinson, political editor of ITV News, explained the difficulties of reporting the Iraq conflict in 2003; his experiences led him to state that he intended, more than ever, to explain the contradictory case.[6] The Neil Report, commissioned in light of the Hutton enquiry, recommended a 'renewed emphasis on core values of accuracy, serving public interest, impartiality, independence and accountability'.[7] Whether such changes will alter the evidence of interventionist propaganda remains doubtful.

The nature of war is likely to remain virtual with technology allowing for the legitimization of conflict. The individual soldier will retain a place in helping the public identify with the positive human elements of conflict, pride, bravery, compassion and loyalty. Propaganda will continue to exist and will overcome any future changes to society and the information system, just as it has survived the move into a mass society and the rapidity of news dissemination. The plethora of news outlets available does nothing to temper the propagandists' message. The five-theme model of conflict propaganda would only seem to be challenged by resilient public opposition. This in itself appears unlikely. In Western political systems immune from an international threat to sovereignty, domestic issues will continue to dominate politics. In this respect, the state–military–media system continues to work effectively at legitimizing conflict.

NOTES

INTRODUCTION

1 The overall and proportional numbers of those British adults (over 15 years old) reading the national newspapers analysed herein fell slightly between 1990–91 and 1999. Despite this the press still enjoyed a wide circulation. For example, in 1991 the daily readership for newspapers stood at around: *The Sun* 3.6 million, *Daily Mirror* 2.9 million, *The Daily Telegraph* 1 million, *The Times* 400,000 and *The Guardian* 400,000. By 1999 the numbers were around: *The Sun* 3.5 million, *The Mirror* 2.2 million, *The Daily Telegraph* 1 million, *The Times* 700,000 and *The Guardian* 360,000. These figures are out of a population total of around 45 million and 46 million persons, respectively. However, this does not provide an exact representation of the press' proliferation. Each newspaper sold is read on average by between 2.4 and 3 people, boosting significantly the overall exposure of each newspaper. These figures were kindly provided without charge by the National Readership Surveys Ltd.

2 The Gulf War of 1990–91 was seen as the last conflict of its type while Kosovo and Afghanistan were deemed to be representative of the likely scale and intricacies of future conflict. However, the second US-led Gulf War proved that such assumptions were not necessarily true.

3 For a discussion of cinema propaganda in this period see Chapman, J., *The British at War. Cinema, State and Propaganda, 1939–1945*, I.B. Taurus, London, 1998.

1 THE THEORY OF PROPAGANDA

1 The remit of this work is essentially an examination of propaganda with reference to the post-1900 era. The book will utilize contemporary propaganda issues with reference to foundations in earlier crises. This should not be taken as an alignment with either of the debates concerning the differences between or continuity of propaganda in the ancient or modern periods; a discussion that is central to the arguments of some writers on propaganda.

2 For a chronological overview of many of the definitions of propaganda, see Culbert, D., Cull, N. and Welch, D. (eds), *Propaganda and Mass Persuasion. A Historical Encyclopedia, 1500 to the Present*, ABC-Clio Inc, California, 2003, pp. 317–25.

3 For a discussion of propaganda stories during the First World War, see Ponsonby, A., *Falsehood in Wartime. Propaganda Lies of the First World War*, Institute for Historical Research, Torrance, California, 1991. Sanders, M. and

Taylor, P., *British Propaganda During the First World War, 1914–1918*, The Macmillan Press Ltd, London, 1982.

4 Lasswell, H., 'The Theory of Political Propaganda', *The American Political Science Review*, Vol. 21, No. 3, August 1927, p. 627.

5 Ibid. p. 631.

6 Lasswell, H., *Politics. Who gets What, When, How*, McGraw-Hill Book Co, USA, 1936, in Lasswell, *The Political Writings of Harold D. Lasswell*, The Free Press, USA, 1951, p. 298.

7 The definitions arrived at were thus: 'Intentional propaganda *is a systematic attempt by an interested individual (or individuals) to control the attitudes of groups of individuals through the use of suggestion and, consequently, to control their actions*; unintentional propaganda *is the control of the attitudes and, consequently, the actions of groups of individuals through the use of suggestion*'. Doob, L., *Propaganda. Its Psychology and Technique*, Henry Holt and Company, New York, 1944, p. 89 (emphasis from the original text).

8 Doob, L., *Public Opinion and Propaganda*, Archon Books, Hamden, Connecticut, 1966, p. 240 (emphasis from the original text).

9 Ibid. p. 54.

10 Ellul, J., *Propaganda. The Formation of Men's Attitudes*, Vintage Books, New York, 1973.

11 Blanco White, A., *The New Propaganda*, Victor Gollancz Ltd, London, 1939.

12 Ibid. p. 11.

13 Carr, E., *Propaganda in International Politics*, Oxford Pamphlets on World Affairs, No. 16, Clarendon Press, Oxford, 1939.

14 Ibid. p. 3.

15 Ibid. p. 4.

16 Ibid. p. 6.

17 Bartlett, F., *Political Propaganda*, Cambridge University Press, 1940.

18 Ibid. p. 2. The debate between the forms of education and propaganda is also raised in discussions. Generally, the line divides thus: Education teaches people how to think, while propaganda teaches them what to think. While this may be a useful distinction between the terminologies of the two words, in reality the distinction appears less clear-cut. As propaganda thrives on embedded cultural assumptions, the state-directed education system can have a role to play in shaping the attitudes of the public as much as it can enable people to question their environment.

19 Ibid. p. 30.

20 Ellul, J., *The Technological Society*, Jonathan Cape, London, 1965.

21 Ellul, 1973, op, cit. p. 61.

22 Jowett, G. and O'Donnell, V., *Propaganda and Persuasion*, Sage Publications, London, 1992, p. ix.

23 Ibid., p. 4.

24 Ibid., p. 4.

25 Mackenzie, J., *Propaganda and Empire. The Manipulation of British Public Opinion, 1880–1960*, Manchester University Press, Manchester, 1984, p. 3.

26 Bartlett, op. cit. p. 43.

27 Taylor, P., *Munitions of the Mind. A History of Propaganda from the Ancient World to the Present Day*, Manchester University Press, Manchester, 1995, p. 6.

28 Robins, K., Webster, F. and Pickering, M., 'Propaganda, Information and Social Control', in Hawthorn, J. (ed.), *Propaganda, Persuasion and Polemic*, Edward Arnold Ltd, London, 1987.

29 Thomson, O., *Easily Led. A History of Propaganda*, Sutton Publishing, Gloucestershire, 1999, p. 5 (italics added).
30 For the theories of Lippmann and Chomsky refer to: Lippmann, W., *Public Opinion*, Free Press Paperbacks, London, 1997. Lippmann, W., *The Phantom Public. A Sequel to 'Public Opinion'*, Macmillan, New York, 1930. Lippmann, W., *The Public Philosophy*, Hamish Hamilton, London, 1955. Herman, E. and Chomsky, N., *Manufacturing Consent. The Political Economy of the Mass Media*, Pantheon Books, New York, 2002.
31 Thomson, op. cit. p. 330.
32 Rampton, S. and Stauber, J., *Weapons of Mass Deception. The Uses of Propaganda in Bush's War on Iraq*, Robinson, London, 2003.
33 Scheer, C., Scheer, R. and Chaudhry, L., *The Five Biggest Lies Bush told us about Iraq*, Akashic Books and Seven Stories Press, New York, 2003. The fives lies identified are; Al Qaeda's ties to Iraq, Iraq's chemical and biological weapons, Iraq's nuclear weapons, the war will be a 'cakewalk' and Iraq as a democratic model.
34 Ibid. p. 169.

2 NEWSPAPERS, THE REPORTER AND THE WIDER CONTEXT

1 The Fourdrinier was the first papermaking machine producing a continuous roll of paper, capable of providing varying sizes. Named after the two English brothers who took up the patent from Frenchman Nicolas Louis Robert, the machine saw paper output increase tenfold and the price reduced significantly. For a discussion, see Clair, C., *A History of Printing in Britain*, Cassell and Company Ltd, London, 1965, p. 208.
2 Koenig's patent for the machine was taken out in Britain in 1810 but little work was carried out on the machine. Later developments meant that *The Times* was first printed by one of Koenig's machines on 29 November 1814. The machine saw production increase from 250 impressions an hour to 1,100. For details see ibid. pp. 212–14.
3 Ellul, J., *Propaganda. The Formation of Men's Attitudes*, Vintage Books, New York, 1973. Lasswell, H., *The Political Writings of Harold D. Lasswell*, The Free Press, USA, 1951.
4 Taylor, P., *Munitions of the Mind. A History of Propaganda from the Ancient World to the Present Day*, Manchester University Press, Manchester, 1995.
5 For details of the history of war reporting, see Knightley, P., *The First Casualty. The War Correspondent as Hero and Myth-Maker from the Crimea to Kosovo*, Johns Hopkins University Press, Baltimore, 2002.
6 For further details see Knightley, P., 'Here is the Patriotically Censored News', *Index on Censorship*, Nos 4 and 5, Vol. 20, April/May 1991.
7 Ignatieff, M., *Virtual War. Kosovo and Beyond*, Vintage, London, 2001.
8 Taylor, P., 'The Military and the Media Past, Present and Future', in Badsey, S., *The Media and International Security*, Frank Cass Publishers, London, 2000, p. 199.
9 Gowing, N., 'Media Coverage: Help or Hindrance in Conflict Prevention', in Badsey, ibid. p. 212.
10 Recent examples of journalists' post-conflict books include; Atkinson, R., *Crusade. The Untold Story of the Gulf War*, Harper Collins Publishers, London, 1994; Bell, M., *In Harm's Way. Reflections of a War-Zone Thug*, Penguin Books, London, 1996; Bishop, P., *Famous Victory. The Gulf War*, Sinclair-Stevenson

Limited, London, 1992; Bishop, P. and Witherow, J., *The Winter War. The Falklands*, Quartet Books Limited, London, 1982; Fialka, J., *Hotel Warriors. Covering the Gulf War*, The Woodrow Wilson Centre Press, 1992; Hastings, M., *Going to the Wars*, Macmillan, London, 2000; Kay, R., *Desert Warrior: Reporting from the Gulf a Personal Account*, Penumbra Books, London, 1992; Simpson, J., *From the House of War. John Simpson in the Gulf*, Hutchinson, London, 1991.

11 Simpson, 1991 op. cit. p. 278 (italics added).

12 Ibid. pp. 301–2.

13 Bell, M., *In Harm's Way. Reflections of a War-Zone Thug*, Penguin Books, London, 1996, pp. 127–8 (emphasis from the original text).

14 Adie, K., *The Kindness of Strangers. The Autobiography*, Headline Books Publishing, London, 2003, p. 246.

15 Hammond, P., E-mail correspondence with author, 8 July 2002.

16 Kay, R., *Desert Warriors. Reporting from the Gulf a Personal Account*, Penumbra Books, London, 1992, p. 77.

17 Ibid. p. 59.

18 Recent academic discussion of the issue corroborates the depiction of war reportage as unobjective. Phillip Knightley and David Welch argue that for much of its history war reportage has failed to be objective. Knightley for his part believes war reportage has been objective only twice, during the Crimean War and Vietnam. Welch argues against any notion of objective war reportage. For this debate see: Knightley, P. and Welch, D., 'Has War Reporting ever been Truly Objective?', *BBC History Magazine*, Vol. 5, No. 6, June 2004, p. 31.

19 Hastings, M., *Going to the Wars*, Macmillan, London, 2000, p. 354.

20 Hastings, 'The Journalist's Struggle to Pierce the Fog of War', *The Daily Telegraph*, 5 February 1991, p. 16.

21 Bell, op. cit.

22 Hammond, P., E-mail correspondence with author, 8 July 2002.

23 Meade, G., 'Hard Ground Rules in the Sand', *Index on Censorship*, Vol. 20, Nos 4 and 5, April/May 1991, p. 7.

24 Goff, P. and Trionfi, B. (eds), *The Kosovo News and Propaganda War*, International Press Institute, Vienna, 1999, p. 14.

25 Thomson, A., in ibid. p. 450.

26 Kieran, M., *Media Ethics. A Philosophical Approach*, Praeger, London, 1997, p. 60. Kieran is currently a lecturer in the philosophy department of the University of Leeds.

27 Bishop and Witherow, op. cit. pp. 150–1.

28 Taylor, P., *War and the Media. Propaganda and Persuasion in the Gulf War*, Manchester University Press, 1998, p. X.

29 The fear of a protracted conflict with an unclear exit strategy, commonly known as 'Vietnam Syndrome', continues to haunt political and military planners.

30 Simpson, J., 'Free Men Clamouring for Chains', *Index on Censorship*, Vol. 20, Nos 4 and 5, April/May 1991, p. 4.

31 This issue will be considered in Chapter 6.

32 MOD, *British Defence Doctrine*, Joint Warfare Publication (JWP), 0–01, p. 417.

33 Billiere, P., *Looking for Trouble*, Harper Collins Publishers, London, 1995, p. 405.

34 *The Life and Death of Colonel Blimp*, The Archers, 1943. The film attempted to demonstrate the need for new thinking during conflict and a new army. 'Blimp' was depicted as outdated, holding the values of a soldier who had come through the Boer War and the Great War. The film shows 'Blimp' finally accepting the need for change. However, the title's reference to David Low's cartoons of the

Evening Standard, deriding officers of the 'old school', and the slightly clouded moral to the story meant that government believed the film depicted the British Army in a negative light, hence initially banning it.
35 Ibid. p. 406.
36 Shalikashvili, J., in Dunsmore, B., *The Next War. Live?*, Joan Shorenstein Center on the Press, Politics, and Public Policy, John F. Kennedy School of Government, Harvard University, Cambridge MA, 1996, p. 9.
37 Shaw, M. and Carr-Hill, R., *Public Opinion, Media and Violence. Attitudes to the Gulf War in a Local Population*, University of Hull, 1991, p. 34. The above quotation also highlights the limitations of simplistic opinion polls, utilized by the media, states and other groups to substantiate legitimacy for their stance. An acknowledgement of support for a conflict can be registered but this does little to enhance the complex understanding or concerns of the public at large.
38 Ignatieff, op. cit. p. 192.
39 Bishop, P., *Famous Victory. The Gulf War*, Sinclair-Stevenson Limited, London, 1992, p. 38.
40 Taylor, P., *Munitions of the Mind. A History of Propaganda from the Ancient World to the Present Day*, Manchester University Press, 1995, p. 208.
41 Taylor, 1998, op. cit. MacArthur, *Second Front. Censorship and Propaganda in the Gulf War*, University of California Press, Berkeley, 1993.
42 Badsey, S., in Badsey, S. and Pimlott, J., *The Gulf War Assessed*, Arms and Armour Press, London, 1992, pp. 226–7.
43 In 1996, Badsey reaffirmed his conclusions that tabloid newspapers had reverted to their original functions as entertainment and advertising providers, while broadsheets acted as a means by which political elites communicated. Badsey, S., 'The Influence of the Media on Recent British Military Operations', in Stewart, I. and Carruthers, E. (eds) *War, Culture and the Media. Representations of the Military in 20th Century Britain*, Flicks Books, Wiltshire, 1996, p. 14.
44 Adie, 2003, op. cit. p. 263.
45 Taylor, P., 'The Military and the Media Past, Present and Future', in Badsey, 2000. op. cit. p. 191.
46 Taylor, P., 'The World Wide Web goes to War, Kosovo 1999', in Gauntlett, D., *Web Studies. Rewiring Media Studies for the Digital Age*, Arnold, London, 2000, p. 196.
47 Stewart, I., 'Reporting Conflict: Who Calls the Shots?', in Badsey, 2000, op. cit. pp. 72–3. Dr Ian Stewart is a Senior Lecturer in the Department of Communications Studies at the Royal Military Academy Sandhurst.
48 Bell, op. cit. p. 28.
49 During the Gulf War the Iraqis attacked the Saudi town of Khafji, taking many Westerners by surprise. The incident will be considered in the proceeding chapter.
50 Mould, D., 'Press Pools and Military-Media Relations in the Gulf War: A case study of Khafji, January 1991', *The Historical Journal of Film Radio and Television*, Vol. 16, No. 2, 1996, pp. 133–4. Professor David Mould is Director of Communication and Development Studies at the University of Ohio.
51 Bell, op. cit. p. 238.
52 Greenslade, R., 'Prejudice, Distortion and the Cult of Celebrity. Is the Press going to Hell in a Handcart?', *Inaugural Lecture at City University*, London, 22 January 2004. http://www.presswise.org.uk/display_page.php?id=656 (accessed 27/08/2004). Greenslade is Chair of Journalism at City University, London.
53 Ibid.
54 Adie, K., 'The Media Portrayal of the Military', in Badsey, 2000, op. cit. p. 52.

55 Ibid. pp. 55–6.
56 Adie, 2003, op. cit. p. 97.
57 *Daily Telegraph*, 15 February 1991, in Taylor, 1992, op. cit. p. 212.
58 Dobkin, B., 'Constructing News Narratives. ABC and CNN Cover the Gulf War' in Denton, R., *The Media and the Persian Gulf War*, Praeger Publishers, Westport, 1993, p. 115.
59 Shaw and Carr-Hill, 1991, op. cit. p. 11.
60 Shaw, M. and Carr-Hill, R., 'Public Opinion and Media War Coverage in Britain', in Mowlana, H., Gerber, G. and Schiller, H., *Triumph of the Image. The Media's War in the Persian Gulf – a Global Perspective*, Westview Press, Oxford, 1992, p. 154.

3 WAR AND THE *GREEN BOOK*

1 Hiro, D., *Desert Shield to Desert Storm. The Second Gulf War*, Paladin, London, 1992.
2 Abdul Karim Kassem led a military overthrow of the monarchy in July 1958. He became head of the new Republic but was himself overthrown and executed by the Ba'ath party in February 1963. For brief details, see *The Columbia Encyclopedia*, Sixth Edition, 2001, www.bartleby.com/65/ka/Kassem-A.html (accessed 6/08/2004).
3 In 1981, as the first major fighting occurred between Iraq and Iran the nominal price of oil per barrel stood at around $38 to $39. Between 1986 and 1989, the price fluctuated between around $11 and $19. The Iraqi invasion of Kuwait saw prices rise to around $32 to $33. Figures from the Energy Information Administration, www.eia.doe.gov/emeu/cabs/chron.html (accessed 3/09/2004).
4 United Nations Resolution 660 (1990), 2 August, www.un.org/Docs/scres/1990/scres90.htm (accessed 6/08/2004).
5 United Nations Resolution 661 (1990), 6 August, 3.c, www.un.org/Docs/scres/1990/scres90.htm (accessed 6/08/2004).
6 Ibid. 9.b.
7 United Nations Resolution 662 (1990), 9 August, 1, www.un.org/Docs/scres/1990/scres90.htm (accessed 6/08/2004).
8 United Nations Resolution 665 (1990), 25 August, 1, www.un.org/Docs/scres/1990/scres90.htm (accessed 6/08/2004).
9 United Nations Resolutions 664 (1990), 18 August, was the first example. Subsequent Resolutions such as 666 (1990), 13 September, then made reference to these requests. www.un.org/Docs/scres/1990/scres90.htm (accessed 6/08/2004).
10 United Nations Resolution 667 (1990), 16 September, www.un.org/Docs/scres/1990/scres90.htm (accessed 6/08/2004).
11 The presentation of such conciliatory attempts will be examined in Chapter 6.
12 United Nations Resolution 678 (1990), 29 November, www.un.org/Docs/scres/1990/scres90.htm (accessed 6/08/2004).
13 Desert Shield and Desert Storm refer to the American codenames for the phases during the conflict. Desert Shield began in September 1990 as forces were deployed in Saudi Arabia on defensive terms in an attempt to halt further advances by Iraq. Desert Storm refers to the commencement of air offensives against Iraq from 16 January 1991. The lesser-known term, Operation Desert Sabre, refers to the initiation and completion of the ground war phase, which began on 24 February 1991. For the British these events fell under the title Operation Granby.

14 In fact, the numbers of troops periodically reported in the media far exceed this figure and often failed to distinguish between total Iraqi numbers and the strength of forces actually present in Kuwait.

15 Taylor, P., *War and the Media. Propaganda and Persuasion in the Gulf War*, Manchester University Press, 1998, p. X.

16 During the Falklands War, the British military were in the position of being able to control the flow of news back to Britain. The geographical location of the islands and the limits of transmission technology meant that journalists' copy was often seriously delayed. The British also controlled the war zone and only allowed journalists from the United Kingdom to accompany its forces. For a discussion of these issues and the personal accounts of reporters operating under these conditions see: Knightley, P., *The First Casualty. The War Correspondent as Hero and Myth-Maker from the Crimea to Kosovo*, Prion Books Limited, London, 2000. Hastings, M., *Going To The Wars*, Pan Books, London, 2001. Eddy, P., Linklater, M. and Gillman, P., *The Falklands War*, Sphere Books Limited, London, 1982. Fox, R., *Eyewitness Falklands. A Personal Account of the Falklands Campaign*, Methuen, London, 1982.

17 For figures and a discussion of the issue see Shaw, M. and Carr-Hill, R., *Public Opinion, Media and Violence. Attitudes to the Gulf War in a Local Population*, University of Hull, 1999.

18 Hudson, M. and Stainer, J., *War and the Media. A Random Searchlight*, Sutton Publishing, Gloucestershire, 1999, p. 209.

19 For a discussion of the development of this myth and a history of Kosovo see Leurdijk, D. and Zandee, D., *Kosovo. From Crisis to Crisis*, Ashgate Publishing Limited, Aldershot, 2001.

20 For an online version of the Dayton Agreement, A/50/790, see http://ods-dds-ny.un.org/doc/UNDOC/GEN/N95/380/71/IMG/N9538071.pdf?Open Element (accessed 6/08/2004).

21 Abrahams, F., 'Humanitarian Law Violations in Kosovo', Human Rights Watch, New York, 1998.

22 Ignatieff, M., *Virtual War. Kosovo and Beyond*, Vintage, London, 2001, p. 13.

23 United Nations Security Resolution 1160 (1998), 31 March, 8. www.un.org/Docs/scres/1998/scres98.htm (accessed 6/08/2004).

24 United Nations Security Resolution 1199 (1998), 23 September, www.un.org/Docs/scres/1998/scres98.htm (accessed 6/08/2004).

25 United Nations Security Resolution 1203 (1998), 24 October, www.un.org/Docs/scres/1998/scres98.htm (accessed 6/08/2004).

26 United Nations, 'Security Council Statement S/PRST/1999/2', 19 January 1999, www.un.org/Docs/sc/statements/1999/sprst99.htm (accessed 6/08/2004).

27 For a discussion of these talks, see Chapter 6.

28 The G8 consists of: Canada, France, Germany, Italy, Japan, Russia, United Kingdom and United States. The group was established to meet regularly and discuss world issues.

29 Bennett, C., E-mail correspondence with author, 15 April 2002.

30 New Labour, *Britain Deserves Better*, Election 1997 Manifesto, www.psr.keele.ac.uk/area/uk/man/lab97.htm (accessed 29/07/2004).

31 Cook, R., 'Robin Cook's Speech on the Government's Ethical Foreign Policy', *Guardian Unlimited*, http://www.guardian.co.uk/indonesia/Story/0%2C2763%2C190889%2C00.html (accessed 6/08/2004). The other three goals were: security for all nations, prosperity for Britain and the maintenance of quality of life in Britain.

32 Gelbard, R., quoted in Shenon, P., 'U.S. Says it Might Consider Attacking Serbs', *The New York Times*, 13 March 1998, p. 10.
33 Amnesty International, *Kosovo. The Evidence*, Amnesty International, London, 1998.
34 United Nations Security Resolution 1160, www.un.org/Docs/scres/1998/scres98. htm (accessed 19/08/2004).
35 Shinoda, H., 'The Politics of Legitimacy in International Relations. The Case of NATO's Intervention in Kosovo', http://www.theglobalsite.ac.uk/press/ 010shinoda.htm (accessed 6/08/2004).
36 Solano, J., 'NATO Press Release', 23 March 1999, (99) 40, www.nato.int/docu/ pr/pr99e.htm (accessed 6/08/2004).
37 Tony Blair, Hansard Debates, House of Commons, 29 March 1999, Vol. 328.
38 Benn, T., 29 March 1999, ibid.
39 Dalyell, T., 31 March 1999, ibid.
40 Chomsky, N., *The New Military Humanism. Lessons from Kosovo*, Pluto Press, London, 1999.
41 Hammond, P., 'Reporting 'Humanitarian' Warfare: Propaganda, Moralism and NATO's Kosovo War', *Journalism Studies*, Vol. 1, No. 3, August 2000a, http:// myweb.lsbu.ac.uk/~hammonpb/2000b.html (accessed 6/08/2004). At the time of writing this thesis Philip Hammond was Senior Lecturer in Media, London South Bank University.
42 Malcolm, N., *Kosovo. A Short History*, Papermac, London, 1998.
43 Ignatieff, M., op. cit, p. 192.
44 Taylor, P., 'WWW1. Kosovo – the First Internet War' in Gauntlett, D. (ed.), *Web Studies. Rewiring Media Studies for the Digital Age*, Arnold, London, 2000, p. 196.
45 Brivio, E., 'Soundbites and Irony. NATO Information is Made in London', in Goff, P. and Trionfi, B. (eds), *The Kosovo News and Propaganda War*, International Press Institute, Vienna, 1999, p. 516. At the time of writing this thesis, Enrico Brivio was the President of the International Press Association.
46 Chomsky, N., 'The Media and The War. What War?' in Mowlana, H., Gerbner, G. and Schiller, H. (eds), *Triumph of the Image. The Media's War in the Persian Gulf – A Global Perspective*, Westview Press, Oxford, 1992, p. 54.
47 Badsey, S., 'The Influence of the Media on Recent British Military Operations', in Stewart, I. and Carruthers, S. (eds), *War, Culture and the Media. Representations of the Military in 20th Century Britain*, Flicks Books, Wiltshire, 1996.
48 Harris, R., *Gotcha! The Media, the Government and the Falklands Crisis*, Faber and Faber, London, 1983, p. 26. For more information regarding the Falklands and the media see Adams, V., *The Media and the Falklands Campaign*, Macmillan, Basingstoke, 1986, and Morrison, D. and Tumber, H., *Journalists at War. The Dynamics of News Reporting during the Falklands Conflict*, Sage, London, 1988.
49 Ibid. p. 16.
50 For discussion on the structure of the news system during the Gulf, see Taylor, 1998, op. cit., pp. 51–9.
51 Tony Matthews, of the MOD's D News Projects, has stated that the *Green Book* as a single, uniform, monograph was not in place during the Gulf War. However, he does state that the press regulations 'would largely have been those within the Green Book'. Interestingly, he also states that the details of the media guidelines during the Gulf War had not been retained. Thus, for the purposes of this discussion the *Green Book* will form the basis for the analysis of media restrictions

in both of the conflicts assessed herein. Correspondence with the author, 5 April 2002.

52 MOD, *Green Book. Working Arrangements with the Media in Times of Emergency, Tension, Conflict or War*, www.mod.uk/news/green_book/foreword.htm (accessed 19/02/2002).

53 Ibid. Main Text, Point Five, www.mod.uk/news/green_book/maintext.htm (accessed 19/02/2002).

54 Media Restrictions, found in Harris, op. cit., p. 26.

55 *Green Book*, op. cit. Annex A.

56 Ibid. Point 9, Main Text.

57 Ibid. Point 34, Main Text, For War Correspondents.

58 Ibid. Point 44, Main Text.

59 Ibid. Point 62, Main Text.

60 Ibid. Point 30, Main Text (emphasis from the original text).

61 Ibid. Point 51, Main Text (emphasis from the original text).

62 Ibid. Point 16, Main Text.

63 Ibid. Point 57, Main Text.

64 Ibid. Point 18, Main Text.

65 Ibid. Point 43, Main Text.

66 Ibid. Point 41, Main Text.

67 Ibid. Point 52, Main Text.

68 Ibid. Point 68, Main Text.

69 Ibid. Point 66, Main Text.

70 Adie, K., in Taylor, P., *War and the Media. Propaganda and Persuasion in the Gulf War*, Manchester University Press, 1992, p. 54.

4 UNCENSORED NEWS, CRITICAL DEBATE?

1 Robins, K., Webster, F. and Pickering, M., 'Propaganda, Information and Social Control', in Hawthorn, J. (ed.), *Propaganda, Persuasion and Polemic*, Edward Arnold Ltd, London, 1987, p. 16.

2 Riddell, P., *Parliament under Blair*, Politico's Publishing, London, 2000, p. 160.

3 Tunstall, J., *Newspaper Power. The New National Press in Britain*, Clarendon Press, Oxford, 1996, p. 1.

4 Robinson, P., 'The Policy-Media Interaction Model. Measuring Media Power during Humanitarian Crisis', *Journal of Peace Research*, Vol. 37, No. 5, 2000.

5 Waldegrave, W., quoted in Michael Knipe, 'British Nurse Freed by Iraq after Kaunda Plea', *The Times*, 17 July 1990, p. 22.

6 Boseley, S. and Taylor, B., 'Daphne Parish Freed by Iraq', *The Guardian*, 17 July 1990, p. 20.

7 Butcher, T. and Muir, J., 'Iraq Frees Nurse after Kaunda Plea', *The Daily Telegraph*, 17 July 1990, p. 1.

8 Teimourian, H., 'Saddam poised to set Iraq on new Political Course', *The Times*, 17 July 1990, p. 13.

9 Hinchcliffe, P. quoted in Victor, P. and Chimbano, C., 'Kaunda Blames Bazoft Death on Britain', *The Times*, 18 July 1990, p. 1.

10 Editorial, 'Beyond the Pale', *The Daily Telegraph*, 19 July 1990, p. 14.

11 Teimourian, H., 'Saddam Launches Attack on his Arab Creditors', *The Times*, 18 July 1990, p. 10.

12 Teimourian, H., 'Iraq Accuses Kuwait of Plundering Key Oilfield', *The Times*, 19 July 1990, p. 11.

13 McEwan, A., 'Experts believe Iraq will stop short of Invasion' and 'Saddam Rhetoric "May Lead to War"', *The Times*, 26 July 1990, p. 9.

14 Hirst, D., 'Kuwait seeks Arab backing in Propaganda War with Iraq', *The Guardian*, 20 July 1990, p. 12.

15 Pugh, D. and Tisdall, S., 'Iraq Masses Troops', *The Guardian*, 25 July 1990, p. 1.

16 Davies, N., 'Iraq's Troops "Won't Budge"', *Daily Mirror*, 26 July 1990, p. 4.

17 Walker, C., 'Fears Rise in Gulf as Iraq "Big Brother" Rattles Sabre', *The Times*, 25 July 1990, p. 11.

18 Bird, C., 'British Monitor Wounded in Kosovo', *The Guardian*, 16 January 1999, p. 16.

19 Black, Ian, 'Serbs Dare West to Raise the Stakes', *The Guardian*, 19 January 1999, p. 13.

20 Editorial, 'Last Resorts', *The Times*, 19 January 1999, p. 23.

21 Editorial, 'Killing Zone', *The Daily Telegraph*, 18 January 1999, p. 21.

22 Wood, M., 'We'll Bomb Serbs', *The Sun*, 20 January 1999, p. 2.

23 Theodoulou, M. and McEwen, A., 'Iraqi Invasion Angers both East and West', *The Times*, 3 August 1990, p. 1.

24 Hirst, D., 'Superpowers Unite on Iraq', *The Guardian*, 3 August 1990, p. 1.

25 Bishop, B., 'Superpowers Unite against Iraq', *The Daily Telegraph*, 3 August 1990, p. 1.

26 McEwen, A., 'Tougher Sanctions set to follow International Outrage', *The Times*, 3 August 1990, p. 2.

27 Thatcher, M., in McEwen, A. and Gumicio, J., 'UN agrees on Mandatory Iraq Sanctions', *The Times*, 6 August 1990, p. 1.

28 O'Brien, C., 'Why Bush is Treating Kuwait as a Modern Pearl Harbour', *The Times*, 9 August 1990, p. 12.

29 Fieldhouse, Lord, 'Press Role in Time of Crisis', *The Times*, 11 August 1990, p. 11. This letter was followed underneath by one from the chairman of the Green Party that sought to confirm that not everyone was behind military intervention.

30 Thurgood, L., 'A Ruthless and Brutal Operator', *The Guardian*, 3 August 1990, p. 2.

31 Comment, 'Halt this Monster Now', *Daily Mirror*, 3 August 1990, p. 2.

32 Solomans, M., '20p. Petrol Prices set to Soar as the Baghdad Beast Seizes Kuwait', *The Sun*, 3 August 1990, p. 1. Kavanagh, T. and Kay, J., 'He's got the Oil World in his Hands', *The Sun*, 3 August 1990, p. 2.

33 Bishop, P., 'We can do Nothing for Kosovo', *The Daily Telegraph*, 19 January 1999, p. 22.

34 Parris, M., 'Apoplexy Passes for Action where Kosovo is Concerned', *The Times*, 19 January 1999, p. 2.

35 Editorial, 'Last Resorts', *The Times*, 19 January 1999, p. 23.

36 Jenkins, S., 'Big Bang Theorist', *The Times*, 20 January 1999, p. 18.

37 Evans, M., 'Europe Vetoes US Ultimatum to Milosevic', *The Times*, 25 January 1999, p. 11.

38 Editorial, 'Gladstone's Shade. Why Kosovo? Why British Troops? Blair Must Explain', *The Times*, 3 February 1999, p. 17.

39 Loyd, A., 'Massacre Bodies become Pawns in Propaganda War', *The Times*, 5 February 1999, p. 17.

40 Woollacott, M., 'Showdown with the Killer', *The Guardian*, 19 January 1999, p. 16.

41 Routledge, P., 'Why Kosovo is not Worth the Life of a Single British Squaddie', *Daily Mirror*, 19 January 1999, p. 2.

42 Editorial, 'Stamp out the Butcher of Kosovo', *Daily Mirror*, 19 January 1999, p. 6.
43 'Nato Warns Serb Beast', *The Sun*, 18 January 1999, p. 2.
44 Routledge, P., 'Crisis in Kosovo. It is not our Fight', *Daily Mirror*, 24 March 1999, p. 5.
45 Robinson, op. cit.
46 Tunstall, op. cit.

5 THE FIVE THEMES OF CONFLICT PROPAGANDA

1 Doob, L., *Public Opinion and Propaganda*, Archon Books, Hamden, Connecticut, 1966, p. 72.
2 Ibid.
3 Ellul, J., *Propaganda. The Formation of Men's Attitudes*, Vintage Books, New York, 1973, p. 93.
4 Lasswell, H., 'The Theory of Political Propaganda', *The American Political Science Review*, Vol. 21, No. 3, August 1927, p. 627.
5 Day, J., 'MOD Briefing', 1 April 1999, www.kosovo.mod.uk/brief010499.htm (accessed 17/05/04).
6 Cook, R., 'MOD Briefing', 13 April 1999, Cook, R., 'MOD Briefing', 11 April 1999, Henderson, D., 'MOD Briefing', 18 April 1999, www.kosovo.mod.uk (accessed 17/05/04). Mr Doug Henderson was the Minister for the Armed Forces.
7 Pascoe-Watson, G. and Parker, N., 'Clobba Slobba', *The Sun*, 25 March 1999, p. 1.
8 Editorial, 'Containing War', *The Times*, 17 January 1991, p. 13.
9 Editorial, 'Deadlock in Geneva', *The Times*, 10 January 1991, p. 13.
10 Extract from Bush speech, 'Bush Tells America why the Waiting had to turn to Battle', *The Daily Telegraph*, 18 January 1991, p. 5.
11 Bird, C., 'Wily Ruler who Thrives on Political Turmoil', *The Guardian*, 24 March 1999, p. 2.
12 Kettle, M., Brummer, A., Bird, C. and O'Kane, M., 'Serb TV Bombed off the Air', *The Guardian*, 23 April 1999, pp. 1–2.
13 Editorial, 'In a Just Cause', *The Times*, 13 August 1990, p. 11.
14 Editorial, 'Democracy Expects', *The Times*, 18 August 1990, p. 11.
15 Thurgood, L., 'A Ruthless and Brutal Operator', *The Guardian*, 3 August 1990, p. 2.
16 Tisdall, S., 'Kuwait Pays the Price for False US Signals to Iraq', *The Guardian*, 3 August 1990, p. 3.
17 Becker, J., 'Baghdad and the Blind Eyes', *The Guardian*, 2 November 1990, p. 9.
18 Woollacott, M., 'Saddam's Words fall on Ready Ears', *The Guardian*, 11 August 1990, p. 1.
19 Comment, 'Paying the Price for Past Error', *The Guardian*, 3 August 1990, p. 16.
20 It is notable though that those countries named for criticism do not include either the United States or Great Britain, although France, a traditionally frosty ally, and the Soviet Union, the old Cold-War enemy, are both mentioned.
21 Comment, 'Choosing the Best Option', *The Guardian*, 6 August 1990, p. 18.
22 Comment, 'Getting Restless in the Gulf', *The Guardian*, 6 November 1990, p. 20.

23 Comment, 'Beyond the Clash of Desert Shields', *The Guardian*, 16 November 1990, p. 22.
24 Young, H., 'Brutal Price that has to be Paid', *The Guardian*, 15 January 1991, p. 19.
25 Comment, 'Power, in the First Few Days', *The Guardian*, 18 January 1991, p. 20.
26 Chomsky, N., 'The Media and the War: What War?', in Mowlana, H., Gerbner, G. and Schiller, H. (eds), *Triumph of the Image. The Media's War in the Persian Gulf – A Global Perspective*, Westview Press, Oxford, 1992, p. 54.
27 Editorial, 'No Soft Options', *The Times*, 4 September 1990, p. 11. Given the newspaper's traditional right-leaning political inclination this criticism of Liberal policy and backing of the Conservative agenda seems wholly understandable.
28 United Nations Resolution 670 reaffirmed previous resolutions and banned sanction-busting flights to and from Iraq.
29 Editorial, 'The Mood Hardens', *The Times*, 27 September 1990, p. 13.
30 Editorial, 'Boycott this Brutal Tyrant', *The Sun*, 2 August 1990, p. 6.
31 Editorial, 'No Hiding Place', *The Sun*, 24 September 1990, p. 6.
32 Comment, 'If War Comes', *Daily Mirror*, 9 August 1990, p. 2.
33 Keegan, J., 'How are we to Stop the March of this Madman?', *The Daily Telegraph*, 4 August 1990, p. 10.
34 For examples see Kaldor, M., 'Bombs Away! But to Save Civilians we must get in some Soldiers', *The Guardian*, 25 March 1999, p. 18, Editorial, 'Defeating Milosevic', *The Guardian*, 25 March 1999, p. 19 and Editorial, 'Rescue the Kosovans', *The Guardian*, 1 April 1999, p. 23.
35 Editorial, 'Nato and Kosovo', *The Times*, 24 March 1999, p. 21.
36 Editorial, 'Clear Targets', *The Times*, 14 April 1999, p. 19.
37 Editorial, 'Half Measures are not Enough', *The Daily Telegraph*, 3 April 1999, p. 25.
38 For example see Editorial, 'Time to Act', *The Sun*, 24 March 1999, p. 8. Perkins, K., 'This Time we Hold Back at our Peril', *The Sun*, 25 March 1999, p. 6. Major General Ken Perkins was *The Sun's* military adviser.
39 Editorial (entitled The Sun Speaks its Mind), 'Don't Send our Troops off to Die', *The Sun*, 5 April 1999, p. 1.
40 Ibid.
41 Editorial, 'Whatever it Takes . . . We Must do it', *Daily Mirror*, 8 April 1999, p. 6.
42 Editorial, 'Nato Must Never let up on Milosevic', *Daily Mirror*, 12 April 1999, p. 6.
43 Editorial, 'Send in the Troops to End Horror', *Daily Mirror*, 14 April 1999, p. 6.
44 Editorial, (entitled Voice of the Mirror), 'Time to Send in Troops', *Daily Mirror*, 23 April 1999, p. 1.
45 Greenslade, R., '*The Sun's* War. A New Britain, A New Kind of Newspaper', *The Guardian*, 25 February 2002, G2 p. 12.
46 Ibid.
47 For example see, Editorial, 'Rebel MPs are Right to Cry Peace', *Daily Mirror*, 26 February 2003, p. 6. Editorial, 'Don't Attack Iraq, Take on North Korea', *Daily Mirror*, 6 March 2003, p. 8. Editorial, 'Don't Drag us into an Illegal War', *Daily Mirror*, 14 March 2003, p. 6.
48 No author cited, 'Countdown to War. Our Front-Line Fact-Finders', *Daily Mirror*, 18 March 2003, p. 15. Editorial, 'He's let us Down . . . He Never Will', *Daily Mirror*, 18 March 2003, pp. 2–3.

49 Editorial, 'Toughest Time is still ahead, PM', *Daily Mirror*, 6 May 2003, p. 10.
50 Ibid.
51 Editorial, 'Sweet Dreams', *The Sun*, 23 April 1999, p. 8 (emphasis from the original text).
52 Ellul, op. cit. p. 38n.
53 Kay, J., '20 Things you didn't know about Butcher of Baghdad', *The Sun*, 3 August 1990, p. 3.
54 Kavanagh, T. and Pascoe-Watson, G., 'Beginning of the End', *The Sun*, 4 June 1999, p. 2.
55 Editorial (by *The Sun* foreign desk), 'Day Saddam Beat Minister to Death', *The Sun*, 5 October 1990, p. 6 (emphasis from the original text).
56 Traynor, I., 'A Talent for Playing with Fire', *The Guardian*, 27 March 1999, p. 5.
57 Reicher, S., 'Running with the Mad Dog', *The Guardian*, 2 February 1991, p. 23. Dr Stephen Reicher was, at the time of the article, Lecturer in Psychology at Exeter University.
58 Theodoulou, M., 'Gulf Tension Rises after Iraq Breaks Off Talks', *The Times*, 2 August 1990, p. 11.
59 Butt, G. and Gribben, R., 'Oil Prices Jump as Iraq – Kuwait Talks Collapse', *The Daily Telegraph*, 2 August 1990, p. 1.
60 Pascoe-Watson, G., 'Raging Fool', *The Sun*, 17 January 1991, p. 7.
61 Kavanagh, T., 'Drunk Slobba', *The Sun*, 26 March 1999, pp. 6–7.
62 Bishop, P., 'Milosevic has a Taste of his own Medicine', *The Daily Telegraph*, 24 March 1999, p. 5.
63 Russell, A., 'Inhuman Logic behind Milosevic's Brutalities puts the Region at Risk', *The Daily Telegraph*, 7 April 1999, p. 6.
64 Mullin, J., 'Saddam "Under Pressure" on TV', *The Guardian*, January 30 1991, p. 2.
65 Such associations with Hitler were also visible in the aftermath of both crises and at times cited by senior figures within the Western establishment. Richard Butler, for example, was leader of the UN Special Commission from July 1997 and has recorded the UN attempts to disarm Saddam Hussein. In this text Butler compares Iraq with Nazi Germany and stresses the similarities between Hussein and Hitler's infamy for using chemical weapons. See Butler, R., *The Greatest Threat. Iraq, Weapons of Mass Destruction and the Crisis of Global Security*, Public affairs, New York, 2000, p. viii and p. xv.
66 Bishop, P., 'Proof of Hitlerian Determination', *The Daily Telegraph*, 3 August 1990, p. 2.
67 Written by 'Our Foreign Staff', 'Press Joins Governments in Condemning "Hitler of Baghdad"', *The Daily Telegraph*, 4 August 1990, p. 2.
68 Brodie, I., 'Bush Warns US to be Prepared for Sacrifices', *The Daily Telegraph*, 21 August 1990, p. 1.
69 Hepburn, I., 'How the 2 Hitlers Compare', *The Sun*, 4 August 1990, pp. 4–5.
70 It is interesting to note that *The Sun* had no reservations about using the positive connotations of the word *blitzkrieg*, possibly because of its swift and efficient connotation. In predicting the impending allied air war against Iraq, the newspaper claimed: 'A third of the blitzkrieg force will be devoted to smashing tarmac roads linking Iraqi soldiers to the front'. Hall, A., '96 Hours to Wipe 'Em Out', *The Sun*, 11 January 1991, p. 2.
71 Comment, 'Halt this Monster Now', *Daily Mirror*, 3 August 1990, p. 2 (emphasis from the original text).

72 Butcher, T., 'The First 50 Days of Lost Opportunities', *The Daily Telegraph*, 12 May 1999, p. 14. In this quotation the newspaper has drawn the distinction between ethnic cleansing and the actual execution of Kosovo Albanians. Ethnic cleansing is often used simply as a blanket term for the execution, rather than the removal, of the Albanian population in much of the press.

73 Robertson, G., 'MOD Briefing', 19 April 1999, www.kosovo.mod.uk/brief190499.htm (accessed 17/05/2004). George Robertson was Secretary of State for Defence.

74 Cook, R., 'MOD Briefing', 13 April 1999, www.kosovo.mod.uk/brief130499.htm (accessed 17/05/2004).

75 Editorial, 'Cause for which the West is ready to fight', *The Daily Telegraph*, 15 January 1991, p. 16

76 Hastings, M., 'After the War: How', *The Daily Telegraph*, 25 February 1991, p. 18.

77 Editorial, 'Uniting for Peace', *The Times*, 7 August 1990, p. 11.

78 Howard, M., 'Gulf: No Time for Sanctions To Bite', *The Times*, 2 January 1991, p. 10.

79 Boyes, R., 'Five Easy Steps to Dictatorship', *The Times*, 24 April 1999, p. 20.

80 Editorial, 'Last Resorts', *The Times*, 19 January 1999, p. 23.

81 Editorial, 'War Crimes', *The Sun*, 2 April 1999, p. 8.

82 Editorial, 'Save these Victims from Tyrant's Evil', *Daily Mirror*, 31 March 1999, p. 6.

83 Comment, 'If War Comes', *Daily Mirror*, 3 August 1990, p. 2

84 Ibid.

85 Brodie, I., 'Chill Memory of being Shot Down Haunts President', *The Daily Telegraph*, 18 January 1991, p. 5.

86 Editorial, 'Rulers of the Sky', *The Sun*, 18 January 1991, p. 6.

87 Ibid.

88 Littlejohn, R., 'Let Baghdad go to Iraq and Ruin!', *The Sun*, 11 February 1991, p. 6.

89 United Nations, *Geneva Convention Relative to the Protection of Civilian Persons in Time of War*, Article 3, www.unhchr.ch/html/menu3/b/92.htm (accessed 25/5/2004).

90 Sanders, M and Taylor, P., *British Propaganda during the First World War, 1914–1918*, The Macmillan Press Ltd, London, 1982, p. 162.

91 Henderson, D., 'MOD Briefing', 18 April 1999, www.kosovo.mod.uk/brief180499.htm (accessed 17/05/2004).

92 Robertson, G., 'MOD Briefing', 19 April 1999, www.kosovo.mod.uk/brief190499.htm (accessed 17/05/2004).

93 Henderson, D., 'MOD Briefing', 30 April 1999, www.kosovo.mod.uk/brief300499.htm (accessed 17/05/2004).

94 Ellul, J., op. cit. p. 212.

95 The reference to premeditated action is in line with British assumptions concerning guilt in the legal process. The existence of a demonstrable premeditated action implies the greater culpability and the legitimacy of tougher sanctions.

96 Comment (open letter from *The Sun* to our troops at war), 'Why We Support You', *The Sun*, 1 April 1999, p. 8 (emphasis from the original text).

97 Lader, P., 'It would have Happened Anyway', *The Daily Telegraph*, 27 April 1999, p. 22.

98 Walker, C., 'Allied Pilots Queue up for "Turkey Shoot" in the Desert', *The Times*, 2 February 1991, p. 3.

99 Kavanagh, T. and Parker, N., '300 Iraqis Die in Tank Blitz', *The Sun*, 31 January 1991, p. 1.
100 Parker, N. and Lee-Potter, A., 'We Spank their Tanks', *The Sun*, 7 April 1999, p. 4
101 Ibid.
102 Sanders and Taylor, op. cit. p. 137.
103 Laurence, C., 'A Reign of Terror and of Torture', *The Daily Telegraph*, 2 November 1990, p. 17.
104 Laurence, C., 'What have they done to Kuwait?', *The Daily Telegraph*, 2 November 1990, p. 17.
105 Lederer, E., 'Doctors tell of Iraqi Murderers of Infants', *The Guardian*, 12 November 1990, p. 10.
106 Tisdall, S., 'Kuwaitis Bear Army Terror', *The Guardian*, 7 February 1991, p. 2.
107 For a discussion of propaganda during the First World War see: Ponsonby, A., *Falsehood in Wartime. Propaganda Lies of the First World War*, Institute for Historical Research, California, 1991. Sanders and Taylor, op. cit.
108 Botton, A., 'We will Fight them on the Airwaves', *The Daily Telegraph*, 26 May 1999, p. 26.
109 Loyd, A. and di Giovanni, J., 'Serbs on Murder Spree', *The Times*, 27 March 1999, p. 1 (Emphasis from the original text).
110 Kiley, S., 'Serbs make Rape a Weapon of War', *The Times*, 6 April 1999, p. 2.
111 Foreign Staff article, 'Women Kidnapped, Raped and Tortured by Soldiers, says UN', *The Daily Telegraph*, 26 May 1999, p. 16.
112 Smucker, P., 'My Mother Died Screaming in my Lap as we Fled across Icy Mountains', *The Daily Telegraph*, 13 April 1999, p. 10.
113 Askill, J., 'Kiddies Shot like Rabbits', *The Sun*, 7 May 1999, p. 7.
114 Arnold, H., 'Tide of Tears', *Daily Mirror*, 30 March 1999, p. 4.
115 Walker, M. and Pick, H., 'Baghdad Calls for Negotiations', *The Guardian*, 1 November 1990, p. 8.
116 Traynor, I. and Steele, J., 'Nightmare of Sealed Trains Returns', *The Guardian*, 1 April 1999, p. 3 (emphasis from the original text).
117 Editorial, 'Displaced People', *The Guardian*, 26 May 1999, p. 19.
118 Editorial, 'Folly and Madness', *The Guardian*, 5 April 1999, p. 15.
119 Ibid.
120 Flynn, B., 'Nazis 1999', *The Sun*, 1 April 1999, p. 6.
121 Comment (open letter from *The Sun* to our troops at war), 'Why We Support You', *The Sun*, 1 April 1999, p. 8. (Emphasis from the original text).
122 Dowdney, M., '1939 or 1999?', *Daily Mirror*, 1 April 1999, p. 1.
123 Drewienkiewicz, J., 'MOD Briefing', 1 April 1999. www.kosovo.mod.uk/brief010499.htm (accessed 17/05/2004).
124 Hammond, P., 'Moral Combat. Advocacy Journalists and the New Humanitarianism', www.sbu.ac.uk/~hammondpb/2002.html (accessed 17/05/2004).
125 Downdney, M., 'Sad's Army is a Total Shambles', *Daily Mirror*, 22 August 1990, p. 5.
126 Harvey, R., 'Saddam's Big Gun Misfires', *The Daily Telegraph*, 6 August 1990, p. 16.
127 Armitage, M., 'Will the Iraqis put up a Fight', *The Times*, 16 January 1991, p. 18.
128 Major, J., Hansard, House of Commons Debates, 17 January 1991, Vol. 183.
129 Evans, M., 'West Stunned by Enormous Scale of Iraqi Fighting Machine', *The Times*, 12 February 1991, p. 2.

130 Perkins, K., 'This Time we Hold Back at our Peril', *The Sun*, 25 March 1999, p. 6.
131 The Maginot Line was the French system of static fortifications, built along her border to protect France from invasion. The Line was widely criticized for its purely defensive nature. Furthermore, its depth and length were greatly exaggerated and these deficiencies were only truly exposed publicly when France fell swiftly to the Germans in 1940.
132 For a discussion of the Maginot Line's influence on British wartime propaganda see Willcox, D., 'The Maginot Line and British Propaganda', Unpublished MA Dissertation, University of Kent at Canterbury, 2000.
133 Fairhall, D., 'Western Military Planners put Feet back on the Ground', *The Guardian*, 24 November 1990, p. 9 and Fairhall, D. and Becker, J., 'Warriors in the Desert', *The Guardian*, 14 January 1991, p. 24.
134 Evans, M., 'Saddam's Maginot Line can be Broken', *The Times*, 24 November 1990, p. 9.
135 Ibid.
136 Evans, M., 'Quick Surge through Obstacles is Vital', *The Times*, 23 February 1991, p. 24.
137 Khafji is a port-town inside Saudi Arabia, which had largely been abandoned due to the crisis. An Iraqi incursion on 29 January 1991 took allied defences by surprise and the attackers were able to hold the town for a considerable amount of time, the newspapers widely reported the figure of 36 hours.
138 Walker, C., 'Strategists Mull over Unexpected Twist in Script', *The Times*, 1 February 1991, p. 2.
139 Evans, M. and Walker, C., 'Iraqi Onslaught Blunted', *The Times*, 2 February 1991, p. 1.
140 Editorial, 'Saddam's Cunning', *The Daily Telegraph*, 1 February 1991, p. 18.
141 Ibid.
142 Ibid.
143 King, J., 'Confusion in the Battle for Khafji', *The Guardian*, 2 February 1991, p. 3.
144 Fairhall, D., Norton-Taylor, R. and Agencies, 'Fresh Tanks Mass as Battles Rage in Saudi Arabia', *The Guardian*, 31 January 1991, p. 1.
145 King, J., 'Confusion in the Battle for Khafji', *The Guardian*, 2 February 1991, p. 3.
146 Walker, M. and Fairhall, D., 'Iraqis Mass for Surge South', *The Guardian*, 1 February 1991, p. 1.
147 Evans, M. and Walker, C., 'Iraqi Onslaught Blunted', *The Times*, 2 February 1991, p. 1.
148 Blanco White, A., *The New Propaganda*, Victor Gollancz Ltd, London, 1939, p. 67.
149 Sanders and Taylor, op. cit. p. 207.
150 Editorial, 'Shades of Suez', *The Times*, 1 January 1991, p. 9.
151 Editorial, 'Europe's Clear Duty', *The Daily Telegraph*, 4 January 1991, p. 16.
152 Comment, 'If War Comes', *Daily Mirror*, 9 August 1990, p. 2 (all emphasis from the original text).
153 Teimourian, H., 'Despot in the Babylonian Tradition, *The Times*, 13 August 1990, p. 10.
154 Comment, 'Mirror Comment', *Daily Mirror*, 15 January 1991, p. 4 (words in brackets added; emphasis from the original text).
155 Editorial, 'No Choice but War', *The Times*, 16 January 1991, p. 19.
156 Ibid.

157 Blair, T., 'Blair sees New World Order in Kosovo Conflict', *The Times*, 12 April 1999, p. 4.
158 Editorial, 'Realities on the Ground', *The Daily Telegraph*, 30 March 1999, p. 29.
159 Editorial, 'No Mercy for the Butcher of Kosovo', *Daily Mirror*, 24 March 1999, p. 6
160 Editorial, 'Evil Tyrant's Threat to all in Europe', *Daily Mirror*, 3 April 1999, p. 6.
161 Kavanagh, T., 'With True Moral Courage, Blair has Seized Control of NATO and Made Himself a Giant of the Free World', *The Sun*, 24 April 1999, p. 6.
162 Editorial, 'Scud Wars', *The Times*, 23 January 1991, p. 15.
163 Littlejohn, R., 'How Hi-Tech Spares Life', *The Sun*, 19 January 1991, p. 6 (emphasis from the original text).
164 Evans, M., 'NATO is Poised to Strike at the Heart of the Milosevic Regime', *The Times*, 1 April 1999, p. 2.
165 Walker, M. and Fairhall, D., 'Iraqis Mass for Surge South', *The Guardian*, 1 February 1991, p. 1.
166 Editorial, 'The Little Things that Mean a Lot', *The Guardian*, 1 February 1991, p. 18.
167 Hastings, M., 'Targeting the Force to Defeat Saddam Hussein', *The Daily Telegraph*, 8 January 1991, p. 14.
168 Evans, M., 'Precision Bombing sends Signal to Arab World', *The Times*, 19 January 1991, p. 2 and Editorial, 'Bombing Iraq', *The Times*, 5 February 1991, p. 11.
169 Editorial, 'Timing for Victory', *The Times*, 11 February 1991, p. 11.
170 On 13 February 1991 allied bombers struck a Baghdad shelter killing hundreds of civilians. The allies insisted that the installation was used for military purposes while the Iraqis claimed it was nothing more than a civil air-raid shelter.
171 Editorial, 'Direct Hit in Amiriya', *The Times*, 14 February 1991, p. 15.
172 Hastings, M., 'The Tragic Price to Pay for Defeating Saddam', *The Daily Telegraph*, 14 February 1991, p. 2.
173 Editorial, 'The Enemy within are a Menace', *The Sun*, 15 February 1991, p. 6.
174 Kavanagh, T., '10 Facts to Damn Hussein', *The Sun*, 14 February 1991, p. 1.
175 Editorial, 'Milosevic is to Blame', *The Daily Telegraph*, 15 April 1999, p. 27.
176 Editorial, 'The Moment NATO Feared', *The Guardian*, 16 April 1999, p. 19.
177 Ibid.
178 Ibid.
179 Ibid.
180 Farrell, S. and Ford, R., 'The Girls who Hope to find Peace in Britain', *The Times*, 24 April 1999, p. 1.
181 *The Times* did carry a critical article on the RTS bombing the following week, once any potential outrage had dissipated. The presentation and treatment of such views, including this article, will be dealt with in the next chapter.
182 Editorial, 'We Stand with Blair', *The Sun*, 24 April 1999, p. 8.
183 Editorial, 'Striking at the Tools of Evil Regime', *Daily Mirror*, 24 April 1999, p. 6.
184 Strauss, J., 'Serbs Gloomy but Defiant after Attack on Chinese Embassy', *The Daily Telegraph*, 10 May 1999, p. 4.
185 Editorial, 'Errors Play into Hands of a Tyrant', *Daily Mirror*, 10 May 1999, p. 6.
186 Solana, J., 'NATO Press Conference', 8 May 1999, www.nato.int/kosovo/press/p990508b.htm (accessed 17/05/2004).

187 Cook, R., 'MOD Briefing', 8 May 1999, www.kosovo.mod.uk/brief080599.htm (accessed 17/05/2004).
188 Ibid.
189 Shea, J., 'NATO Morning Briefing', 9 May 1999, www.nato.int/kosovo/press/b990509a.htm (accessed 17/05/2004). Jamie Shea was NATO's spokesman during the Kosovo Conflict.
190 Henderson, D., 'MOD Briefing', 9 May 1999, op. cit.
191 Comment, 'Mirror Comment', *Daily Mirror*, 18 January 1991, p. 4.
192 Schwarzkopf, N., quoted in article 'There is no way out of there', *The Daily Telegraph*, 28 February 1991, p. 2.
193 Ignatieff, M., *Virtual War. Kosovo and Beyond*, Vintage, London, 2001.
194 Ibid. p. 3.
195 The unnamed airmen are quoted in Coughlin, C., 'Pilots full of Praise for the Planes and the Planning', *The Daily Telegraph*, 18 January 1991, p. 3.
196 Airs, G., 'Geez! It's the Stormin' Norman Star Wars Video', *Daily Mirror*, 19 January 1991, p. 4 (emphasis from the original text).
197 No credited author, 'Who's Who in Wacky Racers, *The Sun*, 12 June 1999, p. 7.
198 Fouque, A., quoted in News in Brief, 'War Phallic', *The Guardian*, 14 February 1991, p. 2.
199 Keegan, J., 'Iraq Moves its Scud Missiles to Kuwait', *The Daily Telegraph*, 22 August 1990, p. 8
200 Keegan, J., 'This Time War will be like Nothing on Earth', *The Daily Telegraph*, 11 January 1991, p. 16.
201 Editorial, 'Crippling Saddam', *The Daily Telegraph*, 29 August 1990, p. 14.
202 Taylor, 1998, op. cit. p. 239.
203 Keegan, J., 'So the Bomber got through to Milosevic after all', *The Daily Telegraph*, 4 June 1999, p. 28.

6 PRESENTING ALTERNATIVE OPINIONS

1 Before the outbreak of the First World War, a Joint Standing Committee was established to facilitate cooperation between newspaper proprietors and the military and government. However, when war broke out the government was no longer willing to accept the notion of voluntary control, hence the emergence of D-Notices. For a discussion of these issues refer to Hopkin, D., 'Domestic Censorship In The First World War', *Journal of Contemporary History*, Vol. 5, No. 4, 1970, pp. 151–69.
2 Rosenblum, M., *Who Stole the News?: Why we can't keep up with what happens in the world and what we can do about it*, John Wiley & Sons Inc, New York, 1993, p. 128. At the time of publication Mort Rosenblum was a special correspondent for the Associated Press, based in Paris.
3 In 1993, the D-Notice system was renamed DA-Notice (Defence Advisory Notices). The present system consists of five standing notices covering the following issues: military operations, plans and capabilities; nuclear and non-nuclear weapons and equipment; ciphers and secure communications; sensitive installations and secure addresses; and finally United Kingdom security and intelligence services and special forces. For further information refer to http://www.dnotice.org.uk/index.htm (accessed 16/06/2004).
4 Lenman, B., *The Eclipse of Parliament. Appearance and Reality in British Politics since 1914*, Edward Arnold, London, 1992, p. 10.

5 The Mass Observation archive (hereafter MOA) at the University of Sussex is best known for the data collated throughout the Second World War. However, the MOA has continued to issue recent directives (the set of guidelines given to respondents that focus their attention on to specific issues and events), one of which solely dealt with the Gulf Crisis as it emerged and developed through 1990 and 1991, while the Kosovo conflict, significantly not meriting a directive of its own, was covered in a general 1999 directive. The information obtained is not representative of society; many of the contributors are elderly, female and middle-class. Furthermore, the respondents are volunteers and as such are in the position to have the time to respond to the directives and demonstrate a willingness to follow current affairs. These elements probably make the respondents more avid followers of current affairs than many members of the general public. However, it is a useful source to take into account when attempting to ascertain, at least from a limited perspective, attitudes towards crises as they were witnessed at the time.

6 The model devised by the pair sought to address the issues of US media behaviour and performance and is not focused on the effects of that behaviour. In short, the model was based upon the notion that the media are firmly embedded within the market system. This system imposes five filters through which information must pass; the five filters are: ownership, advertising, sourcing, flak and anticommunist ideology. Propaganda can then only be effective when it is consistent with the objectives of those controlling the filters. For further discussion of the model refer to Herman, E. and Chomsky, N., *Manufacturing Consent. The Political Economy of the Mass Media*, Pantheon, New York, 1988 and Herman, E., 'The Propaganda Model: A Retrospective', December 2003, www.chomsky.info/onchomsky/20031209.htm (accessed 10/06/2004).

7 Keeble, R., *The Gulf War Myth. A Study of the Press Coverage of the 1991 Gulf Conflict*, Unpublished PhD thesis, City University London, 1996. At the time of writing this chapter Richard Keeble was the Department of Journalism's Director of Research at City University, London.

8 Gowing, N., *Real-Time Television Coverage of Armed Conflicts and Diplomatic Crises. Does it Pressure or Distort Foreign Policy Decisions?* The Joan Shorenstein Barone Center on the Press, Politics and Public Policy, Harvard University, Working Paper 94-1, Cambridge, USA, 1994. When Gowing wrote this paper he was Diplomatic Editor for ITN's Channel Four News.

9 Ibid. p. 26.

10 Robinson, P., 'The Policy–Media Interaction Model. Measuring Media Power during Humanitarian Crisis', *Journal of Peace Research*, Vol. 37, No. 5, 2000, pp. 613–33.

11 Ibid. p. 630.

12 Bellamy, A., 'Reconsidering Rambouillet', *Contemporary Security Policy*, Frank Cass, London, Vol. 22, No. 1, April 2001, pp. 31–56. At the time of writing this article Bellamy was a Lecturer in Defence Studies for King's College London at the Joint Services Command and Staff College. Bellamy is currently a Lecturer in Peace and Conflict Studies, School of Political Science and International Studies at the University of Queensland, Australia.

13 Powell, E., 'A Crusade Built on Sand', *Daily Telegraph*, 19 January 1991, p. 15.

14 As well as global television networks the press is also represented by on-line editions of their newspapers. These websites allow global access to their opinions. The news stories are regularly updated and articles re-written to reflect

developments throughout the day and on occasions this shifts the interpretation of the opinions.

15 Hammond, P., 'Reporting "Humanitarian" Warfare: Propaganda, Moralism and NATO's Kosovo war', *Journalism Studies*, Vol. 1, No. 3, August 2000a, http://myweb.lsbu.ac.uk/~hammonpb/2000b.html (accessed 6/08/2004).

16 Badsey, S., 'The Media, the Military and Public Opinion', in Badsey, S. (ed.), *The Media and International Security*, Frank Cass Publishers, London, 2000, pp. 243–44.

17 Woollacott, M., 'Saddam's Words fall on Ready Ears', *The Guardian*, 11 August 1990, p. 1.

18 Comment, 'Up the Ante and up the Spout?', *The Guardian*, 27 October 1990, p. 26.

19 Editorial, 'Iraq's Naked Villainy', *The Times*, 3 August 1990, p. 11.

20 Almond, P., 'Naval Blockade Likely Reaction', *The Daily Telegraph*, 3 August 1990, p. 2.

21 Keegan, J., 'How are we to Stop the March of this Madman?', *The Daily Telegraph*, 4 August 1990, p. 10.

22 Editorial, 'Comment', *The Daily Telegraph*, 15 August 1990, p. 14.

23 Editorial, 'In a Just Cause', *The Times*, 13 August 1990, p. 11.

24 Ibid. p. 11.

25 Ibid. p. 11.

26 Woollacott, M., 'Setting up Saddam', *The Guardian*, 9 August 1990, p. 17.

27 Fletcher, M., 'Gap Widens between US Rhetoric and the Realities', *The Times*, 18 August 1990, p. 2.

28 The just war theory is traditionally a Christian concept and expounded by Saint Thomas Aquinas. The theory seeks to identify both justifications for going to war and permissible actions once engaged in conflict. For an overview see Moseley, A., 'Just War Theory', The Internet Encyclopaedia of Philosophy, www.utm.edu/research/iep/j/justwar.htm (accessed 10/06/2004) and BBC, 'The Theory of the Just War', http://www.bbc.co.uk/religion/ethics/war/justwarintro.shtml (accessed 10/06/2004).

29 Editorial, 'Crippling Saddam', *The Daily Telegraph*, 29 August 1990, p. 14.

30 Editorial, 'Time for Reflection and Diplomacy', *The Daily Telegraph*, 4 September 1990, p. 16.

31 Editorial, 'Democracy Expects', *The Times*, 18 August 1990, p. 11.

32 Benn, T., 'Parliament should not give Thatcher a Free Hand', *The Guardian*, 6 September 1990, p. 9.

33 Editorial, 'No Soft Options', *The Times*, 4 September 1990, p. 11.

34 Editorial, 'The Mood Hardens', *The Times*, 27 September 1990, p. 13.

35 Editorial, 'Withdraw or Fight', *The Times*, 1 December 1990, p. 17.

36 O'Brien, C., 'Finding a Balance after the Gulf War', *The Times*, 3 January 1991, p. 10.

37 Evans, M., 'Gulf Poker Minus the Ace', *The Times*, 11 January 1991, p. 10.

38 Editorial, 'Gladstone's Shade. Why Kosovo? Why British Troops? Blair must Explain', *The Times*, 3 February 1999, p. 17.

39 Bellamy, 2001, op. cit. p. 31.

40 Ibid.

41 Walker, W., 'OSCE Verification Experiences in Kosovo: Nov 1998–June 1999' in Booth, K. (ed.), *The Kosovo Tragedy. The Human Rights Dimension*, Frank Cass, London, 2001, p. 139. Walker himself has been criticized for hastening the build-up to war through his reaction to the Racak massacre when he used phrases such as 'personal revulsion' and a 'crime against humanity'.

This criticism came from Philip Hammond in his article '"Good Versus Evil" After The Cold War: Kosovo and the moralisation of war reporting', *Javnost/ The Public*, Vol. 7, No. 3, 2000b. www.sbu.ac.uk/philip-hammond/2000a.html (accessed 16/06/2004).

42 For his interpretation of the Rambouillet peace talks see, Chomsky, N., *The New Military Humanism. Lessons from Kosovo*, Pluto Press, London, 1999, Chapter 5.

43 Hammond, 2000b, op. cit.

44 Pilger, J., 'Myth-Makers of the Gulf War', *The Guardian*, 7 January 1991, p. 21.

45 Editorial, 'A War NATO just has to Win', *Daily Mirror*, 26 March 1999, p. 6.

46 Temple Mount in the Old City of Jerusalem is a holy place for both Jews and Muslims. During the incident in question Israeli troops fired on Palestinians killing between 18 and 20 of their number.

47 Hiro, D., *Desert Shield to Desert Storm. The Second Gulf War*, Paladin, London, 1992.

48 Ibid. p. 227.

49 Tisdall, S., 'US Offers to meet Saddam', *The Guardian*, 1 December 1990, p. 1.

50 Editorial, 'Failure in Geneva', *The Daily Telegraph*, 19 January 1991, p. 16.

51 Editorial, 'Shades of Suez', *The Times*, 1 January 1991, p. 9.

52 Rallings, C., Thrasher, M. and Moon, N., 'British Public Opinion during the Gulf War', *Contemporary Record*, Vol. 6, No. 2, Autumn 1992, p. 378.

53 D'Ancona, M., 'Fifth Columnists or Royal Corps?', *Index On Censorship*, Vol. 20, Nos 4 and 5, April/May 1991, p. 8.

54 Connaughton, R., *Military Intervention in the 1990s. A New Logic of War*, Routledge, London, 1992, p. 138.

55 Ibid. p. 148.

56 Billiere, P., *Storm Command. A Personal Account of the Gulf War*, Harper Collins Publishers, London, 1992, p. 63–4.

57 Billiere, P., *Looking for Trouble*, Harper Collins Publishers, London, 1995, pp. 405–6. It is perhaps because of this recognition of the potential power of the media that de la Billiere was to complain about the role of the CNN in Baghdad.

58 Mass Observation reports during both conflicts saw the repetition of those who felt emotionally affected by events. However, this often manifested itself in people feeling confused about what the best course of action should be and often shielded themselves from coverage.

59 Reynolds, P. W., 'Operation Granby or "Once Round the Desert – Go!"', Unpublished letter dated 27 January 1991, The Imperial War Museum, 91/32/1.

60 Laurence, C., 'A Reign of Terror and of Torture', *The Daily Telegraph*, 2 November 1990, p. 17.

61 Laurence, C., 'What will they find in Kuwait?', *The Daily Telegraph*, 22 February 1991, p. 19.

62 For an account of Amnesty International's findings see: Amnesty International, 'Iraq/Occupied Kuwait. Human Rights Violations since 2 August', December 1990.

63 For a discussion of these propaganda issues see Ponsonby, A., *Falsehood in Wartime. Propaganda Lies of the First World War*, Institute for Historical Research, California, 1991.

64 Dr Gisli Sigurdsson is quoted in Walker, C., 'Invaders' Reign of Terror goes on', *The Times*, 11 December 1990, p. 12.

65 Knipe, M., 'Amnesty Details Brutalities of Invaders', *The Times*, 19 December 1990, p. 9 (emphasis from the original text). For the report in question, see Amnesty International, December 1990, op. cit.

66 Dowdney, M., 'Iraqis Gouged out Victim's Eyes', *Daily Mirror*, 19 December 1990, p. 2.

67 The Amnesty International Report uses the figure 300, however the actual evidence of these findings is limited to one page, page 56, of an 82 page document. However, this was the incident most utilized by the press, presumably because of its ability to stir emotion in the reader. Far less relevance was given to adult deaths that occurred as a result of the looting of life-support machines, evidence of which was also contained in the report.

68 Tisdall, S., 'Kuwaitis Bear Army Terror', *The Guardian*, 7 February 1991, p. 2.

69 Kelly, T., quoted in Taylor, P., *War and the Media. Propaganda and Persuasion in the Gulf War*, Manchester University Press, 1992, p. 202.

70 Blair, T., Speech to the Economist Club of Chicago, 22 April 1999, in Ignatieff, M., *Virtual War. Kosovo and Beyond*, Vintage, London, 2001, p. 72.

71 Keohane, D., 'The Debate on British Policy in the Kosovo Conflict. An Assessment', *Contemporary Security Policy*, Frank Cass Journal, Vol. 21, No. 3, December 2000, p. 79. At the time of writing his article Keohane was Senior Lecturer in the School of Politics, International Relations and the Environment at Keele University.

72 Abrahams, F., 'Humanitarian Law Violations in Kosovo', Human Rights Watch, New York, 1998.

73 Abrahams, F. and Bouckaert, P., *Federal Republic of Yugoslavia. A Week of Terror in Drenica. Humanitarian Law Violations in Kosovo*, Human Rights Watch, USA, 1999.

74 Ibid. p. 63.

75 Ibid. p. 76.

76 Human Rights Watch, *Civilian Deaths in the NATO Air Campaign*, Vol. 12, No. 1 (D) February 2000, p. 3.

77 Ibid. p. 2.

78 Cook, R., 'MOD Briefing', 13 April 1999, www.kosovo.mod.uk (accessed 17/05/04).

79 Ibid.

80 Human Rights Watch, *Kosovo. Rape as a Weapon of "Ethnic Cleansing"*. Vol. 12, No. 3 (D), March 2000, p. 8.

81 Amnesty International, *Amnesty International Annual Report 2000. Yugoslavia*. www.web.amnesty.org/web/ar2000web.nsf/countries/445feb9f97b52-b9e802568f2 (accessed 01/10/2002).

82 Amnesty International, 1998, op. cit. p. 15.

83 Amnesty International, December 1990, op. cit. p. 4.

84 Whitely, A., *Human Rights in Iraq and Iraqi-Occupied Kuwait*, 8 January 1991, http://stagrny.hrw.org/reports/1991/IRAQ91 (accessed 01/10/2002).

85 Middle East Watch, *Needless Deaths in the Gulf War. Civilian Casualties during the Air Campaign and Violations of the Laws of War*, New York, 1991, p. 4.

86 Taylor,1992, op. cit. p. 227.

87 Comment, 'Mr Heath takes a Useful Trip', *The Guardian*, 12 October 1990, p. 22.

88 Editorial, 'Traitor Ted!', *The Sun*, 17 September 1990, p. 2.

89 Editorial, 'Batty Benn', *The Sun*, 18 January 1991, p. 6

90 Major, J., quoted in Jones, G. and Lowry, S., 'Allies Prepared for War as Peace Efforts Collapse', *The Daily Telegraph*, 16 January 1991, pp. 1–2.

NOTES

91 Diamond, J., 'Just what will our Lads be Dying for?' *Daily Mirror*, 15 January 1991, p. 4 (emphasis from the original text).
92 Jenkins, S., 'Big Bang Theorist', *The Times*, 20 January 1999, p. 18.
93 Jenkins, S., 'The Real Catastrophe', *The Times*, 24 March 1999, p. 20.
94 Ibid.
95 Jenkins, S., 'Suckers for Punches', *The Times*, 14 April 1999, p. 18.
96 Hume, M., 'The War against the Serbs is about Projecting a Self-Image of the Ethical New Britain Bestriding the World. It is a Crusade', *The Times*, 15 April 1999, p. 22. When writing this article Mick Hume was editor of *LM* magazine.
97 Ibid.
98 Freedland, J., 'The Left needs to Wake Up to the Real World. This War is a Just One', *The Guardian*, 26 March 1999, p. 19.
99 For Keohane's discussion on this issue see: Keohane, D., 'The Debate on British Policy in the Kosovo Conflict. An Assessment', *Contemporary Security Policy*, Vol. 21, No. 3, December 2000, pp. 78–94. Douglas Hogg has been the Conservative candidate for Sleaford and North Hykeham since 1992.
100 Pilger, J., 'What Really Happened at Rambouillett? And What Else is being Kept Under Wraps by our Selective Media?', *New Statesman*, 31 May 1999, p. 15.
101 Keegan, J., 'If Saddam had seen what I have seen he would leave Kuwait Today', *The Daily Telegraph*, 16 November 1990, p. 18.
102 Robinson, S., 'Bush needs a Home Guard for the Gulf', *The Daily Telegraph*, 3 December 1990, p. 18.
103 Holden, W., '"Peace Groupies" Set up Camp', *The Daily Telegraph*, 19 November 1990, p. 12.
104 Letts, Q., 'Paint Protester Misses her Mark', *The Daily Telegraph*, 16 January 1991, p. 13.
105 Comment, 'Mirror Comment', *Daily Mirror*, 11 January 1991, p. 4.
106 Littlejohn, R., 'Richard Littlejohn Column', *The Sun*, 17 January 1991, p. 6.
107 Hastings, M., 'Targeting the Force to Defeat Saddam Hussein', *The Daily Telegraph*, 8 January 1991, p. 14.
108 Hastings, M., 'The Journalist's Struggle to Pierce the Fog of War', *The Daily Telegraph*, 5 February 1991, p. 16.
109 Littlejohn, R., 'TV too Even-Handed', *The Sun*, 19 January 1991, p. 6.
110 'Here is the News from the Gulf', *The Sun*, 15 January 1991, p. 6.
111 Knightley, P., *The First Casualty. The War Correspondent as Hero and Myth-Maker from the Crimea to Kosovo*, Prion Books Limited, London, 2000, p. 481.
112 Nicholls, P., Hansard, House of Commons Debates, 17 January 1991, Volume 183.
113 Editorial, 'Brigadier Bigmouth', *The Sun*, 1 December 1990, p. 6.
114 Billiere, P., *Storm Command. A Personal Account of the Gulf War*, Harper Collins Publishers, London, 1992, p. 112.
115 Major, J., *John Major. The Autobiography*, Harper Collins Publishers, London, 1999, p. 232
116 Thompson, D., 'Church Leaders Unite to Condemn "Unjust War"', *The Daily Telegraph*, 24 November 1990, p. 9.
117 Wheeler, N., 'Reflections on the Legality and Legitimacy of Nato's Intervention in Kosovo', in Booth, K. (ed.), *The Kosovo Tragedy. The Human Rights Dimension*, Frank Cass, London, 2001, p. 160.
118 Laughland, J., 'The War is being Fought to Destroy the Very Principles which Constitute the West. This is not Moral: It is Meglomanic', *The Times*, 22 April 1999, p. 24.

119 Bishop, P., 'We can do Nothing for Kosovo', *The Daily Telegraph*, 19 January 1999, p. 22.

120 Thomson, A., '"Surgical" Strikes are not the Answer', *The Daily Telegraph*, 24 March 1999, p. 24.

121 Routledge, P., 'Why Kosovo is not Worth the Life of a Single British Squaddie', *The Daily Mirror*, 19 January 1999, p. 2.

122 Routledge, P., 'Crisis in Kosovo. This is not our Fight', *Daily Mirror*, 24 March 1999, p. 5.

123 Routledge, P., 'This Evil Barrage Shames Britain', *Daily Mirror*, 26 March 1999, p. 7.

124 Routledge, P., 'Public Split on Air War Widens', *Daily Mirror*, 10 April 1999, p. 7.

125 Editorial, 'No Mercy for the Butcher of Kosovo', *Daily Mirror*, 24 March 1999, p. 6.

126 Editorial, 'Stamp out the Butcher of Kosovo', *Daily Mirror*, 19 January 1999, p. 6.

127 Comment, 'Time to be Tough', *Daily Mirror*, 6 August 1990, p. 2.

128 Gott, R., 'Stop the War. Nato should Lose', *The Guardian*, 10 April 1999, p. 23.

129 Ehrenreich, B., 'Violence is the Victor', *The Guardian*, 22 April 1999, p. 19.

130 Carruthers, S., 'New Media, New War', *International Affairs*, Vol. 77, No. 3, July 2001, p. 680.

131 Goff, P. and Trionfi, B. (eds), *The Kosovo News and Propaganda War*, International Press Institute, Vienna, 1999, p. 16.

132 Parris, M., 'Apoplexy Passes for Action where Kosovo is Concerned', *The Times*, 19 January 1999, p. 2.

133 Bishop, P., 'Air Strikes would show the West's Policy has Failed', *The Daily Telegraph*, 23 March 1999, p. 14.

134 For examples of the *Telegraph* editorial policy see: Editorial, 'Let the Real War Begin', 12 April 1999, p. 19 and Editorial, 'Nato then, Nato now', 23 April 1999, p. 29.

135 Keegan, J., 'The Time has Come for Nato to Sack its Man at the Top', *The Daily Telegraph*, 7 May 1999, p. 28.

136 Editorial, 'Nato's other Opponents', *The Daily Telegraph*, 11 May 1999, p. 23.

137 Eyal, J., 'The Aerosol Myth', *The Guardian*, 24 March 1999, p. 20. At the time of writing this article Eyal was Director of Studies at the Royal United Services Institute, London.

138 Kaldor, M., 'Bombs Away! But to Save Civilians we must get in some Soldiers too', *The Guardian*, 25 March 1999, p. 18 and Hodgson, G., 'America's Obsession', *The Guardian*, 27 April 1999, p. 15.

139 Editorial, 'Time To Act', *The Sun*, 24 March 1999, p. 8 and Editorial, 'Don't Send our Troops off to Die', *The Sun*, 5 April 1999, p. 1.

140 Editorial, 'Spineless Allies must Back Blair', *Daily Mirror*, 20 May 1999, p. 6.

141 Keegan, J., 'So the Bomber got through to Milosevic after all', *The Daily Telegraph*, 4 June 1999, p. 28.

142 Kehoane, op. cit. p. 84.

143 Best, G., 'Saddam's Propaganda Pictures and the Laws of War', *The Daily Telegraph*, 4 February 1991, p. 2. Best was a former Professor of Modern History at Edinburgh University.

144 Editorial, 'Distorted Views', *The Times*, 15 February 1991, p. 22.

145 Kavanagh, T., '10 Facts to Damn Saddam', *The Sun*, 14 February 1991, p. 1.

146 No author cited, 'TV News "Biased"', *The Sun*, 16 February 1991, p. 5.

147 Fox, R., 'Speed of the Message Leaves Truth Trailing Behind', *The Daily Telegraph*, 22 January 1991, p. 2.
148 Billiere, 1992, op. cit. p. 65.
149 Ibid. p. 206.
150 Ibid. p. 261.
151 Human Rights Watch, February 2000, op. cit. p. 8.
152 Editorial, 'Nato's Moral Morass', *The Times*, 28 April 1999, p. 20.
153 Editorial, 'Striking at the Tools of Evil Regime', *Daily Mirror*, 24 April 1999, p. 6.
154 Connaughton, R., *Military Intervention in the 1990's. A New Logic of War*, Routledge, London 1992, p. 148.
155 Wilcox, C., Tanaka, A. and Allsop, D., 'World Opinion in the Gulf Crisis', *The Journal of Conflict Resolution*, Vol. 37, No. 1, March 1993, p. 70.
156 King, A., 'Britons Remain Firm on the use of Force, Says Gallup', *The Daily Telegraph*, 4 December 1990, p. 10.
157 Mckle, D., 'Gender Gap Revealed on Resort to Arms', *The Guardian*, 16 January 1991, p. 1.
158 No author, 'Support Rises for Nato Attacks despite Civilian Casualties', *The Daily Telegraph*, 30 April 1999, p. 1.
159 Mass Observation, Autumn/Winter Directive 1990, Part 2 – The Gulf Crisis, A.001–End, Women A–C, A1473.
160 Mass Observation, Autumn/Winter Directive 1990, Part 2 – The Gulf Crisis, A.001–End, Women, A1473.
161 Mass Observation, Autumn/Winter Directive 1990, Part 2 – The Gulf Crisis, B.001–End, Women, B36.
162 Mass Observation, Autumn/Winter Directive 1990, Part 2 – The Gulf Crisis, B.001–End, Women, B1424.
163 Mass Observation, Autumn/Winter Directive 1990, Part 2 – The Gulf Crisis, A–D, Men, D157.
164 Mass Observation, Spring/Summer Directive 1999, Part 2 – Current Issues, Part 3 – Current Events, Women K–Z, K310.
165 Mass Observation, Spring/Summer Directive 1999, Part 2 – Current Issues, Part 3 – Current Events, Women K–Z, T842 and L1991, Mass Observation, Spring/Summer Directive 1999, Part 2 – Current Issues, Part 3 – Current Events, Men A–Z, K1380.
166 Mass Observation, Autumn/Winter Directive 1990, Part 2 – The Gulf Crisis, A–D, Men, B2392, Mass Observation, Spring/Summer Directive 1999, Part 2 – Current Issues, Part 3 – Current Events, Women K–Z, L2835.
167 Mass Observation, Spring/Summer Directive 1999, Part 2 – Current Issues, Part 3 – Current Events, Women K–Z, M355 and M2629.
168 Mass Observation, Autumn/Winter Directive 1990, Part 2 – The Gulf Crisis, A.001–End, Women, A1473, Mass Observation, Autumn/Winter Directive 1990, Part 2 – The Gulf Crisis, B.001–End, Women, C2079, Mass Observation, Spring/Summer Directive 1999, Part 2 – Current Issues, Part 3 – Current Events, Women K–Z, R2849.
169 Bishop, P., *Famous Victory. The Gulf War*, Sinclair-Stevenson Limited, London, 1992, pp. 45–6.
170 Bishop, P., 'Proof of Hitlerian Determination', *The Daily Telegraph*, 3 August 1990, p. 2 and 'Ominous Calm Underlines Impatience to get on with it', *The Daily Telegraph*, 19 February 1991, p. 3.

171 Antonowicz, A., 'Anything but the Truth', *Daily Mirror*, 23 January 1991, p. 6.
172 Fialka, J., *Hotel Warriors. Covering the Gulf War*, The Woodrow Wilson Centre Press, Baltimore, 1992, p. 10.
173 MOD, 'Kosovo. Lessons from the Crisis, MOD 6/01/00', www.mod.uk/publications/kosovo_lessons/chapter6.htm (accessed 17/07/2003).
174 Bellamy, C., *Expert Witness. A Defence Correspondent's Gulf War 1990–91*, Brassey's, New York, London, 1993, p. xxvii.
175 Kay, R., *Desert Warrior. Reporting from the Gulf, a Personal Account*, Penumbra Books, London, 1992, p. 24.
176 Ibid. pp. 80–1.
177 Burkart, J., 'The Media in the Persian Gulf War. From Carnival to Crusade', in Leslie, P., *The Gulf War as Popular Entertainment. An Analysis of the Military–Media Complex*, Symposium Series Vol. 42, The Edwin Mellen Press, Lewiston, Queenston, Lampeter, 1997, p. 23.
178 Perkins, G., 'Letter to "Tony" Marriot-Smith', unpublished letter dated 8 December 1990, Imperial War Museum, 93/29/1.
179 Bishop, P., *Famous Victory. The Gulf War*, Sinclair-Stevenson Limited, London, 1992, p. 172.
180 Kamali, A., 'The United States–United Nations Coalition in the Persian Gulf: A Critical Evaluation', article in Leslie, op. cit. p. 3.
181 Chomsky, 1999, op. cit. Chapter 1.
182 Ignatieff, op. cit. p. 5.
183 Hastings, M., *Going to the Wars*, Pan Books, London, 2001, p. 349.
184 Shaw, M., *Mediating Denial*, available at www.martinshaw.org/degraded.htm (accessed 30/09/2002).
185 Robinson, op. cit.
186 Gowing, op. cit.

CONCLUSION

1 Ellul, J., *Propaganda. The Formation of Men's Attitudes*, Vintage Books, New York, 1973.
2 Taylor, P., *Munitions of the Mind. A History of Propaganda from the Ancient World to the Present Day*, Manchester University Press, Manchester, 1995.
3 No author cited, 'War in Iraq 2003: Baghdad Dares to Celebrate Faces of War', *Coventry Evening Telegraph*, 9 April 2003, pp. 4–5.
4 Meek, J., Goldenberg, S., Steele, J., Wazir, B. and Wilson, J., 'War in the Gulf', *The Guardian*, 11 April 2003, p. 5. Brigan, B., 'Straw explains the Looting Backlash', *The Daily Telegraph*, 12 April 2003, p. 10.
5 Aaronovitch, D., 'All for One: The Rebirth of Iraq is too Important to be Left in American Hands Alone', *The Observer*, 13 April 2003, p. 27.
6 Robinson, N., 'I Committed an Act of Gross Immaturity by Text', *The Times*, 16 July 2004, p. 21.
7 Cawthorne, A., 'BBC Reforms Journalism Guidelines', 23 June 2004, www.Reuters.co.uk (accessed 22 July 2004).

BIBLIOGRAPHY

Archival sources

Imperial War Museum, London

Ayers, J., 'Diary of an Aid Worker in Albania, 1999', Imperial War Museum 99/37/1.

Boswell, R., 'Letters from HMS Manchester', Imperial War Museum 91/32/1.

Clouston, D., 'Letters from the Persian Gulf, November 1990 – April 1991', Imperial War Museum, 91/32/1.

Ewin, D., 'Certificate of Appreciation', Imperial War Museum 93/30/1.

Kirby, E., 'Letters to the Families of Servicemen during the Gulf War and the Conflict in the Former Yugoslavia 1991–1993', Imperial War Museum 98/16/1.

Levins, H., 'Journals from a Reporter in Bosnia and Kosovo, December 1995–January 2001', Imperial War Museum Sound Archive.

Miscellaneous 2379, 'Baghdad Air Show Cartoon', Imperial War Museum, Misc 154 (2379).

Miscellaneous 2420, 'Poem by Private M. Ferguson', Imperial War Museum Misc 155 (2420)

Miscellaneous 2430, 'Saddam Hussein Face Cartoon', Imperial War Museum Misc 157 (2430).

Miscellaneous 2677, 'Documents Relating to Bosnia-Herzegovina, c1993', Imperial War Museum Misc 176 (2677).

Miscellaneous 2770, 'Work of the Red Cross in Bosnia-Herzegovina, c1994, Imperial War Museum Misc 185 (2770).

Miscellaneous 2962, 'Letter from Lieutenant General Sir Peter de la Billiere to Captain Jong-Ku Yoon, 18th March 1991', Imperial War Museum Misc 202 (2962).

Monro, S., 'Diary from the Persian Gulf', December 1990–March 1991', Imperial War Museum 92/40/1.

Perkins, G., 'Letters from a US Pilot in the Persian Gulf', Imperial War Museum 93/29/1.

Pilbeam, T., 'Letters from Operation Granby, January–March 1991', Imperial War Museum, 94/26/1.

Reynolds, P., 'Letters from Operation Granby, December 1990–March 1991', Imperial War Museum 91/32/1.

Walker, R., 'Diary from Operation Granby, 7th December 1990–23rd March 1991', Imperial War Museum 92/40/1.
Whitticase, R., 'Letters from the Persian Gulf, 2nd January–11th March 1991', Imperial War Museum 91/32/1.

Mass Observation Archive, University of Sussex

Spring/Summer Directive 1999, Part 2 – Current Issues, Part 3 – Current Events, M–O Amalgamated Collection Women.
Spring/Summer Directive 1999, Part 2 – Current Issues, Part 3 – Current Events, A–Z Amalgamated Collection Men.
Autumn/Winter Directive 1990, Part 2 – The Gulf Crisis, A.001–End Women.
Autumn/Winter Directive 1990, Part 2 – The Gulf Crisis, B.001–End Women.
Autumn/Winter Directive 1990, Part 2 – The Gulf Crisis, C.001–End Women.
Autumn/Winter Directive 1990, Part 2 – The Gulf Crisis, A–D Men.

British Library Newspaper Library, Colindale, London

Daily Mirror
The Daily Telegraph
The Guardian
The Sun
The Times

Unpublished sources

Keeble, R., *The Gulf War Myth. A Study of the Press Coverage of the 1991 Gulf Conflict*, Unpublished PhD thesis, City University, 1996.
Willcox, D., 'The Maginot Line and British Propaganda', Unpublished MA Dissertation, University of Kent at Canterbury, 2000.

Gulf War and Iraq: books

Atkinson, R., *Crusade. The Untold Story of the Gulf War*, Harper Collins Publishers, London, 1994.
Baudrillard, J., *The Gulf War did not Take Place*, Indiana University Press, Bloomington, 1995.
Bellamy, C., *Expert Witness. A Defence Correspondent's Gulf War 1990–91*, Brassey's, London, 1993.
Billiere, P., *Storm Command. A Personal Account of the Gulf War*, Harper Collins Publishers, London, 1992.
Bishop, P., *Famous Victory. The Gulf War*, Sinclair-Stevenson Limited, London, 1992.
Brittain, V., *The Gulf Between Us. The Gulf War and Beyond*, Viagro, London, 1991.
Butler, R., *The Greatest Threat. Iraq, Weapons of Mass Destruction and the Crisis of Global Security*, Public affairs, New York, 2000.

Campen, A., *The First Information War. The Story of Communications, Computers, and Intelligence Systems in the Persian Gulf War*, AFCEA International Press, Fairfax VA, 1992.

Cordingley, P., *In The Eye of the Storm. Commanding the Desert Rats in the Gulf War*, Hodder and Stoughton, London, 1996.

Coughlin, C., *Saddam. The Secret Life*, Macmillan, London, 2003.

Cradock, P., *In Pursuit of British Interests. Reflections on Foreign Policy*, John Murray Ltd, London, 1997.

Decosse, D. (ed.) *But was it Just?*, Doubleday, New York, 1992.

Denton, R., *The Media and the Persian Gulf War*, Praeger Publishers, Westport, 1993.

Fialka, J., *Hotel Warriors. Covering the Gulf War*, The Woodrow Wilson Center Press, Baltimore, 1992.

Greenberg, B. and Gantz, W., *Desert Storm and the Mass Media*, Hampton Press, Cresskill NJ, 1993.

Greg, P., *The British Media and the Gulf War*, University of Glasgow Media Group, Glasgow, 1993.

Hiro, D., *Desert Shield to Desert Storm. The Second Gulf War*, Paladin, London, 1992.

Hussein, S., *Social and Foreign Affairs in Iraq*, Croom Helm Ltd, London, 1979.

Johnstone, I., *Aftermath of the Gulf War. An Assessment of UN Action*, Lynne Rienner Publishers Inc, London, 1979.

Kay, R., *Desert Warrior. Reporting from the Gulf, a Personal Account*, Penumbra Books, London, 1992.

Leslie, P. (ed.) *The Gulf War as Popular Entertainment. An Analysis of the Military–Media Complex*, Symposium Series Vol. 42, The Edwin Mellen Press, Lewiston N.Y, 1997.

MacArthur, *Second Front. Censorship and Propaganda in the Gulf War*, University of California Press, Berkeley, 1993.

Morrison, D., *Television and the Gulf War*, John Libbey and Company Ltd, London, 1992.

Mowlana, H., Gerbner, G. and Schiller, H. (eds) *Triumph of the Image. The Media's War in the Persian Gulf – A Global Perspective*, Westview Press, Oxford, 1992.

Norris, C., *Uncritical Theory. Postmodernism, Intellectuals and the Gulf War*, Lawrence and Wishart, London, 1992.

Pimlott, J. and Badsey, S. (eds) *The Gulf War Assessed*, Arms and Armour, London, 1995.

Ridgeway, J., *The March to War*, Four Walls Eight Windows, New York, 1991.

Shaw, M., *Civil Society and Media in Global Crises. Representing Distant Violence*, Pinter, London, 1996.

Shaw, M. and Carr-Hill, R., *Public Opinion, Media and Violence. Attitudes to the Gulf War in a Local Population*, University of Hull, 1991.

Simpson, J., *From the House of War. John Simpson in the Gulf*, Hutchinson, London, 1991.

Smith, H., *The Media and the Gulf War*, Seven Locks Press, Washington, 1992.

Taylor, P., *War and the Media. Propaganda and Persuasion in the Gulf War*, Manchester University Press, 1998.

Taylor, P., *War and the Media. Propaganda and Persuasion in the Gulf War*, Manchester University Press, 1992.

Walsh, J., *The Gulf War did not Happen. Politics, Culture and Warfare post-Vietnam*, Arena, Aldershot, 1995.

Wilcken, P., *Anthropology. The Intellectuals and the Gulf War*, Prickly Pear Press, Cambridge, 1994.

Witherow, J. and Sullivan, A., *War in the Gulf. A pictorial history*, Sidgwick and Jackson, London, 1991.

Gulf War and Iraq: articles and publications

Amnesty International, 'Iraq/Occupied Kuwait. Human Rights Violations since 2nd August', Amnesty International, December 1990.

Article XIX, 'Stop Press. The Gulf War and Censorship', *International Centre on Censorship*, Issue 1, February 1991. Issue 2, May 1991.

D'Ancona, M., 'Fifth Columnists or Royal Corps?', *Index On Censorship*, Vol. 20, Nos 4 and 5, April/May 1991.

Hansard, House of Commons Debates, 17 January 1991, Volume 183.

Knightley, P., 'Here is the Patriotically Censored News', *Index on Censorship*, Vol. 20, Nos 4 and 5, April/May 1991

Lebovic, J., 'Before the Storm. Momentum and the Onset of the Gulf War', *International Studies Quarterly*, No. 38, 1994.

Meade, G., 'Hard Ground Rules in the Sand', *Index on Censorship*, Vol. 20, Nos 4 and 5, April/May 1991.

Middle East Watch, 'Needless Deaths in the Gulf War. Civilian Casualties during the Air Campaign and Violations of the Laws of War', Middle East Watch, New York, 1991.

Mould, D., 'Press Pools and Military-Media Relations in the Gulf War. A Case Study of Khafji, January 1991', *The Historical Journal of Film Radio and Television*, Vol. 16, No. 2, 1996.

No author cited, 'War in Iraq 2003. Baghdad Dares to Celebrate Faces of War', *Coventry Evening Telegraph*, 9 April 2003, pp. 4–5.

Ottosen, R., 'Enemy Images and the Journalistic Process', *Journal of Peace Research*, Vol. 32, No. 1, 1995.

Pilger, J., 'Alternative Reality. Why don't we Hear about what is Happening in the Gulf?' *New Statesman*, 24 May 1991.

Pinter, H., 'Blowing up the Media', *Index on Censorship*, Vol. 21, No. 5, May 1992.

Rallings, C., Thrasher, M. and Moon, N., 'British Public Opinion during the Gulf War', *Contemporary Record*, Vol. 6, No. 2, Autumn 1992.

Simpson, J., 'Free Men Clamouring for Chains', *Index on Censorship*, Vol. 20, Nos 4 and 5, May 1991.

United Nations 'Resolution 678 (1990)', 29 November, www.un.org/Docs/scres/1990/scres90.htm (accessed 1/8/2004).

United Nations, 'Resolution 667 (1990)', 16 September, www.un.org/Docs/scres/1990/scres90.htm (accessed 1/8/2004).

United Nations, 'Resolution 665 (1990)', 25 August, www.un.org/Docs/scres/1990/scres90.htm (accessed 1/ 8/2004).

United Nations, 'Resolution 664 (1990)', 18 August, www.un.org/Docs/scres/1990/scres90.htm (accessed 1/ 8/2004).

United Nations, 'Resolution 662 (1990)', 9 August, www.un.org/Docs/scres/1990/scres90.htm (accessed 1/8/2004).

United Nations, 'Resolution 661 (1990)', 6 August, www.un.org/Docs/scres/1990/scres90.htm (accessed 1/8/2004).

United Nations, 'Resolutions 660 (1990)', 2 August, www.un.org/Docs/scres/1990/scres90.htm (accessed 1/8/2004).

Whitely, A., 'Human Rights in Iraq and Iraqi-Occupied Kuwait', 8 January 1991, http://stagrny.hrw.org/reports/1991/IRAQ91 (accessed 1/10/2002).

Wilcox, C., Tanaka, A. and Allsop, D., 'World Opinion in the Gulf Crisis', *The Journal of Conflict Resolution*, Vol. 37, No. 1, March 1993.

Kosovo: books

Baevich, A., *War over Kosovo. Politics and Strategy in a Global Age*, New York, Columbia University Press, 2001.

Booth, K. (ed.) *The Kosovo Tragedy. The Human Rights Dimension*, Frank Cass, London, 2001.

Buckley, M. and Cummings, S., *Kosovo. Perceptions of the War and its Aftermath*, Continuum, London, 2001.

Carpenter, T., *NATO's Empty Victory*, Cato Institute, Washington, 2000.

Chomsky, N., *The New Military Humanism. Lessons from Kosovo*, Pluto Press, London, 1999.

Clark, H., *Civil Resistance in Kosovo*, Pluto Press, London, 2000.

Daalder, I. and O'Hanlon, M., *Winning Ugly. NATO's War to Save Kosovo*, Brooking's Institute, Washington, 2000.

Drezov, K., *Kosovo, Myths, Conflict and War*, Keeble European Research Centre, 1999.

Goff, P. and Trionfi, B. (eds) *The Kosovo News and Propaganda War*, International Press Institute, Vienna, 1999.

Hammond, P., *Degraded Capability. The Media and the Kosovo Crisis*, Pluto Press, London, 2000.

Hibbert, R., *The Kosovo Question. Origins, Present Complications and Prospects*, David Davies Memorial Institute, London, 1999.

Ignatieff, M., *Virtual War. Kosovo and Beyond*, Vintage, London, 2001.

Judah, T., *Kosovo War and Revenge*, Yale University Press, New Haven, 2000.

Leurdijk, D. and Zandee, D., *Kosovo. From Crisis to Crisis*, Ashgate Publishing Limited, Aldershot, 2001.

Malcolm, N., *Kosovo. A Short History*, Papermac, London, 1998.

Virilio, P., *Strategy of Deception*, Verso, London, 2000.

Waller, W., Gokay, B. and Drezov, K. (eds) *Kosovo. The Politics of Delusion*, Frank Cass, London, 2001.

Weller, M., *The Crisis in Kosovo, 1989–1999*, Pearson/Reuters, London, 2002.

Kosovo: articles and publications

Abrahams, F., 'Humanitarian Law Violations in Kosovo', Human Rights Watch, New York, 1998.

Abrahams, F. and Bouckaert, P., 'Federal Republic of Yugoslavia. A Week of Terror in Drenica. Humanitarian Law Violations in Kosovo', Human Rights Watch, New York, 1999.

Abrahams, F., Staver, E. and Giles, P., 'A Village Destroyed', Human Rights Watch, New York, 1999.

Amnesty International, 'Amnesty International Annual Report 2000. Yugoslavia', www.web.amnesty.org/web/ar2000web.nsf/countries/445feb9f97b52b9e802568f2 (accessed 01/10/2002).

Amnesty International, 'A Broken Circle. "Disappeared" and Abducted in Kosovo Province. Amnesty International Report October 1999', AI Index: Eur 70/106/99.

Amnesty International, 'Kosovo. The Evidence', Amnesty International, London, 1998.

Bellamy, A., 'Reconsidering Rambouillet', *Contemporary Security Policy*, Frank Cass, London, Vol. 22, No. 1, April 2001.

Bellamy, A., 'Is Bombing Serbia Legal?', *Interstate Online*, Issue 54, Spring 1999a.

Bellamy, A., 'Reasons on Bombing Serbia', *Interstate Online*, Issue 54, Spring 1999b.

Caplan, R., 'International Diplomacy and the Kosovo Crisis', *International Affairs*, Vol. 74, No. 4, 1998.

Carruthers, S., 'New Media, New War', *International Affairs*, Vol. 77, No. 3, July 2001.

Cook, R., 'Ministry of Defence Briefing', 8 May 1999, www.kosovo.mod.uk (accessed 17/05/2004).

Cook, R., 'Ministry of Defence Briefing', 13 April 1999, www.kosovo.mod.uk (accessed 17/05/2004).

Cook, R., 'Ministry of Defence Briefing', 11 April 1999, www.kosovo.mod.uk (accessed 17/05/2004).

Dixon, P., 'Britain's Vietnam Syndrome? Public Opinion and British Military Intervention from Palestine to Yugoslavia', *Review of International Studies*, Vol. 26, No. 1, January 2000.

Freedman, L., 'Victims and Victors. Reflections on the Kosovo War', *Review of International Studies*, Vol. 26, No. 1, January 2000.

Grundmann, R., Smith, D. and Wright, S., 'National Elites and Transnational Discourses in the Balkans War', *European Journal of Communication*, Vol. 15, No. 3, 2000a.

Grundmann, R., Smith, D. and Wright, S., 'Infosuasion in European Newspapers', *European Journal of Communication*, Vol. 15, No. 3, 2000b.

Grundmann, R., Smith, D. and Wright, S., 'From the Persian Gulf to Kosovo – War Journalism and Propaganda', *European Journal of Communication*, Vol. 15, No. 3, 2000c.

Hammond, P., 'Reporting 'Humanitarian' Warfare: Propaganda, Moralism and NATO's Kosovo War', *Journalism Studies*, Vol. 1, No. 3, August 2000a.

Hammond, P., '"Good Versus Evil" After the Cold War. Kosovo and the Moralisation of War Reporting', *Javnost/The Public*, No. 3, Vol. 7, 2000b, www.sbu.ac.uk/philip-hammond/2000a.html (accessed 16/06/2004).

Hammond, P., 'The War on TV', *Broadcast Magazine*, 14 May 1999a, www.fair.org/articles/hammond-tv-war.html (accessed 1/08/2004).

Hammond, P., 'A War of Words and Pictures', *The Independent*, 6 April 1999b, www.fair.org/articles/hammond.html (accessed 1/08/2004).

Hansard, House of Commons Debates, 29 March 1999, Vol. 328.

Henderson, D., 'Ministry of Defence Briefing', 30 April 1999, www.kosovo.mod.uk (accessed 17/05/2004).

Human Rights Watch, 'Kosovo: Rape as a Weapon of "Ethnic Cleansing"', Human Rights Watch, Vol. 12, No. 3 (D) March 2000.

Human Rights Watch, 'Civilian Deaths in the NATO Air Campaign', Human Rights Watch, Vol. 12, No. 1 (D) February 2000.

International Crisis Group, 'Reality Demands. Documenting Violations of International Humanitarian Law in Kosovo', International Crisis Group, Brussels, 2000, http://www.icg.org/home/index.cfm?id = 1865&l = 1 (accessed 1/08/2004).

Kadare, I., 'Who owns the Battlefield?', *Index on Censorship*, Vol. 27, No. 3, May/June 1998.

Keohane, D., 'The Debate on British Policy in the Kosovo Conflict. An Assessment', *Contemporary Security Policy*, Vol. 21, No. 3, December 2000.

Lloyd, J., 'Cook Declares Total War on Fascism', *New Statesman*, 3 May 1999.

Ministry of Defence, 'Ministry of Defence Briefing', 18 April 1999, www.kosovo.mod.uk (accessed 17/05/04).

Ministry of Defence, 'Ministry of Defence Briefing', 1 April 1999, www.kosovo.mod.uk (accessed 17/05/04).

Ministry of Defence, 'Kosovo: Lessons from the Crisis', MOD 6/01/00, www.mod.uk/publications/kosovo_lessons/chapter6.htm (accessed 17/07/2003).

Pilger, J., 'What Really Happened at Rambouillett? And what else is being kept under wraps by our Selective Media?', *New Statesman*, 31 May 1999.

Reif, D., 'A New Age of Liberal Imperialism?', *World Policy Journal*, Vol. 16, No. 2, Summer 1999.

Robertson, G., 'Ministry of Defence Briefing', 19 April 1999, www.kosovo.mod.uk (accessed 17/05/2004).

Shaw, M., 'Mediating Denial', www.martinshaw.org/degraded.htm (accessed 30/09/2002).

Shea, J., 'NATO Morning Briefing', 9 May 1999, www.nato.int/kosovo/press/b990509a.htm (accessed 17/05/2004).

Shenon, P., 'U.S. Says it Might Consider Attacking Serbs', *The New York Times*, 13 March 1998.

Shinoda, H., 'The Politics of Legitimacy in International Relations. The Case of NATO's Intervention in Kosovo', www.theglobalsite.ac.uk. (accessed 11/08/2004).

Solano, J., 'NATO Press Conference', 8 May 1999, www.nato.int/kosovo/press/p990508b.htm (accessed 17/05/2004).

Solano, J., 'NATO Press Release', 23 March 1999, (99) 40, www.nato.int/docu/pr/pr99e.htm (accessed 1/08/2004).

Stojanovic, S., 'Spinning Kosovo. Media and Propaganda in a Post Modern World', http://www.balkanpeace.org/library/spinn1.html (accessed 1/08/2004).

United Nations, 'Security Council Statement S/PRST/1999/2', 19 January 1999, www.un.org/Docs/sc/statements/1999/sprst99.htm (accessed 1/08/2004).

United Nations, 'Security Resolution 1203 (1998)', 24 October, http://www.un.org/ Docs/scres/1998/scres98.htm (accessed 11/08/2004).
United Nations, 'Security Resolution 1199 (1998)', 23 September, http://www. un.org/Docs/scres/1998/scres98.htm (accessed 11/08/2004).
United Nations, 'Security Resolution 1160 (1998)', 31 March, http://www.un.org/ Docs/scres/1998/scres98.htm (accessed 11/08/2004).
Weller, M., 'The Rambouillet Conference on Kosovo', *International Affairs*, Vol. 75, No. 2, April 1999.
Youngs, T., Oakes, M., Bowers, P. and Hillyard, M., 'Kosovo. Operation "Allied Force"', *House of Commons Research Paper 99/48*, 29 April 1999.

Propaganda and public opinion theory: books

Bartlett, F., *Political Propaganda*, Cambridge University Press, 1940.
Blanco White, A., *The New Propaganda*, Victor Gollancz Ltd, London, 1939.
Carr, E., *Propaganda in International Politics*, Oxford Pamphlets on World Affairs, No. 16, Clarendon Press, Oxford, 1939.
Doob, L., *Public Opinion and Propaganda*, Archon Books, Hamden, Connecticut, 1966.
Doob, L., *Propaganda. Its Psychology and Technique*, Henry Holt and Company, New York, 1944.
Ellul, J., *Propaganda. The Formation of Men's Attitudes*, Vintage Books, New York, 1973.
Hawthorn, J. (ed.) *Propaganda, Persuasion and Polemic*, Edward Arnold Ltd, London, 1987.
Herman, E. and Chomsky, N., *Manufacturing Consent. The Political Economy of the Mass Media*, Pantheon Books, New York, 2002.
Jowett, G. and O'Donnell, V., *Propaganda and Persuasion*, Sage Publications, London, 1992.
Lasswell, H., *The Political Writings of Harold D. Lasswell*, The Free Press, USA, 1951.
Lippmann, W., *Public Opinion*, Free Press Paperbacks, London, 1997.
Lippmann, W., *The Phantom Public. A Sequel to 'Public Opinion'*, Macmillan, New York, 1930.

Propaganda and public opinion history: books

Auckland, R., *Aerial Propaganda Leaflets*, The Psywar Society, Leeds, 1992.
Chapman, J., *The British at War. Cinema, State and Propaganda, 1939–1945*, I.B. Taurus, London, 1998.
Cole, R., *Propaganda in Twentieth Century War and Politics. An Annotated Bibliography*, Scarecrow Press, London, 1996.
Culbert, D., Cull, N. and Welch, D. (eds) *Propaganda and Mass Persuasion. A Historical Encyclopedia, 1500 to the Present*, ABC-Clio Inc, California, 2003.
Mackenzie, J., *Propaganda and Empire. The Manipulation of British Public Opinion, 1880–1960*, Manchester University Press, 1984.

Ponsonby, A., *Falsehood in Wartime. Propaganda Lies of the First World War*, Institute for Historical Research, California, 1991.

Rampton, S. and Stauber, J., *Weapons of Mass Deception. The Uses of Propaganda in Bush's War on Iraq*, Robinson, London, 2003.

Sanders, M. and Taylor, P., *British Propaganda during the First World War, 1914–1918*, The Macmillan Press Ltd, London, 1982.

Scheer, C., Scheer, R. and Chaudhry, L., *The Five Biggest Lies Bush Told us About Iraq*, Akashic Books and Seven Stories Press, New York, 2003.

Taylor, P., *British Propaganda in the Twentieth Century. Selling Democracy*, Edinburgh University Press, 1999.

Taylor, P., *Global Communications, International Affairs and the Media since 1945*, Routledge, London, 1997.

Taylor, P., *Munitions of the Mind. A History of Propaganda from the Ancient World to the Present Day*, Manchester University Press, 1995.

Thomson, O., *Easily Led. A History of Propaganda*, Sutton Publishing, Gloucestershire, 1999.

Media and war history: books

Adams, V., *The Media and the Falklands Campaign*, Macmillan, Basingstoke, 1986.

Adie, K., *The Kindness of Strangers. The Autobiography*, Headline Books Publishing, London, 2003.

Arnett, P., *Live from the Battlefield. From Vietnam to Baghdad*, Bloomsbury, London, 1994.

Badsey, S. (ed.) *The Media and International Security*, Frank Cass Publishers, London, 2000.

Bell, M., *In Harm's Way. Reflections of a War-Zone Thug*, Penguin Books, London, 1996.

Billiere, P., *Looking for Trouble. An Autobiography. From the SAS to the Gulf*, Harper Collins Publishers, London, 1995.

Bishop, P. and Witherow, J., *The Winter War. The Falklands*, Quartet Books Limited, London, 1982.

Connaughton, R., *Military Intervention in the 1990's. A New Logic of War*, Routledge, London, 1992.

Curran, J. and Guervitch, M., *Mass Media and Society*, Arnold, London, 2000.

Curran, J. and Seaton, J., *Power Without Responsibility. The Press and Broadcasting in Britain*, Routledge, London, 2000.

Dunsmore, B., *The Next War. Live?*, Joan Shorenstein Center on the Press, Politics, and Public Policy, John F. Kennedy School of Government, Harvard University, Cambridge MA, 1996.

Eddy, P., Linklater, M. and Gillman, P., *The Falklands War*, Sphere Books Limited, London, 1982.

Fox, R., *Eyewitness Falklands. A Personal Account of the Falklands Campaign*, Methuen, London, 1982.

Gauntlett, D. (ed.) *Web Studies. Rewiring Media Studies for the Digital Age*, Arnold, London, 2000.

Gowing, N., *Real-Time Television Coverage of Armed Conflicts and Diplomatic Crises. Does it Pressure or Distort Foreign Policy Decisions?* The Joan Shorenstein Barone Center on the Press, Politics and Public Policy, Harvard University, Working Paper 94-1, Cambridge MA, 1994.

Harris, R., *Gotcha! The Media, the Government and the Falklands Crisis*, Faber and Faber, London, 1983.

Hastings, M., *Going to the Wars*, Pan Books, London, 2001.

Herman, E., *Beyond Hypocrisy. Decoding the News in the Age of Propaganda*, South End Press, Boston MA, 1992.

Herman, E. and Chomsky, N., *Manufacturing Consent. The Political Economy of the Mass Media*, Pantheon, New York, 1988.

Hudson, M. and Stainer, J., *War and the Media. A Random Searchlight*, Sutton Publishing, Gloucestershire, 1999.

Kieran, M., *Media Ethics. A Philosophical Approach*, Praeger, London, 1997.

Knightley, P., *The First Casualty. The War Correspondent as Hero and Myth-Maker from the Crimea to Kosovo*, Prion Books Limited, London, 2000.

Lynch, J., *Reporting the World*, Conflict and Peace Forums, Berkshire, 2002.

Morrison, D. and Tumber, H., *Journalists at War. The Dynamics of News Reporting During the Falklands Conflict*, Sage, London, 1988.

Rosenblum, M., *Who Stole the News?. Why we can't keep up with what happens in the World and what we can do about it*, John Wiley & Sons Inc, New York, 1993.

Schlesinger, P., *Media, State and Nation. Political Violence and Collective Identities*, Sage Publications Ltd, London, 1991.

Stewart, I. and Carruthers, S. (eds) *War, Culture and the Media. Representations of the Military in 20th Century Britain*, Flicks Books, Wiltshire, 1996.

General: books

Chandler, D., *Rethinking Human Rights. Critical Approaches to International Politics*, Palgrave, Basingstoke, 2002.

Clair, C., *A History of Printing in Britain*, Cassell and Company Ltd, London, 1965.

Ellul, J., *The Technological Society*, Jonathan Cape, London, 1965.

Lenman, B., *The Eclipse of Parliament. Appearance and Reality in British Politics since 1914*, Edward Arnold, London, 1992.

Lippmann, W., *The Public Philosophy*, Hamish Hamilton, London, 1955.

Major, J., *John Major. The Autobiography*, Harper Collins Publishers, London, 1999.

Riddell, P., *Parliament Under Blair*, Politico's Publishing, London, 2000.

Tunstall, J., *Newspaper Power. The New National Press in Britain*, Clarendon Press, Oxford, 1996.

General: articles/publications

BBC, 'The Theory of the Just War', http://www.bbc.co.uk/religion/ethics/war/justwarintro.shtml (accessed 10/06/2004).

Carruthers, S., 'New Media, New War', *International Affairs*, Vol. 77, No. 3, July 2001.

Cawthorne, A., 'BBC Reforms Journalism Guidelines', 23 June 2004, www.Reuters. co.uk (accessed 22/07/2004).

Freedman, L., 'Why the West Failed', *Foreign Policy*, No. 97, Winter, 1994–95.

Greenslade, R., 'Prejudice, Distortion and the Cult of Celebrity. Is the Press going to Hell in a Handcart?', Inaugural Lecture at City University, London, 22 January 2004. http://www.presswise.org.uk/display_page.php?id=656 (accessed 27/08/2004).

Herman, E., 'The Propaganda Model: A Retrospective', December 2003, www.chomsky.info/onchomsky/20031209.htm (accessed 10/06/2004).

Hopkin, D., 'Domestic Censorship in the First World War', *Journal of Contemporary History*, Vol. 5, No. 4, 1970, pp. 151–69.

Knightley, P. and Welch, D., 'Has War Reporting ever been Truly Objective?', *BBC History Magazine*, Vol. 5, No. 6, 2004.

Lasswell, H., 'The Theory of Political Propaganda', *The American Political Science Review*, Vol. 21, No. 3, August 1927.

Ministry of Defence, 'British Defence Doctrine', Joint Warfare Publication (JWP), 0–01.

Ministry of Defence, 'DA-Notice', http://www.dnotice.org.uk/index.htm (accessed 16/06/04).

Ministry of Defence, *Green Book. Working Arrangements with the Media in Times of Emergency, Tension, Conflict or War*, www.mod.uk/news/green_book/foreword. htm (accessed 19/02/2002).

Moseley, A., 'Just War Theory', The Internet Encyclopaedia of Philosophy, www. utm.edu/research/iep/j/justwar.htm (accessed 10/06/2004).

New Labour, *Britain Deserves Better*, 1997 Election Manifesto, www.psr.keele. ac.uk/area/uk/man/lab97 (accessed 29/07/2004).

Robinson, P., 'The Policy-Media Interaction Model. Measuring Media Power during Humanitarian Crisis', *Journal of Peace Research*, Vol. 37, No. 5, 2000.

Ritchie, J., 'Covert Propaganda in the Cold War', *Interstate Online*, Issue 50, Spring 1997.

Shaw, T., 'The Information Research Department of the British Foreign Office and the Korean War, 1950–53', *Journal of Contemporary History*, Vol. 34, No. 2, 1999.

United Nations, 'Geneva Convention Relative to the Protection of Civilian Persons in Time of War', Article 3, www.unhchr.ch/html/menu3/b/92.htm (accessed 25/5/2004).

INDEX

226

Printed in the United Kingdom
by Lightning Source UK Ltd.
118073UK00001BB/5